Cognitive Systems and the Extended Mind

PHILOSOPHY OF MIND

SERIES EDITOR
David J. Chalmers, Australian National University

Cognitive Systems and the Extended Mind

ROBERT D. RUPERT

OXFORD

UNIVERSITY PRESS

2009

OXFORD
UNIVERSITY PRESS

Oxford University Press, Inc., publishes works that further
Oxford University's objective of excellence
in research, scholarship, and education.

Oxford   New York
Auckland   Cape Town   Dar es Salaam   Hong Kong   Karachi
Kuala Lumpur   Madrid   Melbourne   Mexico City   Nairobi
New Delhi   Shanghai   Taipei   Toronto

With offices in
Argentina   Austria   Brazil   Chile   Czech Republic   France   Greece
Guatemala   Hungary   Italy   Japan   Poland   Portugal   Singapore
South Korea   Switzerland   Thailand   Turkey   Ukraine   Vietnam

Copyright © 2009 by Oxford University Press, Inc.

Published by Oxford University Press, Inc.
198 Madison Avenue, New York, New York 10016

www.oup.com

Oxford is a registered trademark of Oxford University Press

Library of Congress Cataloging-in-Publication Data
Rupert, Robert D.
Cognitive systems and the extended mind / Robert D. Rupert.
    p.   cm.—(Philosophy of mind)
ISBN 978-0-19-537945-7
1. Cognition.   2. Cognitive science.   I. Title.
BF311.R864 2009
121—dc22   2008052862

9 8 7 6 5 4 3 2 1

Printed in the United States of America
on acid-free paper

To Kristy,
with love

Preface

This book reacts to the situated movement in cognitive science (Robbins and Aydede 2009), which emphasizes the contribution of the environment and the nonneural body to human thought. In preparing my earliest published paper on the topic (Rupert 1998), I hoped to harness situated views to my own ends: the development of a causal–historical theory of mental representation. That work led to a more general interest in situated cognition, an interest that, during the academic year 2000–2001, dominated my research. At that time I was Visiting Assistant Professor at Texas Tech University (TTU). I stayed on at TTU for four additional years, where this project was nurtured, alongside others, by the unstinting intellectual support of my colleagues Edward Averill and Aaron Meskin. My foremost thanks go to them. Concerning the manuscript itself, I extend special thanks to Kenneth Aizawa and David Chalmers. Ken gave me detailed comments on many of the chapters in parts I and II, and, as series editor, Dave provided helpful advice on all aspects of the project, including content, organization, strategy, and style.

Many others have participated with me in this discussion, in various ways through various media, or have supported the endeavor in some other substantive manner. In this regard, I would like to thank Fred Adams, Colin Allen, Michael L. Anderson, Murat Aydede, David B. Barnett, Len Boonin, Sara Rachel Chant, Andy Clark, Jonathan Cohen, Robert Cummins, Howard Curzer, Nic Damjanovic, Carl Gillett, Bob Hanna, Chris Heathwood, David Hilbert, Bryce Huebner, Susan Hurley, Dan Kaufman, Sungsu Kim, Walter Kintsch, Colin Klein, Douglas Kutach, Clayton Lewis, David Lindy, Joseph Long,

William Lycan, Leslie Marsh, Richard Menary, Michael Mozer, Jay Newhard, Alva Noë, Josh Osbun, Ben Pageler, Robert Pasnau, Michael Peirce, John Perry, Philip Robbins, Kristen Rupert, Nicholas Rupert, Luka Ruzic, Richard Samuels, Fred Suppe, John Sutton, Mariam Thalos, Jonathan Weinberg, Rex Welshon, Michael Wheeler, Robert Wilson, and Taduesz Zawidski. (I apologize to anyone I have forgotten!)

I have presented many of the ideas in this book at conferences and departmental colloquia: Mountain-Plains Philosophy Conference, 2001; Pacific Division American Philosophical Association (APA), 2002; TTU; British Society for the Philosophy of Science, 2006; Central Division APA, 2006; University of Washington, Seattle; University of Colorado, Boulder (CU-Boulder); Extended Mind II Conference; Joint Session of the Mind and Aristotelian Societies, 2006; Annual Summer Interdisciplinary Conference, 2006; Society for Philosophy and Psychology, 2006; 4-E Conference, 2007; University of Missouri-Columbia; and University of Illinois at Chicago. Thanks to the various audiences for their probing questions and insightful remarks. In addition, I have had the pleasure of discussing situated cognition with students in a number of my classes at TTU and CU-Boulder; I am grateful to the students for their genuine engagement and for some fine term papers on situated cognition, especially from Todd Banus and Dirk Keaton.

Financial backing is among the most important kind of support. Accordingly, I wish to thank the National Endowment for the Humanities for a Fellowship for College Teachers, which allowed me to work full-time on the manuscript during the 2005–2006 academic year. Thanks also to CU-Boulder for providing additional financial support during the tenure of the fellowship. I would also like to acknowledge the more general support, some of it financial in nature, of the administration and senior Philosophy faculty at TTU: thanks to Jane Winer, Fred Suppe, Howard Curzer, Danny Nathan, Walt Schaller, and Peder Christiansen for ensuring that the junior faculty had plenty of encouragement and resources to pursue their research projects. May the lonesome plains of the Llano Estacado continue to provide a place for young philosophers to flourish.

On a more personal note, I thank my immediate family for their support and inspiration: Kristy, Amy, Cass, and Nick Rupert; Joyce Alexander and Bill Rupert, Jr.; and Bud and Diane Watson. Thanks also to the kids from Burien—especially Aaron Parker, Steve Purcell, Barb Turner, Steve Youngs, Kip Sheldahl, Eric Dushoff, and Rick Rhemke—for thirty fabulous years.

This book draws from the following published papers: "Coining Terms in the Language of Thought: Innateness, Emergence, and the Lot of Cummins's Argument against the Causal Theory of Mental Content," *Journal of Philosophy* 98 (October 2001): 499–530; "Challenges to the Hypothesis of Extended Cognition," *Journal of Philosophy* 101 (August 2004): 389–428; "Innateness and the Situated Mind," in P. Robbins and M. Aydede (eds.), *Cambridge*

Handbook of Situated Cognition (Cambridge: Cambridge University Press, 2009), pp. 96–116; "Realization, Completers, and Ceteris Paribus Laws in Psychology," *British Journal for the Philosophy of Science*, March, 2007: 1–11; and "Review of *Embodiment and Cognitive Science*," by Raymond Gibbs, August, 2006 (http://ndpr.nd.edu/review.cfm?id=7443).

Contents

Cognitive Systems and the Extended Mind

I

Introduction: The Mind, the Computer, and the Alternatives

1.1. The Mind as Computer

Most humans, at one time or another, reflect on the relation between mind and body. The motivation for doing so varies, from concern about an afterlife to questions about mental health to simple curiosity. Regardless of motivation, certain questions consistently arise: Do humans have a nonphysical soul, spirit, or mind? If so, can it exist apart from a human body? Do our beliefs, desires, memories, and fears reside in this immaterial element? When the mind's eye takes a certain perspective on the world, what thing takes that perspective? Human behavior seems to originate in an inner arena of directly experienced thoughts, which eventuate in commands—to the body to act, the voice to speak. What entity looks into that arena and purposefully issues these commands? Is that entity the essence of the person, the thing that makes the individual who he or she is?

This territory is ripe for metaphysical inquiry, for instance, into the nature of immaterial substance, its exercise of free will, and its power to control the body. Emboldened by the impressive track record of natural science, however, many philosophers reject the entire notion of nonphysical minds, souls, or spirits. Belief in such entities is, it is suggested, the stuff of folk superstition, of a piece with belief in life force, witches, or tree spirits (Churchland 1981).

Does the scientific approach offer a more compelling and well-grounded image of the human mind? As the twentieth century progressed, neuroscience, linguistics, computer science, and cognitive psychology—core disciplines of what has come to be known as cognitive science—provided grounds for increasing optimism. Of course, the details were not fully worked out, but these sciences produced parade results together with a guiding metaphor: the mind as a computer. The emerging computational view seemed to show how human thought can proceed by a series of steps in a concrete machine (Ernst and Newell 1969). On this view, the existence of mental states is no more a metaphysical conundrum than the existence of computing machines. The mind is a program; the brain, its hardware. There *is* a sense in which a program exists independently of its particular physical form. Nevertheless, this does not entail the existence of a nonphysical substance in which the program inheres; every instance of a given program takes physical form, for example, as encodings on a disk. For a given human, then, having a mind amounts to having a brain organized so as to move properly through the steps in a problem-solving recipe—whether the problem is playing chess or making sense of someone else's speech.

The computer model sheds less light on the nature of the self or free action, but this, it is widely thought, can be ignored. If the computer model can explain all of human behavior, selves can be set aside. The self is nothing more than the collective dispositions of the program and the data stored in the brain. Decision-making programs operate over goal-states; given an active goal-state (e.g., to go to the movies), the decision-making algorithm determines which command becomes active (e.g., to look up movie times online). Intentional action amounts to no more than the physical implementation of such a command. Computing, together with some nontrivial engineering, accounts for the observed wonders of human intelligence: reasoning, language use, decision-making, categorization, perception, theory-construction, and the rest. First-person reports of free will and the "what it's like" of consciousness take a backseat to the properly scientific explanation of the data.

This view of the mind strongly influenced at least two generations of philosophers, including Hilary Putnam, Jerry Fodor, and Ned Block, among many others. Nevertheless, criticisms of the computer-based research program in cognitive science appeared early (Dreyfus 1992/1972), and the critical voices have grown only louder and more numerous. The point of this book is to make sense of many of those voices. Some voices object to the very idea that human thought should be conceived of a series of problem-solving steps of the sort that can be specified by a computer program. These voices urge the replacement of the computer model with alternative metaphors: an ongoing dance between the brain, nonneural bodily resources, and environmental structures. Other voices accept some version of the computer-based approach but reject the idea that the *brain* is the computer, opting instead for a more expansive vision of the hardware, perhaps including materials beyond the boundary of the body (Clark and Chalmers 1998).

As the preceding suggests, the critical choir does not sing in unison (Wilson 2002; Rupert 2004; Clark 2008a). Below, I elaborate on the range of unorthodox views. Let us pause to note, though, the distance we have come from the questions listed at the outset. This book does not consist in an investigation of the soul, spirit, or immaterial mind. Rather, my primary question of interest—"Where in the physical world is human cognition?"—presupposes that human thought processes are part of the natural, physical order. In more technical terms, we embark presently on a critical tour through the study of what is known as situated cognition: the ways in which the brain, body, and environment work together to produce intelligent behavior. This book represents an attempt to understand the relative contributions of these various physical factors and to identify the most promising conceptual framework in which to cast those contributions.

1.2. Alternatives: The Varieties of Situated Cognition

Our understanding of human cognition stands at a crossroads, it is frequently claimed; the time has come for a revolution, a paradigm shift, a reenvisioning of ways to think about human thought (Varela, Thompson, and Rosch 1991; van Gelder 1991, 1995; Thelen and Smith 1994; Clark 1997; Brooks 1999; Lakoff and Johnson 1999; Wheeler 2005; Gibbs 2006; Spivey, Richardson, and Zednik 2009). This revolution will sweep away the outdated picture of the human mind as software run on the machine of the brain. Instead, human cognition will be revealed as the emergent activity of a larger, more-encompassing system, as the product of the brain, body, and environment working together (Gibbs 2006). Moreover, this new understanding of human cognition may reveal the nature of cognition itself, thus grounding a general science of cognition.

In the "The Extended Mind," Andy Clark and David Chalmers (1998) make a provocative case for revolution. Research on the use of external resources (e.g., Kirsh and Maglio [1994]) shows that human cognition depends heavily on, and is deeply intertwined with, aspects of the environment beyond the boundary of the human organism. Clark and Chalmers argue that there is no principled reason to distinguish, in kind, the external parts of this sort of process from the bodily portions of it. Thus, we should transcend our existing tendency to treat cognition as an activity solely of the brain or of the organism; instead, we should take human cognition—and with it, the human mind and self—to extend into the world beyond the boundary of the organism. As Clark and Chalmers put it, "Once the hegemony of skin and skull is usurped, we may be able to see ourselves more truly as creatures of the world" (1998, 18).

Call this the 'extended view': the view that human cognition—to some substantial degree—literally includes elements beyond the boundary of the human organism.[1] Arguments for the extended view take a variety of forms, many of which are examined in detail in due course. For now, let us look a bit more closely at Clark and Chalmers's reasoning. Take a given mental state, for example, the belief that Nixon was not impeached. Presumably, in any individual who holds this belief, it takes some physical form or other. Normally, this is assumed to be a state of the person's brain. Imagine, though, a physical state of the environment that plays the same role in a person's mental life as we would expect a neurally encoded mental state to play: it drives speech, inference, and planning. Why should we not consider such a physical state to be one of the subject's beliefs, physically encoded in the external world? If there are such states, then, there is a perfectly literal sense in which the person's mind extends into the environment beyond the boundary of the body. To claim otherwise would manifest nothing more than internalist prejudice.

Clark and Chalmers focus mostly on this sort of hypothetical case, imagining that there exists a memory-impaired person, Otto, who stores information in a notebook, which information plays a role just like the average person's beliefs play. From this book's standpoint—focused as it is on the sciences of the mind—such hypothetical cases are of only marginal interest. Nevertheless, the empirical literature seems to reveal many such states, suggesting that the extended view applies to a substantial portion of actual human cognition (Clark 2003). Consider the much discussed case of inattentional blindness (Simons and Levin 1997). Human perceptual processing makes information about the environment available to cognitive mechanisms that implement a wide range of cognitive functions, from scientific reasoning to the physical navigation of the immediate environment. How rich is this informational packet at a given moment in perceptual processing? Empirical evidence seems to show that much of the time, the information is far less detailed than one might expect; it is nothing like a high-resolution snapshot of the immediate environment (O'Regan 1992; Churchland, Ramachandran, and Sejnowski 1994; Simons and Levin 1997; but compare Silverman and Mack 2006). Rather, at any given time, the subject stores only a small amount of information, along with knowledge of how to get further information from the external world when that information would be useful.

These developments in the science of visual perception seem to provide real-world evidence of the kind of functional parity to which Clark and Chalmers draw our attention via hypothetical examples. Parts of the external world—the objects in our environment—play the same role in cognitive processing as certain neural states play: both the external objects and the neural states carry information that cognitive processing makes use of when needed for reasoning, navigation, and so on. Thus, extended states appear in a substantive role in

---

1. The literature contains a variety of labels and associated acronyms designating this view: 'HEC', for the 'hypothesis of extended cognition'; 'EC', for 'extended cognition'; and 'ECH', for the 'extended cognition hypothesis'.

at least one important domain of human cognition: visual perception. Taken at face value, this establishes the extended view.

The revolt against the orthodox approach—according to which the mind is the computing brain—comes in other forms, however. An alternative to the extended view takes human cognition to rely heavily on the environment but, nevertheless, to be bounded by the human organism. According to this *embedded* view,[2] typical cognitive processes depend, in surprising and complex ways, on the organism's use of external resources (McClamrock 1995, especially part two), but cognition does not literally extend into the environment. The embedded view is radical in its own way, for it recommends a decidedly different approach to the study of human cognition: do not look so much at the internal processes of computation or association but instead at the way the structure of the subject's environment facilitates the success of whatever internal cognitive processes occur. Humans might, for example, be capable of analyzing large amounts of data or of working carefully through an argument, if need be. Typically, though, the human subject relies on shortcuts and heuristics that are valid (enough!) in her immediate environment. Cognitive scientists should not spend their time trying to model the former style of processing when it is much more likely that humans are engaging in the latter.

Consider, for example, what has sometimes been called the law of small numbers (Tversky and Kahneman 1971), the view that a small numbers of observations provides the basis of legitimate generalization about the properties of the kind of item observed. When applied, the law of small numbers can easily deliver erroneous conclusions, as any statistics textbook will make clear. Given the suboptimal status of the law of small numbers, one might expect successful human thinkers to eschew it. Nevertheless, in certain environments—perhaps the ones that humans typically find themselves in—adhering to the law of small numbers makes much better use of one's resources than does careful statistical inference (Kornblith 1993, chapter 5). For example, if relatively homogeneous kinds fill one's environment, generalization on even a few samples is fairly reliable and frees up time to engage in other productive activities; in the typical evolutionary environment, if a single plant specimen with highly articulated, ovoid leaves and small red berries provides sustenance, then the next plant with highly similar appearance probably does as well. Therefore, it is no surprise to find that most humans make mistakes in their statistical reasoning of the sort that one would expect from believers in the law of small numbers.

The preceding example illustrates the dependence of much of our reasoning on the environmental context. Many of the examples that motivate

---

2. Sometimes this view is referred to as the 'hypothesis of embedded cognition', or 'HEMC' (Rupert 2004; Clark 2007; Clark 2008b; and Wilson and Clark 2009); compare Clark's discussion (1997, 105–6) of "catch-and-toss" styles of explanation.

embedded cognition have, however, a more interactive flavor. Visual processing of the sort described above in connection with the extended view also suggests the embedded view; in fact, some authors do not carefully distinguish between the two views when drawing theoretical morals from evidence of highly interactive visual processing (O'Regan 1992; Ballard, Hayhoe, Pook, and Rao 1997). On the embedded interpretation of this data, on-the-fly visual extraction of information from the environment does not render the external source of that information a literal part of the human cognitive system, but it does speak against certain strategies in the study of visual processing. Do not try to find the place in visual cortex where a highly detailed model of the immediate environment is constructed; rather, focus on the mechanisms controlling the serial extraction of small amounts of information from the environment.

The *embodied* view of cognition (Glenberg 1997; Barsalou 1999; Gibbs 2006) fills out our menu. On the embodied view, human cognition bears a privileged relation to distinctively bodily processes. By leaving this privileged relation unspecified, the embodied view provides a large tent (Wilson 2002; Shapiro 2004, chapter 7, 2007), but here is one important strand. Our fundamental concepts pertain directly to the physical body; other concepts are, in some important way, an extension of those fundamental bodily concepts (Lakoff 1987). For instance, the concept of something as abstract as a number might be constructed wholly from experiences of tapping out a beat with one's foot or physically lining up and pressing together the five fingers on one hand and the five fingers on the other.

Proponents of the embodied view also emphasize the context-dependent effects of sensory experiences and motor routines on cognitive processing. How quickly or reliably one categorizes a test item or draws an inference from some stimulus can depend very heavily on the subject's current bodily experiences. Consider the following result (Klatzky, Pellegrino, McCloskey, and Doherty 1989). Subjects are first tested to discover which verbal cues they associate most closely with the physical act of pinching. Subjects are then exposed to a verbal cue highly associated with pinching just prior to the administration of a standard semantic categorization task, in which the subject is asked to determine as quickly as possible whether a given phrase makes sense. If the phrase in question describes an action such that, were it carried out, would involve pinching, then the associated cue acts as a prime, significantly speeding up the subject's judgment of sensibility.

In contrast to the extended and embedded approaches, the embodied view alone assigns no specially active role to the environment in human cognitive processing. Nevertheless, given that sensory and motor processing themselves involve interaction with the environment, it is no wonder that philosophers and cognitive scientists tend to group the embodied view together with the extended and embedded ones.

1.3. Looking Ahead

The data and theoretical arguments that impress proponents of situated cognition go well beyond what is reviewed in the preceding section, as becomes clear in due course. Given the wide-ranging and complex nature of the relevant empirical research, it is no surprise that situated theorists respond with a variety of proposals. A resolution of the matter may have to wait on practicing cognitive science; perhaps cognitive science will, in the end, deliver definitive results or develop analytic tools that unify the data within a single theoretical framework. Such developments do not occur in a vacuum, however. At each stage in the evolution of cognitive science, we should attempt to make sense of where we have gotten, partly in hopes that doing so will facilitate progress. In this vein, I think the philosopher faces an at least threefold challenge: (1) to judge the bearing of the existing data on the individual situated views, as well as on the orthodox view; (2) to sort out the relations among the various theoretical views, situated and otherwise; and (3) to extract from the discussion of (1) and (2) whatever answers cognitive science can give to traditional philosophical questions.

It would be foolhardy to attempt fully to meet this threefold challenge in a monograph—or perhaps in a lifetime. The extended view offers the most radical of the three situated approaches, and consequently, in two of the book's three major divisions, I focus particularly on its prospects. In part I, I argue that the relatively durable cognitive system—the integrated collection of capacities and mechanisms that causally contributes to the production of cognitive phenomena—provides the most plausible line of demarcation between what is cognitive and what is not. The materials of cognitive-scientific explanation—information flow, computation, transformation of activation vectors, and dynamical evolution—pervade the universe; only by focusing on integrated cognitive architectures do we arrive at distinctively cognitive explanations. Given that this integrated system typically appears within the boundary of the human organism, cognition does not extend beyond that boundary, at least not in the substantive way supposed to lead to paradigm shift in cognitive science. I argue further that this systems-based account of cognition explains the success of a wealth of research, on such phenomena as memory, theory of mind, language acquisition, visual processing, conceptual development, reading comprehension, and visual neglect. The investigation of these and other cognitive phenomena has proceeded fruitfully by treating the systems of interest as organismically bounded. My description of the cognitive system, and its correlative appearance within the boundary of the human organism, explains why this organismically focused methodology has proven so fruitful. Finally, to the extent that we can derive conclusions in philosophy of mind from cognitive science, I conclude that, at least at present, we should adopt a nonextended view of the cognitive mind and self.

Having made a case for a nonextended outlook, part II critically surveys arguments in support of the extended view. My reactions to these arguments vary nearly as much as the arguments do, but these reactions often appeal to the reasoning of part I. Cognitive science offers independent reason to posit a (contingently!) nonextended human cognitive system; the interaction between the human cognitive system, so conceived, and its environment accounts satisfactorily for the results that impress proponents of the extended view: therefore, even as a gloss of cases in which the environment makes a striking contribution to cognitive phenomena, the extended view constitutes an unnecessarily extravagant and undermotivated interpretation of the data.

Part III explores the merits of the embedded and embodied views. Here I focus largely on ways in which these approaches depart from or overlap with the orthodox view, that is, the view inspired by the computer model of the mind. For most of part III, the ideas of computation and representation take center stage, the specific subject matter ranging from the innateness of concepts to the action-oriented nature of mental representations to the ontological status of computational models. I conclude that much of the computer-inspired approach survives; it does so by incorporating the genuinely important insights of the embodied and embedded views, while defusing, on principled grounds, the antagonistic rhetoric sometimes associated with situated views. Call this co-opting, if you will, but the vision is, I think, promising and has not been pursued sufficiently in the literature.

1.4. Strategy and Methods

1.4.1. Slaying the Cartesian Beast?

At places, the preceding sections emphasize differences between the extended, embedded, and embodied approaches. This might strike the reader as odd, given many authors' apparent enthusiasm for the full range of situated views (see, e.g., Clark [1997]; Rowlands [1999]; Wheeler [2005]; Gibbs [2006]). Do the various situated views exhibit greater theoretical unity than my discussion thus far allows? Does it serve any important purpose to place the three views under a single rubric?

As they are often presented, the three views share an enemy, and that may be reason enough to group them together, at least in some contexts. Imagine that orthodox cognitive science stands as a monolithic research program, unwilling to concede any part of the cognitive domain. Assume, in contrast, that the situated research program is more pluralistic, allowing that an extended view give the correct explanation of some cognitive phenomena, an embedded account of others, and an embodied account of still others. With the stage thusly set, any chink in the orthodox armor will be a boon to all situated approaches. If, for example, an embedded account of some cognitive phenomena wins the day, this seems to improve, however slightly, the outlook for other situated approaches in their attempts to explain distinct cognitive phenomena.

Fair enough, but the lumping together of extended, embedded, and embodied views can just as well muddy the dialectical waters. Conceived of as general frameworks for the study of human cognition, the extended and embedded views are mutually exclusive: it cannot be true *both* that the human cognitive system consists partly of elements beyond the boundary of the organism (the extended view) and that the human cognitive system is organismically bounded but carries out its cognitive work by subtle and complex exploitation of environmental structures (the embedded view). Moreover, even if one is inclined toward pluralism, an extended and an embedded model cannot both be true of a single cognitive process—else there is a single cognitive system that both extends beyond the boundary of the organism and does not. Interestingly, though, there may be cases in which an embedded approach illuminates the activity of an extended cognitive system, by directing our attention to the way in which that extended system interacts with objects beyond its extended boundary during cognitive processing. With equal ease, however, an embedded approach can be joined to a model that places cognition entirely in the computing brain.

Notice a similar flexibility to the embodied approach. An understanding of the way in which the fine details of bodily structure participate in cognitive processing might supplement either an extended, embedded, or entirely orthodox view.[3] If human cognition extends beyond the body's boundary, it is partly via the human body's collaboration with environmental materials—a collaboration so close as to create an extended cognitive system. The correct explanation of how these alliances form most likely appeals to the fine structure of the body that allows it to mesh neatly with environmental structures. The embodied approach might also be wedded to an embedded one. It is natural to think that if the embedded view is correct—if cognition depends heavily on the timely exploitation of external structure—the fine structure of human bodies is explanatorily relevant. Given the body's role as interface between brain and world, we should expect the fine structure of the body to facilitate the efficient exploitation of external structure. All the same, the embodied view might contribute most fruitfully to orthodox cognitive theorizing. Consideration of the fine details of the body may help us to determine which functions the brain computes over which neurally realized representations—nothing more. Thus, it could turn out that extended and highly embedded views are false, even though fine-grained features of the human body ramify through human cognitive processing.

---

3. On some readings of the embodied approach, it works against the extended program (Clark 2008a)—a further reason not to group situated views together uncritically.

The preceding discussion is not merely academic. As becomes clear in chapter 2, my critical approach to the extended view depends on the availability of its embedded (and to some extent embodied) cousin. Moreover, part III recommends a conciliatory reading of both the embedded and embodied approaches as they relate to orthodox, computational cognitive science. None of this makes sense under the motif of an epic struggle that pits a unified antiorthodox front against the Cartesian nemesis, now in its contemporary computational guise. Since, as I hope to convince the reader, the discussion to follow does make good sense, the epic motif serves little dialectical purpose.

1.4.2. The Scope of the Situated View

Two further preliminary points concern the scope of the situated view. Advocates for various situated approaches sometimes claim only a conceptual or prejudice-removing mission (Rowlands 1999, 12, 15, 149, 172; Noë 2004, 210, 218; Clark 2008b, 136). They mean to show only that our cognitive models *need not* be representational, computational, or organismically internalist. We should be willing to consider other possibilities, it is claimed (and perhaps this motivates the grouping together of various situated approaches: any attack on the orthodoxy furthers the goal of expanding our conceptual horizons). To my mind, this is an excessively modest goal; any right-thinking philosopher or cognitive scientist should be willing to consider such possibilities in the abstract—such willingness is, I take it, part of the job description. Why should anyone think, a priori, that when the mind or cognitive system takes physical form, it must be in one location rather than another? An appreciation of the abstract possibilities does not, however, give us any positive reason to endorse one particular theoretical framework in cognitive science.

In contrast to the consideration of mere possibilities, I hope to understand human cognition in its paradigmatic forms. Many advocates for a situated approach to human cognition claim that their outlook applies to the core aspects of our cognitive selves (Rowlands 1999; Wheeler 2005; Gibbs 2006); that working cognitive science should be grounded, in the first instance, in the extended view of cognition (Hutchins 1995); and that shifting to the extended view will change cognitive science root and branch (Haugeland 1995). Such views concern the appropriate framework for studying core cognitive phenomena, that is, those central to what we recognize as intelligent behavior: language use, memory, inference, theory construction, and the like. As a philosopher of cognitive science, my interests lie here. Given this focus, however, claims about rarely used tele-controlled or assistive devices (Clark 2003) or about conceptually possible Martian minds (Clark 2005) are beside the point. They bear on the current discussion only if they reveal something about the central aspects of human cognition as they should be studied on the ground.

1.4.3. Philosophy of Cognitive Science and Philosophy of Mind

It may be clear, then, that the book you now hold is a work in the philosophy of science, philosophy of cognitive science, in particular. It is also an attempt to draw philosophical morals from our best cognitive science; as such, it is a study in the philosophy of mind. If our clearest pretheoretical conception of the mind distinguishes the mind from what it controls or uses, *and* our best cognitive science yields a nexus of integrated cognitive capacities that interact with other resources as they are encountered, *and* this nexus is instantiated in the human organism, then, other things being equal, cognitive science has—so far as it can—told us where the mind is located. Of course, this sort of reasoning presupposes results from philosophy of cognitive science: that our best cognitive science rejects extended cognition and instead embraces an organismically bounded package of integrated cognitive capacities that utilize environmental resources on an ad hoc basis. Establishing this will be the primary task of part I, but we should not lose sight of questions regarding the location of the mind, as it is conceived of pretheoretically.

In light of these remarks, one might wonder how the present project fits into the larger scheme of philosophical inquiry. On the one hand, readers who take completed cognitive psychology to issue the final word about human cognition might take the arguments presented here to bear strongly on questions about the ultimate nature of the human mind and self: these arguments show that, to the best of our knowledge, the human (cognitive) mind and self is organismically bounded. On the other hand, some philosophers will withhold such judgments—even if they find my central arguments persuasive—for such philosophers' methodological commitments assign no special authority to science. On their view, we discover the nature of the self, the mind, and cognition, by reflecting on our concepts. Accordingly, the cognitive self is simply whatever answers to the appropriately refined commonsense concept of a self that reasons, believes, etc. This analytic (as it is called) approach can countenance distinct scientific conceptions of the self, the mind, or the cognitive system, but such conceptions must be marked as products of a separate enterprise, one that tells us only of some technical, newly defined notion of, for example, the cognitive self.

This analytic-cum-ecumenical view has its merits, and much of what I say in this book should be of interest to those who accept it. On a less ecumenical note, though, I am inclined to give precedence to the scientific project. If an analytic philosopher insists that, by conceptual necessity, a mind must have properties P, Q, and R, yet cognitive science implies that minds do not have all of those properties, I am willing to concede the word 'mind' to the analytic philosopher. At the same time, if our best science of the phenomena normally associated with minds says the things responsible for such phenomena lack one of the properties P, Q, or R, the analytic philosopher should accept elimination as a cost of my linguistic concession; that is, she should accept that minds do not exist. This is not the radical claim it might seem, because in the case as I am imagining it, cognitive science tells us that there are things exactly like minds—let us say, minds*—except that they lack one of the properties conceptually necessary of minds. This 'strategy of the asterisk' serves to remind us that no easy *modus tollens* follows from the scientific elimination or heavy-duty revision of an everyday commitment (the conclusion of the *modus tollens* being "science is therefore wrong"). Cognitive science might tell us that minds are very different from what the average person had thought; but so long as we keep in mind that science preserves, for example, minds*—things that are very much like minds—the rejection of the scientific results looks dogmatic and naïve, a refusal to admit that a folk definition (even one produced by the reflective folk) has turned out to have no strict application to the actual world. After all, we should not be surprised if it turns out that common sense or shared culture has hit on concepts that do not accurately describe what, in fact, exists in the natural world.

1.5. The Book's Conclusions

This chapter has previewed the book's overarching themes and clarified its goals and methods. A variety of theoretical approaches—extended, embedded, embodied, and orthodox—offer competing explanations of cognitive psychology's central phenomena. Framed by this menu of competing views, the chapters to follow examine both concrete results and theoretical considerations in cognitive science to see whether they provide any reason to reject or supplement the orthodoxy, and to see whether adopting any aspect of the situated approach yields distinctive and substantial benefits. As we embark upon this inquiry, we should be prepared to embrace some aspects of the situated program while rejecting others.

In the end, I reach definite, but tentative, conclusions about cognitive science. I reject the extended view given the current state of the evidence. In contrast, both the embedded and embodied views add something important to our understanding of human cognition; in their plausible forms, though, neither approach constitutes as radical a departure from rules-and-representations-based cognitive science as their proponents often suggest. In addition, I arrive at tentative, conditional conclusions about the human mind and self: insofar as we trust cognitive science to reveal the location of the human mind and self, cognitive science offers no reason at present to think these extend into the environment.

PART I

The Thinking Organism

2

Principles of Demarcation

Part I builds a case against the extended view, a case that depends partly on the development of an alternative. The case rests on two main lines of reasoning. The first focuses on the need for a principle of demarcation. If the debate about extended cognition is to be of substance, there must be a genuine distinction between what is cognitive and what is not. Thus, we should want to identify what Frederick Adams and Kenneth Aizawa call the "mark of the cognitive" (2001, 46). Principles of demarcation that most clearly deliver an extended view are implausible or unmotivated—or so I argue. A well-motivated alternative identifies cognition with the activity of a certain kind of integrated system, which appears mostly, if not always, within the human organism.

The second line of reasoning adds a seemingly insurmountable challenge to the extended view. The systems-based approach I favor jibes with and helps to explain the experimental practices that ground many successful research programs in cognitive psychology. Thus, there is reason to posit such systems. In addition, the systems-based view accounts naturally for the data that inspire the extended approach. In contrast, any version of the extended view that accounts for the success of orthodox research in cognitive psychology seems to do so only by aping the structure of a nonextended approach. Therefore, to the extent that the cognitive systems I identify are organismically bounded, a nonextended view wins out on the basis of conservatism and simplicity.

The present chapter examines principles of demarcation on which proponents of the extended view rely, either explicitly or implicitly. I argue against these principles, thereby setting the stage for the development of my systems-based criterion in chapter 3, as well as the presentation of the two arguments described above. chapter 4 then criticizes a prominent interpretation of the extended view—one cast solely in terms of extended vehicles or realizers—to which my arguments might not seem to apply.

2.1. The Challenge of Demarcation

Environmental factors affect human thought and problem-solving; this much is beyond dispute. Sometimes the environment forces constraints upon cognizers. If a wall stands between the subject and an object of interest, the subject must abandon at least one information-gathering strategy: immediate visual inspection. In other cases, humans put existing features of the environment to cognitive use: "Red sky at night, sailor's delight." In still other cases, humans intentionally alter the environment so as to facilitate problem-solving: they write notes to themselves.

How, then, does the extended view depart from common sense and cognitive-scientific orthodoxy? Proponents of extended cognition tend to emphasize the active nature of the environment's role; it contributes in an ongoing and interactive way to the production of cognitive phenomena (e.g., language-use, perception, theory-construction, and reasoning—or, perhaps better, the observable effects we associate with these processes). Rearranging tiles on a Scrabble rack, for instance, helps players to see which words those tiles can form (Clark and Chalmers 1998, 8). The physical arrangement and movement of the tiles thus seem to be a genuine part of the cognitive, problem-solving process.

What, though, distinguishes a genuinely cognitive contribution from one that is not—one that is, as one might say, merely causal? Consider the following cases:

Case One. John is fascinated by ancient Greece. He conceives of himself as an heir to ancient Greek culture. He frequently thinks and talks about ancient Athens, the Peloponnesian War, and the like. Clearly, these are forms of cognitive behavior, among the *explananda* of cognitive science. Moreover, John's thought and talk about ancient Greece depend at least indirectly on a complex set of causal connections to ancient Greek buildings, authors, leaders, and so on. In some instances, for example, when John has many books spread in front of him, written by various authors who have been causally affected in various ways by ancient Greek culture, physical elements of ancient Greece influence John's thought process in a multifaceted and ongoing way.

Case Two. Visual perception in natural light clearly counts as a cognitive phenomenon; computational theories of vision exemplify orthodox cognitive science (Marr 1982; Palmer 1999). The sun contributes in a distinctive and nontrivial way to every such act of perception.

Case Three.   In cases of visual perception, the object seen also contributes distinctively and nontrivially to the cognitive outcome; for instance, a tree that the subject sees causally contributes to her avoidance of the tree when walking in its vicinity.

Case Four.   A human uses a calculator to figure the tip on her bill at a restaurant. She pushes a few buttons, and the desired amount is displayed. As in many cases of the use of external resources, the restaurant patron intentionally and reflectively deploys a special-purpose system—a tool—to help her to accomplish a goal to the achievement of which the tool is specially suited.

Case Five.   An artist uses a sketch pad in a highly interactive way so as to facilitate the creation of a product she could not wholly envision in a single cognitive act. She sketches a bit, and the result of that sketching itself suggests worthwhile additions to the sketch, and so on, through numerous iterations (Clark 2003, 76–77).

The cases farther down the list—Cases Four and Five, in particular—may well involve extended cognition; it is not clear (perhaps these are to be treated as spoils to the victor). It does seem clear, however, that cognitive science gains nothing from the treatment of the earlier cases as examples of extended cognition. John's cognitive system, of fairly recent arrival, does not literally include the nonexistent columns, roads, or political institutions of ancient Greece, two and a half millennia removed from John. Only a fantastical view of no experimental import could hold otherwise. Regarding Case Two, the sun's contribution is acknowledged by all extant theories of vision, including nonextended approaches; saying that the sun is, moreover, a literal part of human cognition adds nothing but new labels to the theory of vision. An observed tree is typically fairly close to the perceiver in space and time, and thus it may seem more natural to treat the seen tree as part of human cognition. Nevertheless, what positive reason do we have to think of the tree as literally part of a human cognitive state, system, or process? When a human sees a tree and describes it later to others, it seems to be a paradigmatic case of a cognitive system's getting information from and about something else, something beyond the cognitive system.

The preceding list of cases raises a general challenge: to delineate cognition. The purpose of the list should not be misunderstood, though. It is not an absolute requirement that a principle of demarcation respect the specific judgments I have made about Cases One through Three. Various theoretical virtues might come into play and may, in the end, favor a principle with odd-sounding implications. Let us turn, then, to such virtues, which I present in the form of desiderata for a principle of demarcation.

Desideratum One.   Any revisionary principle for delineating cognition should offer more than new labels for existing categories. Assume that existing practice regularly distinguishes between two significantly different kinds of state, one considered cognitive and the other not. A theorist then proposes a principle of demarcation. When applied, this principle supports an overall approach to cognition that appeals to the same theoretically important distinction ensconced in existing practice; but this new principle entails only one further claim: that things in both categories are cognitive. Conservatism recommends that, other things being equal, we not bother relabeling the categories. (I sometimes refer to the accusation that a view fails to satisfy Desideratum One as the 'mere-semantics' objection, using 'mere-semantics' in the everyday, pejorative sense.)

Desideratum Two. Any principle of demarcation should motivate whatever new entities it introduces. Imagine that we have in hand an entrenched way of explaining data concerning cognition, including the data that most impress proponents of extended cognition. Consider a newly offered explanation that includes all of the entities, categories, and distinctions invoked by the existing approach, but which rests on a principle of demarcation entailing the existence of further entities—new composite systems, for instance. Other things being equal, the offer should be politely declined, and the principle of demarcation in question rejected.

Desideratum Two derives from a principle of simplicity. Admittedly, it is often difficult to measure the relative simplicity of theories; as a result, simplicity is often shunned as a general principle of theory choice. In certain cases, however, simplicity issues a clear verdict. If two theories embrace structurally equivalent explanations (with or without the same labels), but one of those theories simply tacks on commitment to an additional kind of entity, of no causal significance, then the relative simplicity comparison is straightforward.

Desideratum Three. The making of new theoretical commitments in the sciences should purchase empirical progress. If a principle of demarcation entails revisionary results when applied, that principle should make a distinctive contribution to the practice of cognitive science. Proponents of extended cognition might try indirectly to satisfy the first two desiderata by satisfying this one: that is, they might try to show that their principle of cognitive demarcation is not mere verbiage or extraneous complication by demonstrating that their proposed recasting of cognition advances the empirical enterprise. This positive contribution could take various forms, ranging from innovative experimental designs that produce new effects (or otherwise impressive data) to a more unified or explanatorily powerful theoretical interpretation of existing results.

2.2. Extension-Friendly Principles of Demarcation

2.2.1. *The Causal Principle*

Here is a candidate principle of demarcation that clearly favors the extended view: a state or process is cognitive if and only if it contributes causally, in a distinctive and nontrivial way, to the production of some cognitive phenomenon (Wheeler and Clark 1999, 110; Clark 2003, 40, 72–73, 75, 78; Wheeler 2004, 703).[1] I refer to this as the 'causal principle', but we should not lose sight of the qualifications built into it: not just any old cause of a cognitive phenomenon counts as cognitive; the cause must contribute in a nontrivial and distinctive way. It is difficult to make precise the requirement of nontriviality, but as the reader shall see, it does no harm to leave this matter to intuition. The requirement that a contribution be distinctively cognitive excludes such factors as the presence of oxygen or the force of the earth's gravitational field (cf. Wilson [2004, 109–10]). These ubiquitous factors arguably contribute to all human physical and biological phenomena; they provide preconditions for the appearance of cognition without themselves being cognitive.

The casual criterion lacks initial plausibility. When applied to Cases One, Two, and Three, it delivers what seem to be patently incorrect verdicts. In Case One, the causal criterion entails that parts of ancient Greece are literal components of John's cognitive system. With regard to Case Two, the causal criterion counts the sun as part of various humans' cognitive systems or as among their cognitive states; for each time a human sees in natural light, the sun contributes causally, distinctively, and nontrivially to the perceptual outcome (or whatever behavioral phenomena—say, successful navigation—the perceptual process is thought to facilitate). Similar remarks apply to Case Three, that of the very object seen.[2]

Application of our desiderata does not improve the lot of the causal principle. Orthodox cognitive science recognizes the following, theoretically important categories: (a) background conditions, (b) the set of organismically bounded, cognitively relevant states and capacities, (c) extraorganismic tools used by the organism to accomplish cognitive tasks (e.g., a hand-held calculator), (d) extraorganismic factors that the organism gains information about in cognition (e.g., an object seen), and (e) remaining extraorganismic factors (e.g., the sun) that causally facilitate cognition but that do not fall into category (c) or (d). The causal principle thus seems to do one of two things: either it extends, by stipulation, the label 'cognitive' from (b) to (c), (d), and (e), thus failing to satisfy Desideratum One; or

---

1. I have cast the causal principle in biconditional form, giving it the shape of a comprehensive principle of demarcation. As is the case with all of the principles I consider, the causal principle need state only sufficient conditions for something's being cognitive in order to be of use in arguments for the extended view. Except where explicitly noted, this distinction plays no role in the debate.

2. Compare Adams and Aizawa's observation that "the mere causal coupling of some process with a broader environment does not, in general, thereby, extend that process into the broader environment" (2001, 56; see also Adams and Aizawa [2007, chapter 6, 2009]; Butler [1998, 218]; Block [2005]).

it adds extra entities or properties (e.g., a new cognitive system) on top of the ontology of (a)–(e), by joining elements from the various categories and dubbing the result a 'cognitive system', even though the introduction of this entity serves no cognitive-scientific purpose; in which case, Desideratum Two goes unsatisfied.

In reaching such definite conclusions about the causal principle's relation to Desiderata One and Two, I have presupposed that the principle does not measure up with respect to Desideratum Three. A principle's apparent violation of conservatism and simplicity is, however, no violation if the principle anchors significant progress on the empirical front. It is not so easy to show that the causal principle and the extended view it supports fail to advance cognitive-scientific theory or research, relative to simpler or more conservative approaches. Much of what appears in later chapters carries this burden. In this subsection, I hope only to have motivated a general concern that the extended view is extravagant, as well as an interest in the exploration of further candidate principles of demarcation.

2.2.2. Epistemic Dependence

Advocates for the extended view sometimes emphasize the explanatory relevance of the causal processes at issue (Hurley 2001, 6; Noë 2004, 222; Wheeler 2005, 80–81, 134, 201, 207, 237; Chalmers 2008). An epistemic principle of demarcation seems to stand behind such claims: a state or process is cognitive if and only if it helps to explain the occurrence of a cognitive phenomenon.

This appeal to explanatory relations does not effectively ground the extended view. Consider how the explanatory principle would apply in another domain. As it happens, the house I live in has a cracked foundation. The builders' choices—their beliefs, interests, or dispositions—may well explain the cracked foundation. Perhaps the builders chose inferior materials or were distracted when constructing the forms into which cement would be poured. Surely, though, this would not establish that the builders have any of a house's architectural properties or that the builders are part of the underlying physical substrate of a house. We can explain how the builders left their causal stamp on the house without assuming that the builders themselves instantiate architectural properties, as opposed to being the mere causes of architectural properties. The physical substrate of my house's property of having a cracked foundation is right *there*, running along the basement wall. Imagine that the builders have died since constructing my house. Does the explanatory principle entail that my house's state of being structurally unsound is partly located where the builders' corpses are? Or that the past mental states of these now deceased people are part of the physical substrate my house's property of being structurally unsound? This way lies gratuitous metaphysical mystery.

The widely discussed context-sensitivity of explanation (van Fraassen 1977; Lewis 1986, 226–27) adds further cause for concern. One can explain an event *e* by citing one or more of the other events that contributed causally to *e*'s occurrence. The causal history of an event is, however, typically rich and varied. Given the variety of possible explanatory contexts, almost anything causally related to *A could be* explanatorily relevant to *A* in some context or other. Thus, even if distinctiveness is required of potential *explanans*, it invites gratuitous causal spread to reason from "*B* is explanatorily relevant to *A*" to "*B* exhibits the properties (e.g., cognitive properties) exhibited by or associated with *A*" or to "*B* constitutes, realizes, implements, or is part of the physical substrate of *A*."

Unless the proponent of the explanatory principle can give us special reason to think explanation-based demarcation holds in the limited domain of cognition, we should reject the general intuition behind the explanatory principle, as well as the explanatory principle applied specifically to cognition. The explanatory principle redraws the category of the cognitive in a way that leads to odd results (reference to the sun, e.g., helps to explain perception in natural light) and does so without changing standard cognitive-scientific practice.

The defender of extended cognition who is inclined toward an epistemic principle might instead focus on understanding: *B* is cognitive if and only if a full understanding of some cognitive phenomenon requires cognizance of *B* (Millikan 1993, essays 7–9; Haugeland 1995, 16; Clark 2001, 153; Gibbs 2006, 11, 24, 41–42, 49, 225). This suggestion faces problems similar to those raised above about explanation. To understand fully some particular act of human visual perception in natural light, one must understand the contribution of the sun, perhaps including the sun's past contribution to evolutionary processes (why not?). A principle of epistemic dependence thus seems to entail the unnecessarily mysterious claim that a particular act of human perception is physically constituted or realized by the sun—and perhaps even by long-past evolutionary processes—or that there is a single cognitive system consisting of the human and the sun (Rupert 2004, 395–96).

Notice the whiff of circularity about this principle. What is understanding, if not a species of cognition? If understanding is a species of cognition, the principle has the form "x is cognitive if and only if it is related in the right way to a certain form of cognition." Perhaps the circularity (or regress) lurking here is not invidious, but the proponent of the understanding-based principle has her work cut out for her in explaining why. Note, too, that if explanation is understood in psychological terms—as occurring only when a certain form of cognition occurs—then the first version of the epistemic principle faces an analogous problem of circularity (or regress).

2.2.3. *Metaphysical Necessity and Sufficiency*

Philosophers often address theoretical question in terms of metaphysical dependence relations, in particular, relations of metaphysical necessity and sufficiency. Might an appeal to such relations ground an extension-friendly principle of demarcation?

Let me begin by illustrating the concepts. It is metaphysically necessary for a number's being even that it be divisible by two with no remainder (i.e., be a number n, such that $n = 2k$, where k is an integer); it is impossible—in an absolute sense—for a number to be even without being divisible by two with no remainder. It is metaphysically sufficient for something's being water that it be pure H_2O; no matter what the possible circumstances, any sample of pure H_2O is automatically water. (These are offered as illustrations only; undoubtedly, some philosophers take exception to them.)

Now, consider the role that a metaphysical dependence relation should play in the debate over extended cognition. Given the dialectical structure of the present discussion, a useful principle of demarcation must meet two constraints. First, it must delineate a category more restrictive than those categories determined by the causal (or epistemic) principle. This seems especially clear from the standpoint of cognitive science. In respect of the typical cognitive outcome, too many states of the environment contribute causally and distinctively to its production, and, moreover, their causal contribution is acknowledged by existing nonextended approaches. Second, if the principle is to support an extended view, it must, when applied, deem a substantial amount of extraorganismic processing to be part of human cognition. In what follows, I consider various versions of the metaphysical approach, arguing that none satisfies both of these demands.

Here, then, is a necessity-based principle of demarcation: something is cognitive if and only if its obtaining is metaphysically necessary for the obtaining of some particular cognitive explanandum (in other words, the latter could not possibly have occurred absent the former, where 'could not possibly' is interpreted in an absolute sense). We should, I think, question the scientific importance of such an approach. Why should cognitive science characterize its theoretically important categories (cognition, in this case) via heavy-duty modal notions such as metaphysical necessity? Other empirical sciences do not appear to do so. Admittedly, scientists sometimes say things of the following sort: "Being negatively charged just *is* to be attracted to things of positive charge." Such claims, however, characterize the (supposed) essence of one kind or property in terms of its causal relation to *other* kinds or properties. It is not as if negative charge's being essentially related to positive charge confers positive charge on things with negative charge!

These are deep philosophical waters, however, and it may be best to set aside this naturalistic qualm, for a related concern goes more directly to the heart of the matter. An attempt to identify the metaphysically necessary conditions for a given cognitive phenomenon to occur yields little extended cognitive processing. Any given cognitive phenomenon—a particular utterance, for instance—in fact was produced by a certain range of causal contributors, but why think that any of them was absolutely necessary for the phenomenon to have occurred? If none of them is necessary, then, a fortiori, none of the contributors located beyond the boundary of the organism is necessary.

Think of this complaint as a dilemma, involving two ways to understand possibility. Philosophers often take alterations in the laws of nature to be possible; this view of possibility constitutes the first horn of the dilemma. On this view, no causal contributor is necessary to, say, a particular utterance, because in some possible situation, with different physics and chemistry and the like, different factors suffice to bring about the utterance. It may seem ridiculous to consider such possibilities, but if the laws of nature were sufficiently different, then the utterance in question might be produced by the fluttering of the subject's hair! In response, proponents of the extended view might characterize cognitive outcomes so narrowly that they cannot be produced by any other causes or conditions than the ones that actually produced them: we might characterize an utterance in such fine-grained detail that any utterance not produced by precisely its real-world causes does not count as the same phenomenon. This, however, seems to reduce the necessity-based criterion to a version of the causal principle; it is a roundabout way of saying, "What actually brought about this behavior is necessary for it." Thus, this approach is mired in some of the same problems as the causal principle: the sun is deemed a literal component of the cognitive process of visual perception in natural light. Therefore, the first horn of the dilemma either yields too little extended cognition or too much, depending on how the cognitive phenomena are characterized.

The second horn restricts consideration to possibilities consistent with the laws of nature. This provides one way to understand some of Alva Noë's claims (2004, 218–25) about perceptual experience. He sometimes talks in terms of necessary contributions to cognitive outcomes (ibid., 220) and in terms of what material substrate the cognitive outcome supervenes on (ibid., 218)—ways of talking that, in the philosophical literature, often carry heavy-duty modal commitments. Nevertheless, according to Noë, it is an empirical matter to discover what is necessary for the brain to do its cognitive work (ibid., 218); and when Noë claims that duplication of the brain may require duplication of the physical environment (at least some environment or other—225, n. 8), he seems to rest his claims on empirical consideration of what we know to be true about the way in which bodily processes interact with the environment to produce neural structure and cognitive outcomes. This approach, however, treats as metaphysically necessary precisely those causal factors that our best cognitive science treats as causally required given our laws of nature.

This suggests a principle of nomological necessity (i.e., necessity in relation to laws of nature): something is cognitive if and only if it is nomologically necessary for the occurrence of a cognitive outcome. This approach, too, seems to yield either too little extended cognition or too much. Presumably, many different physical processes would suffice to bring about the same cognitive phenomenon, in which case, no specific external contributor is nomologically necessary for the production of the phenomenon. A subject's speech might be tightly linked to the contributions of her interlocutor; nevertheless, many possible interlocutors saying many different things could cause the subject to utter the same response, consistent with the laws of nature. One could deny this reading of the possibilities, and claim instead that the speaker's utterance has such specific characteristic that the very external conditions that helped to produce it are the only external conditions that could have done the trick. I see no reason, however, to think that this approach excludes the contribution of the sun, the object seen, etc.

To be fair, Noë is often interested in a different question: whether a perfect duplicate of a subject's brain could have conscious experience in total isolation (i.e., in the absence of a physical environment). The correct answer here may be "no," for it may be nomologically necessary that some external stuff or other exists in order for perceptual experience to occur. Yet, although this point might help Noë to defeat a popular argument for an internally oriented view of conscious experience, it offers no aid to the proponent of the extended view. Grant Noë that the internalist should not simply assume that a brain could exist in the same state absent a physical context; but what use is it to the cognitive scientist to claim that cognition itself therefore consists in the operation of the brain together with some indistinct stuff or other? In other words, showing that any particular brain state can occur only in some range of physical environments does not deliver a plausible, extension-friendly principle of demarcation that applies in particular cases. We should not want to say the visual perception consists in neural activity together with the full range of physical contexts at least one of which must be present; on such a view would, some nonpresent contexts—the ones in the range that do not in fact contribute to the experience in question—become a literal part of the subject's current experience! The only plausible development of this thought tells us to choose, from the entire set of physical contexts, the one that actually causally contributed, and to say that this is part of the cognitive process. This truly does reconstitute the metaphysical necessity principle as the causal one, however, bringing all of the causal principle's problems in its train.

Now consider a criterion of metaphysical sufficiency: something is cognitive if and only if it is metaphysically sufficient for the occurrence of some cognitive phenomenon. This principle suffers from problems similar to those faced by the necessity-based principle. Assume the range of possible situations includes ones in which the laws of nature are different. If this is so, then virtually anything could cause anything. No particular contributor to a causal outcome is metaphysically sufficient for that cognitive phenomenon, because no contributor is such that, in any situation in which it appears, the cognitive phenomenon in question also appears. For any given set of factors that in fact contributes to an actual cognitive outcome, there is some possible situation in which it has none of the effects it has in the real world. All possible sets of laws of nature must be considered, and thus in keeping with at least one of those sets, the factors in question produce some results very different from the actual cognitive phenomenon they produced in the real world.

The straightforward refinement of the sufficiency criterion focuses on sufficiency relative to the actual laws of nature. For our purposes, however, this kind of sufficiency does not differ in any important way from causal sufficiency. After all, sufficiency relative to the laws of nature provides a common—if not entirely satisfactory—way to explain causality. Thus, the metaphysical approach seems to have nothing distinctive and plausible to offer the proponent of the extended view.

At first blush, it might seem to help to combine the two factors—metaphysical necessity and sufficiency—but this approach makes little progress. If we treat possibilities liberally, virtually nothing external is among the necessary and sufficient conditions for the appearance of a given cognitive phenomenon, for the reasons given above. If, instead, we understand possibility narrowly, holding the laws of nature fixed, there seem to be too many ways to produce a given outcome, so very little is necessary; thus, very little is necessary and sufficient. If one instead decides to treat outcomes as especially fragile—that is, having their identity determined by their highly specific, fine-grained characteristics (perhaps including what caused them)—then the result is lots of necessity but not much sufficiency, unless the causal contributors are also characterized in this fine-grained way. In that case, however, the factors in question simply reduce to factors that actually caused the cognitive outcome in question—and the discussion returns to the causal principle and its problems.

2.2.4. *Clark and Chalmers's Four Criteria*

In support of the extended view, Clark and Chalmers develop the hypothetical case of Otto. A review of this case, and Clark and Chalmers's diagnosis of it, might help to identify the mark of the cognitive. Otto is a victim of Alzheimer's disease, who uses a notebook in much the same way most people use their internal memories. When he comes by a piece of useful information, he enters it into his notebook. Imagine now that Otto would like to go to the Museum of Modern Art (MoMA) in Manhattan. Otto looks in his notebook, for there he has recorded MoMA's location: it is on 53rd Street, just east of the Avenue of the Americas. Upon finding the information, Otto and his notebook head off for an afternoon of art appreciation.

Clark and Chalmers claim that, given the way Otto treats the information in his notebook—given the role it plays in Otto's cognitive economy—Otto literally believes MoMA is on 53rd Street, even before he looks it up. His disposition toward that piece of information, recorded in his notebook, does not differ significantly from the average New Yorker's disposition toward her nonoccurrent—that is, not currently active or present to consciousness—but neurally encoded belief that MoMA is on 53rd Street. In such cases as Otto's, Clark and Chalmers claim, "belief is simply not in the head" (1998, 14).

This captures the flavor of some of Clark and Chalmers's reasoning in support of the extended view: the externally stored information plays the functional role of a nonoccurrent belief, and thus Otto has an extended belief. This style of argument is examined in more detail in chapter 5. At present, though, I am interested only in extracting a principle of demarcation from the view. Clark and Chalmers list four features of Otto's use of his notebook that, on their view, ground the notebook's cognitive status:

> First, the notebook is a constant in Otto's life—in cases where the information in the notebook would be relevant, he will rarely take action without consulting it. Second, the information in the notebook is directly available without difficulty. Third, upon retrieving information from the notebook he automatically endorses it. Fourth, the information in the notebook has been consciously endorsed at some point in the past, and indeed is there as a consequence of this endorsement. (1998, 17)

I should emphasize that Clark and Chalmers do not offer these conditions as a general theory of nonoccurrent belief or memory. These conditions are meant to generalize to some extent, though. Furthermore, given how influential Clark and Chalmers's discussion has been (and given everyone's need for a principle of demarcation), it may be worthwhile to see what kind of mileage can be gotten out of these conditions.

Here, then, is a possible principle of demarcation (although, again, not one that Clark and Chalmers explicitly endorse): Something is cognitive if and only if it meets all four conditions. Even when recast generically, Clark and Chalmers's set of criteria seem too narrowly focused to delimit cognition; for even after removing reference to Otto and his notebook, the conditions are geared specifically to nonoccurrent belief. Nevertheless, there are at least two reasons to pursue the present line of inquiry. First, it seems easy enough to imagine how Clark and Chalmers might adapt their criteria to other kinds of cognitive state, memory and perception, for example (cf. Donald [1991, 309], on memory). Second, a large amount of modeling in cognitive science, from the explanation of our linguistic capacities to the account of our understanding of others, invokes information-bearing states, irrespective of whether those states fit into pretheoretical categories such as *belief, perception,* or *memory* (or *knowledge*—cf. Chomsky [1980, 69–70, 90–92]). Thus, so long as Clark and Chalmers's criteria are adequate to the generic case of information-bearing cognitive states, they may well cover the fundamental ground of interest in cognitive science. So, although the discussion to follow continues to focus on nonoccurrent belief, the reader should bear in mind the broader potential of Clark and Chalmers's suggestion.

Consider now an objection, focusing specifically on the role of the fourth criterion, the 'past-endorsement criterion' as Clark and Chalmers sometimes call it. Here is my concern, in outline: The proponent of the extended view has good reason to embrace the past-endorsement criterion; the first three criteria can be satisfied too easily. Yet, adopting the past-endorsement criterion under-cuts the motivation for the extended view: not only does the resulting picture fit equally well into an embedded view of cognition; the thrust of the past-endorse-ment criterion—the privileging of an internal process of endorsement—sug-gests the embedded view more strongly than it does the extended one.

An example will help to develop this dilemma. Prevalent in modern society are telephones, including cellular telephones, and a system of directory service. Given these facts, the first three criteria imply that virtually every adult, Otto included, with access to a telephone and directory service has true beliefs about the phone numbers of everyone whose number is listed. The directory assis-tance operator is a constant in Otto's life, easily reached; when the information would be relevant, it guides Otto's behavior; and Otto automatically endorses whatever the operator tells him about phone numbers. It is absurd, however, to say that Otto has beliefs about all of the phone numbers available to him through directory assistance (i.e., beliefs of the form, "John Doe's phone num-ber is ###-####"), so long as he remembers how to dial up the operator. To say he does would be to depart radically from the ordinary use of "belief." Choose at random a person with a listed phone number such-and-such; assume, plau-sibly enough, that Otto has never consciously entertained the idea that that person's number is such-and-such; we have no apparent grounds for thinking that Otto has an accurate belief that the person's phone number is such-and-such; yet, the principle of demarcation under consideration deems cognitive the inscription of the number in the phone book (or its encoding in the phone company's database).

Clark and Chalmers's first three criteria violate Desideratum One: con-strued as a principle of demarcation, the first three criteria entail a gratuitous relabeling of a process—becoming interested in a person's number, taking out the cell phone and dialing operator assistance, etc.—already understood well enough as a cognitive system's use of noncognitive resources. No causal-explanatory or other theoretical advantage accrues to this relabeling. Thus, if Clark and Chalmers's conditions for nonoccurrent belief are to be worked into a principle of demarcation, inclusion of the past-endorsement criterion seems well advised.

On the other hand, at least the three following considerations speak against the inclusion of the past-endorsement criterion. Clark and Chalmers (1998, 17) themselves raise the first problem: a person can acquire ordinary, nonextended beliefs through processes of which she is not consciously aware; since it would be arbitrary to make the past-endorsement criterion necessary for extended belief, but not nonextended belief, it is best to give up said criterion.

Second, adopting the past-endorsement criterion undermines what is sup-posed to be one of the most important theoretical implications of the extended view: that there is no reason to assign special status to the boundary between organism and environment. If an extended (or any) belief requires conscious endorsement in order to be a genuinely held belief, and conscious endorsement is ultimately an internal process (i.e., one that takes place within the organismic boundary), then the organismically bounded subject is privileged in a deep sense, after all. If a subject's "external" memory or belief-content must be endorsed by organismically internal consciousness, it becomes more difficult to motivate the choice of an extended view over an embedded one; there is less reason to view external marks and objects as anything more than tools used by the mind, as opposed to parts of it. We can grant that cognition often involves intimate interaction with its environment. Given, however, that internal consciousness provides the ultimate source of cognitive authority, it seems quite natural to say that the thinking subject, traditionally conceived of, is *using* those external resources.

In rejoinder, it might be suggested that conscious awareness is itself a property of an extended system. Perhaps, but this engenders a pair of complications. First, the proponent of extended cognition now owes us an extended theory of *conscious acts*. Second, the rejoinder appears to forfeit the generality of Clark and Chalmers's criteria. If Clark and Chalmers's fourth criterion is sometimes satisfied (along with the others) by extended acts of conscious endorsement, Clark and Chalmers need an additional principle of demarcation to cover cases of extended conscious endorsement. What makes these acts cognitive?

Advocates for the extended view might get around the problem in a number of ways, but none of them strike me as particularly promising. For example, Clark and Chalmers might deny that acts of consciousness are cognitive; in which case, their cognitive status would need no vindication. I do not see how this suggestion will fit into the scientific project of which the extended view is meant to be a part, and so I bracket it. Alternatively, Clark and Chalmers might attempt a multistep approach to conscious endorsement. On such a view, any extended act of consciousness is part of a process that was at some point grounded by an act of unproblematic, internal conscious endorsement. Perhaps, an advocate for the extended view will someday work out such a theory of consciousness in detail, but further discussion of the topic seems quixotic at present.

One might instead require only that the internal subject be *causally responsible* for the creation of the external marks or patterns that serve as memory traces in the external store, without requiring conscious acts. It is difficult to see, though, how adding this condition inoculates the criterion at issue against the relevant problem-cases. The subject might be causally responsible for creating information-expressing marks without differing in any substantive way from our phone-equipped Otto. Under the right circumstances, one can, for instance, create an enormous database by the mere stroke of a key, and these could be circumstances in which Clark and Chalmers's first three criteria are satisfied (as, it would seem, could be Clark's criterion [1997, 217] of personal tailoring—the data might have been compiled from the Internet by a search program that takes personalized inputs). We might try some sort of compromise, say, requiring that the subject grasp the data's meaning. Nevertheless, even if this grasp need not be conscious, the problem of internal privilege persists.

Third, I am concerned that, with regard to our desiderata, the four-criterion set does no better than the three-condition set. On the former view, for something to be cognitive, it must be encoded in a way that makes it reliably available to, while also having been endorsed by, a trusting internally instantiated control system. In the case of external resources, this is the orthodox picture with labels changed. The standard picture holds that there are some internal functions—more or less distributed in nature—that control the way in which the organism gains access to external resources. It does no work to introduce criteria that, when applied, rule those external resources to be cognitive, without changing the structure of cognitivist explanation.

The preceding critical discussion focuses entirely on the conscious-endorsement criterion, but the others face difficulties as well. Many states that normally count as nonoccurrent beliefs or memories fail to satisfy Clark and Chalmers's other three criteria (Rupert 2004, n58). They are not readily accessible, do not guide action even when their content would be relevant, and (more clearly for memories than nonoccurrent beliefs) are not always treated as trustworthy by the subject of those states. Many memories and beliefs do not spring to mind when they would be relevant—we simply "forget to remember"—and sometimes we cannot call them to mind even when we want to, the result being that we often act without considering the content of our relevant nonoccurrent beliefs or memories (or information-bearing states, more broadly speaking); and some genuine memories are not treated as reliable by the agent that has them because, for example, they are accompanied by a feeling of uncertainty.

In summary, then, Clark and Chalmers's diagnosis of Otto's case does not provide a plausible principle of demarcation, for many reasons. The criteria are not sufficiently general. They are too conservative, excluding internal information-bearing states that are uncontroversially cognitive (both for the reasons I have given and for the one that Clark and Chalmers give). Moreover, they face the dilemma of being too liberal in certain respects without the fourth criterion and being too embedded-friendly (thereby running afoul of our desiderata) when the fourth criterion is included.

2.3. The Parity Principle

Resistance to the extended view is often claimed to manifest nothing more than internalist prejudice (Clark 2003, 43; Spivey, Richardson, and Fitneva 2004, 163), a sort of arbitrary conservatism. Proponents of the extended view sometimes attempt to defuse this alleged prejudice, thereby securing a fair hearing for the extended view, by appealing to the Parity Principle (Clark 2005, 2–3, 2008b). Clark and Chalmers's original formulation of the Parity Principle, not yet so-named, runs as follows:

> If, as we confront some task, a part of the world functions as a process which, *were it done in the head*, we would have no hesitation in recognizing as part of the cognitive process, then that part of the world *is* (so we claim) part of the cognitive process. (1998, 8)

I sympathize with the motivation behind the Parity Principle. After all, why should it matter where a process takes place? If that process instantiates cognitive or mental properties when it is over *here*, why should things change simply because it is now over *there*?

By book's end, I hope to have convinced the reader that my rejection of the extended view does not flow from an irrational location-based bias, but instead rests on solid, fair-minded arguments. In the present section, though, I have a more modest goal: to show that the Parity Principle cannot serve as a plausible principle of demarcation. Before proceeding, though, I should make it absolutely clear that, as in the case of the four criteria considered above, Clark and Chalmers do not explicitly offer the Parity Principle as a principle of demarcation. Clark sometimes presents it as a way to break down internalist prejudice, a job that can be accomplished via its successful application to a single case, without any presumption that it correctly delimits cognition across the board; alternatively, Clark sometimes treats the Parity Principle as an intuition pump, a way to prime certain functionalist intuitions (more on which in chapter 5). For his part, Chalmers (2008) sometimes focuses on parity of causal role, without any special reference to our judgments or reactions; this approach also has a functionalist flavor. Nevertheless, Clark and Chalmers's endorsement of the Parity Principle is as close as they come to offering a principle of demarcation; and in the absence of any other plausible, extension-friendly principle, it is worth while to evaluate the Parity Principle as a candidate principle of demarcation.

In what follows, I raise four objections to the Parity Principle considered as a principle of demarcation. Some of these seem serious, yet perhaps inconclusive (particularly if we take the Parity Principle to offer only a sufficient condition for something's being cognitive). The final objection, however, appears to show outright that the Parity Principle has no substantive role to play in a theory of cognition, and the objection does this in a way that directs our attention to cognitive systems, the subject of chapter 3.

My first objection concerns the limited scope of the Parity Principle. Consider that many supposedly extended cognitive processes involve ongoing interaction with the environment: a robot's use of a lighted triangle on the wall of an arena to effect navigation (Wheeler 2005), the subtle interplay between organism and the object of perception (Beer 2003; Noë 2004), or a person engaged in the hitch-free use of a tool—a hammer, keyboard, or sketchpad, for instance (Clark 2003). When applying the Parity Principle, the operative question is "If this process were to occur in the head, would we consider it cognitive?" If "yes," the process is cognitive; if "no" (or "indeterminate"), the process is not. When it comes to these interactive processes, though, I cannot see that the answer is a definite "yes," partly because the question simply is not clear. In the case of a robot tracking a light so as to move toward it, what is to be included in the antecedent of the Parity Principle's counterfactual? That is, what are we to imagine is taking place inside a person's (or robot's) head? Is it the interaction between the robot and the mounted, lighted triangle? Are the walls of the room in the head? The structure of the room? An actual lightbulb or LED? Such problems worsen when we turn to ongoing perceptual interaction with a large object, such as a building. Are we supposed to ask what would happen if a large building were in someone's head and the surface of the building were emitting photons that stimulate the subject's retinae? By what process does such stimulation work? Has the brain been rewired? And how can a building be in a person's head without causing the person's death? And so on.

The clearest way to refine the Parity Principle's counterfactual test appeals to the cognitive status of the various properties of external items: assume that all and only the cognitive aspects of an interactive process take place in the subject's head. This line of response is off limits to Clark and Chalmers, though, for it presupposes the very distinction—between cognitive and noncognitive—that the Parity Principle is meant to mark.

So far as I can tell, any other plausible refinement of the Parity Principle places many interactive processes outside the realm of the cognitive. Clark and Chalmers can, of course, bite the bullet here, claiming that such interactive processes are not examples of extended cognitive processing. This, however, would pit their tendency to apply 'cognition' against the intuitions of a great many other extended theorists who take certain kinds of interactive processes to be premier examples of extended cognition (e.g., Thelen and Smith [1994]; van Gelder [1995]; Haugeland [1995]; Beer [2003]; Noë [2004]; Wheeler [2005]). Thus, the Parity Principle either delivers the wrong answer or an answer at odds with the intuitions of many theorists who advocate for the extended view, without offering the sort of theoretical insight into the nature of cognition that might resolve the disagreement.

My second objection emphasizes the theoretical thin-*ness* of the Parity Principle. A true principle of demarcation should reveal something about the theoretically important properties of cognitive processing. In contrast, the Parity Principle asks nothing more than that we react to a counterfactual—one dealing primarily with location. Admittedly, the process of posing and reacting to these counterfactuals might plumb a subject's inchoate sense of what makes a process cognitive. I object, though, to what the process leaves hidden: an account of the distinctive and theoretically central characteristics of cognition—the sort of thing that would resolve the disagreement among proponents of extended cognition as to whether the Parity Principle gets things right in the case of such interactive processes as the seeing of a building.

My third objection questions the very point of plumbing our intuitive reactions to the Parity Principle's counterfactuals. The extended view concerns cognition as a scientifically important property or kind. Thus, if the Parity Principle's purpose is to tease out the implications of our concept of cognition, we should question its value. If we are asking about the average subject's reaction to the Parity Principle's counterfactuals, this process surely is irrelevant, given present concerns. Why think the average person—even the average philosopher—has a concept of cognition that is both determinate and internally articulated? Besides, the concept of cognition is a theoretical construct, like the concept of computation or of a connectionist network. The average person's intuition-based applications of 'cognition', even the well-informed theorist's reactions, should not be trusted to reflect the *actual* structure of cognition—unless, of course, the subject has in hand the correct theory of cognition.

Think of my concern in a slightly different way. The Parity Principle divides the universe into the categories of the cognitive and noncognitive, but only when those properties are understood as response-dependent, that is, as nothing more than properties of being responded to in certain ways by humans. Thus, the two categories appear merely to be *things that have the property of eliciting the judgment 'cognitive' from humans (under such-and-such conditions)* and *the things that do not*. These hardly seem like the kind of properties to build a science of cognition on (unless, of course, one is constructing that specific aspect of a theory of cognition that deals with human categorization of things as cognitive). Moreover, given the lack of agreement on these judgments, even among proponents of extended cognition, there are multiple response-dependent distinctions in play, one corresponding to each group's set of dispositions. The application of the Parity Principle begins to look more like part of an exploration of the variations in one group's range of judgments than it does a way to identify all of the processes—the cognitive ones—that share a natural property of scientific importance.

A pair of caveats are in order. Admittedly, certain intuitive judgments are indispensable in the initial stages of the cognitive-scientific enterprise, for example, judgments that group together various phenomena—language use, decision-making, mathematical problem-solving, etc.—as the ones to be explained by cognitive science. Nevertheless, the structure of the explanations of these phenomena, and the theories that ground such explanations, should not be products of conceptual analysis. Standard scientific methods determine how we should draw theoretically important distinctions between different parts—for example, the cognitive and noncognitive—of those explanations.

Consider, too, the Parity Principle's logical force. If the Parity Principle is meant to convey only a sufficient condition for something's being cognitive, then its failure to apply to some supposedly paradigmatic cases of extended cognition causes no difficulty. If something passes the Parity Principle's test, it achieves cognitive status; but other things might achieve cognitive status on other grounds. This allows the Parity Principle to avoid some of the objections leveled above—the one concerning disagreement among extended theorists, in particular—but it exacerbates other concerns, the complaint about theoretical thinness, for example.

My final objection brings this theoretical thin-ness back into the spotlight. The problem is that the Parity Principle takes no account of independent reasons for locating the cognitive system in one place rather than another. For comparison, consider a lone neuron in preparation. It may be that, were the neuron in my head, it would have the property *being part of my brain* (and such related properties as *being a contributor to large-scale neural processing*), and we would recognize it as such. Nevertheless, in the dish, it is not part of my brain. As an organ, the brain is a physically and functionally integrated system, and something can have the capacity to be part of that system without actually being part of it. The antecedent of this instance of the Parity Principle is plausibly true: if the neuron were in my skull, we would regard it as part of my brain. (Absent further information concerning how the neuron might have gotten into my skull, the most plausible chain of events in which the neuron lands in my skull is one in which the neuron has been physically and functionally integrated into my brain. Why else would it be there?) At the same time, the consequent is false: the lone neuron in preparation is not part of my brain.

This phenomenon is not limited to neural or cognitive contexts. For example, the same act of shooting a gun—performed by the same person in the same geographical location—can instantiate military properties or not, depending on the social and political context. Whether or not the shooting has military properties depends on whether it occurs as part of certain kind of social-political system: a war.

Thus, a generalized Parity Principle should be rejected outright. It is simply not true that, in general, a thing recognized as P in one location therefore has P regardless of its location. Location does not matter *if P is the sort of property that typically survives a change in location*. Lots of properties, however, do not, as a general rule, survive such changes. The Parity Principle is thus deeply uninformative. It warns us not to be biased by unexpected location, but only if the location makes no difference; the location makes no difference, however, only if change in location is not correlated with change in the status of the item or process in question. Thus, when applying a generalized Parity Principle to any particular property, we can have confidence in the Parity Principle's verdict only if we already know whether the property in question is the sort of property that survives a change in location; and here the Parity Principle falls completely silent.

Consider how this concern applies in the cognitive domain. I suspect (and will argue in chapter 3) that something is cognitive if and only if it is part of an integrated cognitive system; I suspect, too, that for humans this integrated system typically appears inside the head. Thus, it may be that some external states or processes would be recognized as cognitive were they in the head, but only because if they were in the head, they would most likely be integrated into the cognitive system. We might think, "Were that process located in the head, it would be part of the cognitive system," precisely because we have independent grounds for thinking the cognitive system is in the head and for thinking that, were the external process in the head, it would be incorporated into that integrated, internal system. This is all consistent with the process's not being part of the cognitive system when external, and thus not cognitive when located outside the organism. This reasoning does not demonstrate the falsity of the Parity Principle, so much as it shows that we can have little confidence in its naive application. Depending on what features actually make something cognitive and how much we know about these features, our reactions to the Parity Principle's counterfactuals might or might not track the cognitive.

At this point, some readers might suspect that I have treated the counterfactual conditionals incorrectly, that, for instance, in the nearest possible world in which the neuron in question is in my head, it is *not* integrated into my brain; for in that world, someone has merely slipped the cell inside my skull (or it appeared there miraculously), without the neuron's being integrated into my brain. Assume further that, in the situation in question (or in the actual world—depending on how precisely we are to read the Parity Principle), we know the neuron is not integrated into the brain and that not being integrated precludes its having brain-properties. Given these assumptions, my objection might seem to lose its force. When the neuron is in my head we do not "recognize" it to be, and thus we would not treat the neuron as having brain-properties; and thus, the counterfactual in question (the antecedent of the Parity Principle) comes out false, and the brain-property version of the Parity Principle does not incorrectly yield the result that the lone neuron has such brain-related properties as *contributing to communication between neural ensembles*.

The careful treatment of such counterfactuals would take us too far afield. Notice, however, the central flaw in this rejoinder. It rests on the assumption that our counterparts in the relevant possible situations know, not only the status of the neuron as it appears in my head, but also the bearing of that status on the neuron's brain-related properties. The rejoinder has force only because it is assumed that we have in hand a correct (enough) theory of large-scale neuronal processing, a theory telling us that a neuron cannot participate in large-scale neuronal processing unless it is physically integrated, in the right sort of way, into the workings of the brain. Thus, the rejoinder fails; for I am worried that, absent a fairly deep and well-confirmed account of cognition, we can have no confidence in the application of the Parity Principle. This concern stands, and the rejoinder itself helps to show why. Application of the Parity Principle tracks what it is intended to track only when the subjects in question have in hand a fairly rich and accurate theory of the domain to which the Parity Principle applies; in the absence of such understanding, the Parity Principle cannot reliably delineate that domain. I conclude, then, that the Parity Principle alone does not demarcate cognition.

2.4. Conclusion

Throughout this chapter, I have honed a challenge to the extended view: its proponents must formulate a principle that (a) distinguishes between what is cognitive and what is not, (b) is likely to count a significant number of extended processes or states among the cognitive, and (c) meets our three desiderata. In order to evaluate the promise of the extended approach, I extracted various principles of demarcation from the literature supporting the extended view, but with negative results. What to put in place of these flawed principles? I recommend a systems-based criterion: a state or process is cognitive if and only if it is a state of, or process occurring in, mechanisms that are elements of the integrated set members of which contribute causally and distinctively to the production of cognitive phenomena. This principle is the focus of chapter 3.

3

Cognitive Systems and Demarcation

The extended view appears most compelling when we attend to the causal production of individual instances of cognitive phenomena. If we take our theoretical cue from token cognitive results—a single subject's exhibiting one kind of cognitive behavior on a single occasion—then it might seem as if the various causal contributors are on par with each other. This, however, misconstrues standard explanatory practice in cognitive science, and in science more generally. We best explain a token outcome—whether a specific instance of human behavior or the crumbling of a specific bridge—by adverting to properties exhibited by the objects, animals, or systems involved and the general relations holding among those properties. Virtually no human speaks only once in her life; when a person does speak, it is explained by whatever explains her general capacity for speech. Thus, cognitive science's explananda include such things as the acquisition of speech and the regularities in subjects' verbal output. Of course, we would like to explain single instances of cognitive behavior; but to do so effectively, we must identify the capacities involved, their distinctive characteristics, and the supporting mechanisms, the operation of which explain single instances of behavior (cf. Wilson [2002, 630]). Such persisting capacities also explain the ways in which some of the capacities in a given integrated collection change over time: certain persisting features of the integrated cognitive system over a given period of time explain why it loses or gains other relatively persisting properties—in development, for example—partly in response to interactions with the environment. I propose, then, that in our search for a

theoretically rich principle of demarcation, we take a cue from successful explanation in cognitive psychology: cognitive phenomena are produced distinctively
by the persisting collections of capacities, mechanisms, skills, and abilities that
play a privileged role in successful cognitive psychological explanation.

Here is the plan for this chapter. First I argue that many successful research
programs in cognitive psychology presuppose the existence of a persisting, relatively unified, and organismically bounded cognitive system. I then give an
account of those persisting systems, which I work into a principle of demarcation. This systems-based view explains the success of the research programs
in question, and this fact grounds an argument in favor of the systems-based
view, as well as a complementary pair of arguments against the extended view.
The later sections respond to a series of extension-friendly rejoinders.

3.1. The Success of Cognitive Psychology

So far as I can tell, cognitive psychologists take little interest in claims of the
form "x is cognitive if and only if x has properties P, Q, and R." Nevertheless, a
good deal of successful research in cognitive psychology presupposes persisting, integrated systems as objects of interest; such systems are the relevant
explanatory constructs—the subjects of experimental investigation and the
properties of which explain the data. Many fruitful research programs have
produced robust results by systematically placing human organisms in a variety of situations and recording their responses. A research program produces
robust results when those results exhibit regular patterns. Such regularity can
amount to (a) consistency in results as the concrete experimental design varies; (b) consistent correlation between variations in results and variations in
abstract properties of the materials used, a correlation insensitive to crosscut-
ting variations in the materials used; or (c) regularity in the changes of patterns
of response (where concrete materials used can vary at each stage) as a function
of past experience or age of the organism. In cases where robust results are
achieved, the most straightforward explanation appeals to reappearance of the
organismic system with its persisting properties; these include higher-order
properties of being likely to change first-order properties in certain regular
ways as the result of aging or experience.

Visual perception provides a straightforward illustration. The organismically bounded subject can be placed in a wide variety of perceptual circumstances and will, highly reliably, have a sensory experience of the kind of object
with which she interacts, regardless of its constituent materials or her particular view of it. If placed in front of a medium-sized chair in reasonably good
light, she will report seeing a chair, regardless of whether it is made of metal,
rattan, or tinker-toys. Why? Presumably, it is because the organism, which
serves as a constant factor across these circumstances, itself instantiates certain

properties: a collection of persisting physical properties, the integrated interaction of which explains why the subject's reported perceptions are a regular function of what she causally interacts with in the environment.

Now consider the role of the persisting system in the investigation of human capacities for memory and language use. Such work normally presupposes that the subjects of investigation are persisting organismically bounded systems. Some such studies are explicitly longitudinal (Bahrick 1979, 1984). In other cases, the work is not longitudinal but is concerned specifically with the way in which an organismically bounded capacity leads to predictable results as environmental circumstances vary. Marsha Lovett, Larry Daily, and Lynne Reder (2000) provide an elegant example of this sort of research. Working within the ACT-R framework (Anderson, Bothell, Byrne, Douglass, Lebiere, and Qin 2004), Lovett et al. first run an experiment to estimate individual differences in short-term memory capacity—amount of source-activation, in particular. Then, using the source-activation value estimated for each subject, Lovett et al. make highly accurate, zero-parameter predictions of the performance of individual subjects on a significantly different experiment (in the first case, the modified digit-span, or MODS, task; in the second case, the n-back task). One would not expect this impressive result if Lovett et al. had excluded some important part of the cognitive system as they transferred their subjects from one experimental context to the next. In a similar vein, Morton Gernsbacher and David Robertson (2005) have found a significant correlation between capacities to understand narratives delivered in various forms: pictorial, verbal, or written. This demonstrates the persistence of a more general, complex capacity to understand narratives, a capacity that operates in various circumstances on various kinds of material.

Consider now a developmental case, the trajectory of children's performance on the false-belief task, which measures the child's ability to attribute beliefs to other agents when the child knows those beliefs to be false (Wimmer and Perner 1983; Perner, Leekham, and Wimmer 1987; Astington 1993; Nichols and Stich 2003). This task produces incredibly robust results (Wellman, Cross, and Watson 2001).[1] Whether experimenters use puppets, stories, cutouts, or live action, success rates on the task are consistent by age, as is the developmental trajectory. Some factors, such as the inclusion of deception in the story, can enhance performance on the false-belief task. Nevertheless, the effects are of the depiction of deception, not of the particular materials used; deception's effect is itself highly robust. Thus, the best explanation of this consistent performance across environmental changes adverts to certain persisting (but also maturing) capacities of the organism: its way of representing, and

---

1. The robustness of the trajectory of children's performance on the false-belief task does not, however, show that the task provides a litmus test for the child's possession of a theory of mind (Bloom and German 2000, Birch and Bloom 2003). My discussion in no way presupposes that successful performance on the false-belief task is a necessary and sufficient condition for the possession of a theory of mind.

processing the representation of, deception. Research on the false-belief task has also been highly fruitful, leading to developments in the understanding of autism (Baron-Cohen, Leslie, and Frith 1985; Baron-Cohen 1995), the child's understanding of goal-directed behavior and mental states (Gergely, Nádasdy, Csibra, and Biró 1995; Meltzoff 1995; Repacholi and Gopnik 1997; Woodward 1998), and the acquisition of language (Bloom 2000, chapter 3).

Examples are not limited to cognitive psychology. A similar pattern appears throughout the cognitive sciences. For instance, Jon Driver and Jason Mattingly (1998) describe a range of findings on parietal neglect that are robust and theoretically fruitful. Patients with right-parietal damage fail to register much of what comes into their left visual hemifield (particularly when they attend concurrently to stimuli in the right visual hemifield). Interestingly, these patients also neglect the left sides of objects that appear entirely in their right visual hemifield. As Driver and Mattingly describe the research, "This form of 'object-based' neglect has now been found in numerous cases, by separate research groups using various tasks...It also fits with findings of object-segmentation effects on visual attention in normal human subjects" (ibid., 19, references excluded). This point appears to generalize to many aspects of the neuroscientific investigation of color vision, motion vision, and the what- and where-systems. In the area of robotics, one finds the following claim made by Husbands, Harvey, and Cliff (1995): "We have shown it is possible to evolve dynamical network controllers plus visual morphologies that produce simple robust autonomous behaviours across a range of related environments" (103). Their work is sometimes taken to support the extended view (Wheeler 2005), but their summary seems to provide better support for an embedded view: the behavior in question is the behavior of a physically bounded agent and is a function of that bounded agent's capacity to navigate in a range of related, but varied, environments.

In this case, as well as the others discussed, there is a natural explanation of the persistence of the relevant capacities: they are physically realized, and the persisting organism provides their integrated, physical substrate; the organism as an integrated physical entity appears in the various circumstances of interest, and *its* persistence explains the persistent appearance of the integrated set of cognitive capacities realized by the organism. That there is a set of such integrated cognitive capacities explains why it is fruitful to subject the same physical organism to varied stimuli. If there were not an integrated, organismically bounded cognitive system, the robustness of results and fruitfulness of such research programs would be a mystery. If the operative cognitive system in these cases were an extended one, the functionally important parts of which change as various external stimuli contribute to cognitive outcomes, we should expect our contrary assumption—of a system that persists across cases—to produce a hodgepodge of perplexing results. This is not, however, what we find in a wide range of research programs in various areas of cognitive science.

In this section, I have emphasized the extent to which the presupposition of a persisting, organismically bounded collection of cognitive capacities has proven fruitful. This phenomenon stands in need of explanation, and I shall argue that my systems-based approach does the job. In addition, I have set the stage for an argument against the extended view: either the extended view does not explain this phenomenon very well, or to the extent that it does, it simply apes the structure of the systems-based view.

Before moving on, I should flag what I have *not* been out to show in this section. I have not claimed that, if the extended view is true, there must be a distinctively extended-cognition-based explanation of *every* cognitive phenomenon; it is consistent with the extended view that some cases of cognitive behavior are explained entirely by appeal to properties instantiated inside the organism. Neither do I claim that cognitive psychology has been anything close to universally successful. Rather, my intention has been to establish the utility of what I take to be cognitive science's fundamental explanatory construct: the persisting set of integrated capacities that contribute, distinctively and nontrivially, to the production of cognitive phenomena.

3.2. The Systems-Based View

3.2.1. In Outline

In their production of cognitive phenomena, such mechanisms as short-term memory, linguistic processing, and visual shape recognition are mutually integrated in a way that they are not integrated with the typical external resource. When one reads, the mechanisms that ground all three of these skills are active. When one listens to someone else talk, one draws on only the first two skills, unless listening partly involves processing the lip-movements of the speaker, in which case all three capacities are implicated. Typing involves all three skills, plus motor planning. All four are active when writing on the chalkboard. And so on. As I see things, then, a genuinely cognitive mechanism contributes to the production of a wide range of cognitive phenomena, across a variety of conditions; it contributes causally, as an element in shifting but heavily overlapping collections of various mechanisms of similar standing, to the production of cognitive phenomena. A given kind of cognitive performance may depend very heavily on a specific kind of external resource, say, a piece of chalk. Nevertheless, that resource may not be cognitive, precisely because it is not part of the integrated cognitive system: it does not contribute causally to the production of a wide range of cognitive phenomena, across a variety of conditions, working together in an overlapping way with a variety of other mechanisms of similar standing.

The cognitive status of individual states, then, derives from the relation between those states and the integrated, persisting cognitive system. Put as a principle of demarcation: a state is cognitive if and only if it consists in, or is realized by, the activation of one or more mechanisms that are elements of the integrated set members of which contribute causally and distinctively to the production of cognitive phenomena. What about processes? As discussed in the empirical literature (in contrast, say, to the writings of process philosophers), processes are causally connected series of states. A *process*, or a proper part of a process, is cognitive, then, if and only if all of its component states are cognitive (where this includes states that constitute the contribution of architecturally basic operations—Pylyshyn [1984]).

Computation, the flow of information, dynamical sub-systems—the various raw materials of cognitive scientific explanation—permeate the universe. The integrated cognitive architecture and its properties provide for the clearest and most plausible distinction between, on the one hand, cognition as a natural kind and, on the other hand, pandemic, only sometimes cognition-related computation, information-flow, and dynamical interaction.

3.2.2. A Technical Elaboration

I propose to sharpen the idea of integration by deploying somewhat technical machinery. Readers who prefer not to wade through technicalities can skip to the next subsection without losing hold of the argument's main thread. Bear in mind, though, that the present subsection offers the most detailed interpretation of talk about integration.

Consider, then, a more precise characterization of what it is for a set of resources to be integrated. Each token instance of cognitive behavior (alternatively, each act of completing a cognitive task) in a given subject involves the causal contribution of certain mechanisms, abilities, or capacities,[2] factors that make a causal contribution distinctively to the production of the cognitive *explananda* in question. Thus, for a given subject at a given time, there exists a set of mechanisms, capacities, external resources, etc. each of which has contributed distinctively to that subject's cognitive processing on at least one occasion. For each such type of mechanism, relative to each kind of cognitive phenomenon that it helps to produce, there is a conditional probability (determined by relative frequency, if by nothing else) of its use relative to each of the other mechanisms, abilities, etc. in the set, as well as a conditional probability of its use relative to each subset thereof. These conditional probabilities can be rank ordered. Assume that mechanisms A, B, and C have contributed distinctively to cognitive processing in the subject in question at least once

2. It is a difficult problem to individuate kinds of mechanism, ability, capacity, etc. This is a general problem, faced by all parties to the debate. Note that the extended view may be advanced by a coarse individuation of kinds of external resource, thus allowing any given kind of external resource to contribute to a wider range of cognitive results. Doing so, however, compromises many arguments used to support the extended view: those that cite human dependence on the fine-grained physical characteristics of the cognition-supporting environment.

(but not necessarily to the same token process). Now assume that, given the history of the co-contribution of A, B, and C, $P(C \mid A\&B) = 0.7$; then the set {A, B, C} goes on the list as a 0.7 (relative to some particular kind of cognitive outcome) and will likely come in ahead of many other sets (for a particular subject at a particular time). The same set might also appear at a different place in the ordering because, for instance, $P(A \mid B\&C)$ does not equal 0.7 relative to the same kind of cognitive outcome. Moreover, given the variety of kinds of cognitive outcome, the same sets appear on the list many more times, most likely with many different associated probabilities. Next, consider the likelihood of a natural cutoff between the higher probabilities and lower ones, a gap that separates highly co-contributing mechanisms from those that are less so. (In the absence of a significant gap in the ordering, 0.5 would seem to mark the relevant cutoff point.) Now count the number of times each type of mechanism appears on the list of sets with higher conditional probabilities (i.e., those sets above the significant gap on the list); these frequencies themselves exhibit a rank ordering, and a natural cutoff (another significant gap) separates those mechanisms that appear frequently on the list—that is, are highly interdependent and heavily co-employed—from those that appear rarely. This indicates which mechanisms are part of the integrated set to be identified with the cognitive system and which are, in contrast, resources used by the cognitive system.

One further condition is needed in order to effect a perceptual (or input-level) screening-off: if a resource or mechanism causally affects only one or a very small number of other mechanisms, and achieves a high integration score simply on account of that effect, then the resource or mechanism is struck from the list of integrated elements. The sun contributes to a wide range of cognitive outcomes, but does so only by stimulating retinal cells, and so the perceptual screening-off condition excludes the sun from the integrated cognitive system. Presumably, the proponent of the extended view does not—no matter how enlarged the cognitive system is—wish to do away with distinctively perceptual mechanisms, that is, mechanisms that contribute to cognitive processing via their sensitivity to proprietary signals (considered physically) from the environment. Thus, I think it is fair to include this condition.

A mechanism's measuring up in the way I have described may not constitute its status as part of an integrated cognitive system. Nevertheless, so long as a subject has a fair amount of experience in the world, this measure is, I submit, highly correlated with, and thus at least diagnostic of, integration.

3.2.3. *The Virtues of the Systems-Based View*

The systems-based principle of demarcation has a number of virtues. Most importantly, it (1) accounts for successful practice in cognitive psychology, (2) does so in a way that respects and can explain the data that impress proponents of extended cognition, and (3) satisfies the desiderata for a principle of demarcation. With regard to (3), the systems-based proposal recognizes all of the standard categories of entities causally participating in cognition, without unnecessary relabeling (Desideratum One). Additionally, it distinguishes in a natural way between cognitive and noncognitive systems, states, and processes, without introducing extraneous entities into the cognitive scientific ontology (Desideratum Two). Furthermore, given that the systems-based principle is not particularly revisionary, it need not demonstrate any special payoff for the cost of its adoption. It is consistent with, in fact it explains, an approach already entrenched on the basis of its empirical success; and this success justifies whatever revisionary implications the systems-based view might have.

Notice, too, that the systems-based principle delivers sensible verdicts when applied to our illustrative cases: it naturally accounts for the noncognitive status of ancient Greek columns, the sun, and the tree seen; they are not components of any integrated cognitive system.

Moreover, the systems-based view allows, as it should, for developmental variation in a given subject's cognitive system. It also allows for variation among cognitive systems from one subject to the next and, on a larger scale, from typical members of one culture or society to typical members of another.

In addition, the systems-based view supports the general conception of intelligent behavior that motivates cognitive-scientific inquiry. A central trait of intelligent behavior is its flexibility. The systems-based view nicely captures the distinction between flexibly deployed cognitive mechanisms and the dedicated, and apparently unintelligent, nature of mere tools, reflexes, and canned responses. Given their status as special-purpose mechanisms, the latter typically are not part of the integrated cognitive system; they do not contribute to the production of a wide range of cognitive phenomena, across a variety of conditions, appearing as causally relevant elements in various overlapping collections of mechanisms of similar standing.

3.3. Two Arguments against the Extended View

How does the systems-based principle bear on the primary issue at hand, that is, the status of the extended approach in cognitive science? For reasons given above, I suspect that external resources do not constitute part of the typical human's cognitive system, for they are not effectively integrated into the human cognitive system. In terms of my technical diagnostic, these external resources either fail to appear in sets determined by higher conditional probabilities or, if they do appear, they fail to appear in very many of these, their being dedicated to the solution of specific problems. If this is correct, the typical human's integrated cognitive architecture is instantiated internally and the study of extended cognition constitutes no revolution in cognitive science. Nevertheless, this conclusion is not given a priori; neither is it based on a fetish for the bodily boundary, contrary to suggestions made by Clark (2007). It is the result of an attempt to make sense of existing cognitive-scientific success and to thereby locate an empirically respectable principle of demarcation.

On one way of reading the situation, then, my brief against the extended view might end with the following argument:

ARGUMENT FROM DEMARCATION

Premise 1.   The systems-based principle of demarcation provides the only plausible criterion of demarcation in the field.
Premise 2.   The systems-based principle places human cognition inside the organism, either entirely or in the main.
Conclusion. Therefore, we should, provisionally, reject the extended view.

I take this argument to be very strong, and versions of it reappear throughout parts I and II. Chapter 1 surveys the most prominent pro-extension principles of demarcation in the literature, finding them all deficient. Nevertheless, readers sympathetic to the extended view will almost certainly think the Argument from Demarcation goes too quickly; perhaps the extended revolution will, and should, occur, even in the absence of any deep principle of demarcation. Thus, it is worth developing a second argument that focuses more, or at least more explicitly, on empirical methodology. (I am not abandoning discussion of demarcation; both arguments are important.)

Of central importance is the ability of the systems-based approach to accommodate the insights of the situated research program; systems of interrelated capacities manage the subtle interaction with the environment and the use of environmental structures to achieve cognitive goals. An integrated cognitive system of the right sort can support a variety of forms of interactive cognitive processing; the system might exploit tools, environmental signs, and input from other people, and it might employ various heuristics the utility of which depends on environmental regularities. Accordingly, I think the systems-cum-nonextended view offers what proponents of extended cognition want: a principled motivation for the investigation of highly interactive, time-dependent cognitive processing, as well as a theoretical framework within which to makes sense of that research.

In contrast, consider how badly at least one kind of extended view—one that appeals to a causal principle of demarcation—handles the success of the various research programs in question. Advocates for the extended view often emphasize the short-lived nature of extended cognitive systems: they are created on the fly, they are soft-assembled (Wilson and Clark 2009), or they involve the organism's perceptual interaction with an object (Noë 2004). Such extended systems are too short-lived (Wilson 2002), however, to account for the kind of successful research reviewed above. There are virtually no external resources that subjects consistently use across conditions in the relevant experimental paradigms. Thus, an extended-cum-causal view makes little sense of the standard practice of tracking the behavior of individual organisms, or kinds thereof, across time, in a variety of different settings; for the extended-cum-causal view implies that different cognitive systems come into existence each time the external resources change.

Here we have the makings of an argument against the extended view, an argument to be reinforced in the sections to come, and given a more complete formulation at the beginning of chapter 4:

ARGUMENT FROM EMPIRICAL SUCCESS AND METHODOLOGY

Premise 1.   The systems-based view accounts naturally for the success of many research programs in cognitive psychology.

Premise 2.   The systems-based view also accounts naturally for the data that impress the proponents of the extended view.

Premise 3.   Approaches that yield the extended view either accomplish only the second goal or fall to criticisms having to do with conservatism, simplicity, and explanatory power.

Conclusion.   Thus, we should accept the systems-based view—and the not particularly extended outlook it contingently supports—and reject the extended view.

Many chapters' work will be needed to support the argument's premises. By stating the argument here, if only in a preliminary form, I hope better to shape and motivate the remainder of this chapter and to set the stage for much of the later discussion. Despite the argument's sketchiness, the primary challenge should be clear: The proponent of the extended view must make sense of the standard methodology on which many successful research programs have been based, and she must do so in a way that offers something useful to cognitive science—not mere relabeling or the superfluous construction of extraneous systems.

Notice the extent to which the two arguments survive variation in the precise description of organismically bounded cognitive systems. We know it is fruitful to treat the organism as containing some kind of persisting cognitive system. The more detailed our account of this system, the more convincing may be the resulting principle of demarcation; nevertheless, the principle of demarcation can be couched in somewhat less definite terms than those spelled out above: a state is cognitive if and only if it is a state of whatever makes up the organismically bounded system presupposed by the sorts of successful research programs reviewed above. Similar remarks apply to the Argument from Empirical Success and Methodology. We could replace all talk of the systems-based view, and with it the details concerning integrated capacities and their underlying mechanisms (and the conditional probabilities of their being co-active), and preserve the gist of the argument. In both cases, such replacement yields a less illuminating result. Nevertheless, substantial arguments against the extended view remain.

3.4. Extension-Friendly Rejoinders

3.4.1. *Organism-Centered Cognition*

The proponent of the extended view might account for the success of mainstream psychological research by focusing on the organism. Organisms make an important contribution to the construction of various short-lived cognitive systems, many of which are extended. Thus, it is natural to study the persisting organism, and it is no surprise that such study produces solid results, given the consistent way in which the organism contributes to the creation of relatively short-lived cognitive systems. (This rejoinder is inspired by Clark's endorsement [2007, 192] of what he labels 'HOC', short for 'the hypothesis of organismically centered cognition'.)

This organism-centered view forfeits the distinctive vision of the extended approach. What is the enduring structure that possesses cognitive capacities that develop over time and explain various forms of behavior? The organism, and it now holds a fundamentally privileged position, at least relative to the research in question. Other bits can be included in what we call cognitive systems, but only because of these bits' causal interaction with the organismic systems—that is, only because the organism, via its cognitive capacities, recruits various materials for use in the production of cognitive phenomena. One might insist on an extended gloss of the situation, but the vision offered is much more in the spirit of an embedded view (cf. Rupert [2004]): the organism is the seat of cognition and locus of control (Butler 1998, 180–81, 212; Wilson 2004, 197–98).

Consider, too, how recruitment is supposed to occur. Organismic mechanisms interact with the environment and, as a result, change states in such a way as to create extended cognitive systems. Yet, in a host of cases that clearly do not involve extended cognition—even, I would guess, by the lights of proponents of the extended view—human organisms rely on many of the same mechanisms (e.g., those involved in perception of far distant objects). Such cases include the experimental paradigms used in connection with the successful orthodox research programs. Absent a convincing principle of demarcation that assigns cognitive status to the recruitment process but not the garden-variety exercise of internal mechanisms, the embedded view wins out, by the following argument. The garden-variety processes do not extend cognition; the advocate for the extended view has no principled basis for distinguishing them in kind from those involved in the recruitment process; therefore, the recruitment processes do not extend cognition.

The theoretical virtues also cut against the organism-centered-yet-extended view. The discussion of traditional research programs in cognitive psychology establishes the utility of some kind of organismic cognitive system. Much of the interesting work in cognitive science explores and should explore further the ways in which that persisting organismic system interacts with the extraorganismic factors during garden-variety as well as (allegedly) extension-creating interactions with the environment. To call some of the external factors 'cognitive' seems to be an exercise in relabeling. Both sides in the debate are committed to the existence of organisms with a distinctive role. Both sides must explain how the organism's cognitive states interact with external materials to produce cognitive phenomena. The organism-centered-yet-extended view adds the label 'cognitive' to some of the external materials, to no apparent end. (Or, depending on how the extended view is articulated, it might add otiose systems, the supposedly extended ones.)

3.4.2. Abstract Properties and Extended Systems

The Argument from Empirical Success and Methodology depends on the claim that the extended view does not give a natural and independently motivated account of the success of organism-centered cognitive psychology. In response, the defender of extended cognition might downplay variations in materials across experimental contexts. She might argue that an extended system persists across experimental contexts because the external materials, even though they vary tremendously, instantiate the same abstract properties. For example, in the case of the false-belief task, a variety of experimental materials—involving puppets, story-boards, etc.—instantiate such abstract properties as *believing the chocolate is in the drawer* and *wanting to deceive his brother*. Thus, there is no purely internal package of cognitive resources that persists in the subject and is of special causal-explanatory importance; rather, certain externally instantiated, abstract properties remain constant across contexts and are part of the privileged collection of cognitive resources.

Proponents of the extended view should be unhappy with this tack, for at least two reasons. First, consider a contrast. In the case of organismically located capacities, there is a persisting basis—the brain, perhaps—for the continued presence of the system's capacity. In the case of the proposed extended systems, however, there is no such basis of persistence. The various external materials might, on various occasions, instantiate the same abstract properties, but these various property-instantiations have no shared physical basis. The puppet show does not share any persisting physical basis with the story read, so the various instantiations of the abstract property *deception* do not appear to be part of a single persisting resource or system.

Second, and more importantly, this defense of the extended approach runs strongly counter to most extant arguments in support of extended cognition;

those arguments emphasize the specific material contexts of cognition: the specific form of the external resources and of the physical body, and the way those physical forms interact (e.g., Clark [2006a, 2006b]). If the defender of the extended view appeals to abstract properties instantiated by various stories, puppet shows, etc., she shifts our attention away from the specific material conditions of cognitive processing—and how they contribute causally to the production of cognitive behavior—and in doing so, she raises difficult questions concerning the organism's ability to track such abstract properties.

One obvious proposal holds that the organism becomes sensitive to these abstract properties by representing them; this, however, invites standard internalist, or at least an embedded, explanation of the processing involved. If representations of the abstract properties appear in the cognitive system, it is gratuitous to count the properties themselves or their environmental instantiations as part of the cognitive system. Worse still for the rejoinder under consideration is the way in which the representations detach from the actual property-instantiations in the environment. In many of the experimental contexts, the abstract property on which the subject's behavior is premised (say, the presence of deception in a story) is not actually instantiated. The materials used merely cause the subject to represent the situation as involving deception (paper cutouts cannot literally deceive anyone). Furthermore, experimental contexts aside, it is common place that humans have and act on false beliefs in everyday life. In many such cases, the properties falsely represented as instantiated in the environment—the ones that, according to the present rejoinder, act as part of the extended package of cognitive resources—do not appear at all!

3.4.3. Growing and Shrinking Systems

Perhaps persisting cognitive systems can grow and shrink; in which case, traditional research in cognitive psychology might investigate persisting systems that are not limited by the boundary of the organism. On this view, the persisting cognitive system grows to encompass environmental items under certain circumstances; then, upon detachment from that environmental item, the cognitive system shrinks back to organismic size (or smaller). Lots of experimental work can now be interpreted as an attempt to see in what ways and under what conditions the human cognitive system grows and shrinks. Insofar as some successful research does investigate an organismically bounded system, it is one that expands and contracts under other conditions; the system may remain organismically bounded when participating in false-belief experiments, for example, but nevertheless expands when, say, solving math problems using pencil and paper.

The growing-and-shrinking rejoinder is no stronger than the two others already discussed. The individuation of such cognitive systems rests on the continuity of the organism. Furthermore, growing and shrinking occurs only when certain kinds of cognitively interesting interaction with the world take place. The standard approach accounts for these cases by describing causal interaction between the organism and its environment, interaction that proceeds in the way it does largely in virtue of the organismically instantiated cognitive capacities. Thus, there is a simpler and more conservative explanation of the cognitive phenomena available in these cases.

Consider also the learning that occurs during the organism's interaction with the environment. The system that learns algebra, partly by listening to a lecture, later works out particular problems with pen and paper. The most plausible explanation of such learning adverts to effects of the interaction *on the organism*. In most cases, this seems the only explanatory option; for in most real-life cases, only the organism persists as the material in which interaction can leave its causal stamp. Thus, both the organismically bounded view and the growing-and-shrinking view tell essentially the same organismically centered story about interaction and its cognitive role and about the cognitive properties of the organism changed during learning; such a story also explains changes over time in the pattern of organism's interactions with the world, that is, changes in the patterns of alleged growing and shrinking. In sum, the growing-and-shrinking hypothesis handles the data only by the trivializing strategy of recreating the form of standard explanations within its own framework, at no apparent gain, thus violating simplicity and conservatism. To make matters worse, the growing-and-shrinking strategy rests on no plausible principle of demarcation.

3.5. The No-Self View

3.5.1. Cognitive Systems without Robust Selves

This section considers a direct criticism of my positive, systems-based view. If the systems-based picture can be undercut, then my two arguments against the extended view collapse. The charge is that my systems-based view reifies the subject, mind, or self in an objectionable way,[3] a concern that I shall now develop in more detail.

On one view of cognition, associated with the work of Daniel Dennett (1991), cognition does not take place in some privileged entity or location. There is no distinct thing, the Central Meaner, that confers meaning on states, rendering them cognitive. Neither does a state become cognitive by taking the stage on the Cartesian Theatre (a place in the brain or nonphysical mind where a subject's mental activity all comes together). Instead, cognition is merely the instantiation of a variety of cognitively relevant properties, occurring in various locations, causally interacting to produce the behavior we identify as intelligent.

---

3. David Chalmers raised this objection; see also Clark (2007, 191).

The items instantiating cognitively relevant properties are not limited a priori; they could range from bits of neural cortex to inscriptions on paper.

Return to the case of Otto and his notebook. Regarding any particular inscription, the notebook instantiates certain information-related properties, while parts of the organism instantiate various other cognitively relevant properties: the latter might be properties of parts of the visual system or the limbic system. These various events or property-instantiations causally interact to produce the notebook user's intelligent behavior. In Clark and Chalmers's example, Otto and his notebook head off to the Museum of Modern Art. We might *talk* of persisting persons, selves, or systems, but from the standpoint of cognitive science, it is convenient talk only. Really, there is only a distribution of various instantiations of cognitive properties, pertaining, for example, to computation and representation, which together account for the behavior cognitive scientists would like to explain. This general view—call it the 'no-self' view—is true to much of the data, and it might be the only way to avoid commitment to a Central Meaner, a Cartesian theatre, or a nonphysical self-substance (Dennett 1991; Clark 2003, 136). If, in contrast, the systems-based view entails the existence of a Central Meaner, a spooky nonphysical substance, or a Cartesian Theatre, the systems-based view is false, for no such things exist.

In the present context, the no-self view is something of a red herring. My discussion of systems in no way appeals to, or entails, the existence of a mysterious self-substance or a single place in the brain (or mind) where all cognition comes together. Contra Clark's recent claim, my arguments do not presuppose that external resources do "their work only by parading structure and information in front of some thoughtful neural overseer" (2007, 191). Instead, I hold that the persisting cognitive subject is a theoretical construct, a hypothesized set of relatively stable cognitive capacities, states, or abilities (or their underlying mechanisms). This sort of thing is rooted in the idea of a cognitive architecture (Pylyshyn 1984; Anderson 2007): the set of primitive representations and operations that function together to produce what we take to be intelligent behavior. This is not to say that the systems-based view *precludes* an architecture with a strong central executive; the systems-based view can accommodate such a picture. My point is simply that the systems-based view makes no very specific commitment to the architecture's control structure; control within an integrated system could be highly distributed, or it could be centralized.

I suspect that my use of 'subjects' has misled some interpreters. When I use the term in connection with psychological research and persisting systems, I have in mind the dry language of methodology sections ("there were fifty seven subjects, all undergraduates enrolled in Introduction to Psychology"); in this context, 'subject' means little more than "warm body that can be reidentified over time." To many readers, however, the language of 'subjects' is likely to suggest a more philosophical notion: the subject as the seat of phenomenal consciousness or as the root of subjectivity. This more philosophical conception in turn brings to mind the illusion of a Central Meaner or Cartesian theatre. This is a mere misunderstanding, though, easily set straight. According to the systems-based view, a cognitive system is an explanatory construct: a collection of mechanisms (or capacities rooted in those mechanisms) the coordinated operation of which plays a distinctive role in accounting for cognitive phenomena. Nothing about this conception of a cognitive system entails a single perspective in the mind's eye or a magical source of meaning or anything of the like (nor, by the way, any special unity or determinacy of conscious experience).

3.5.2. The No-Self View and Arguments against the Extended Approach

The preceding should suffice as a defense of the systems-based view. Nevertheless, the suspicion may remain that the no-self view is somehow superior to the systems-based view, and furthermore that the no-self view supports the extended approach. In this section, I argue that, to the contrary, the commitments of a plausible no-self view dovetail nicely with my two primary arguments against the extended approach.

On the no-self view, cognitive-scientific explanation appeals only to the distributed instantiation of cognitive properties: information, computation, dynamical flow, activation patterns, and the like. These quantities appear far and wide, however, throughout the universe. Thus, a plausible no-self view must endorse a principle of demarcation, one that differentiates between, for example, the ubiquitous flow of information and dynamical evolution and, in contrast, processes that are genuinely cognitive.

Think the challenge in this way. Assume for the sake of argument that, at least in certain circumstances, the human cognitive system includes external resources—when solving a math problem using pencil and paper, for example. The problem-solving process might also include such causal contributors as a teacher's act of writing down a problem to be solved or a broker's voice coming over the phone—causal influences that pose the problem and may provide updated information as the cognitive system is working on it. These extra-systemic causal influences certainly instantiate some cognitively relevant properties: information transmission, computational processing, and dynamical flow. Yet, they are not part of problem-solver's cognitive system. Thus, the advocate for extended cognition needs a principle of demarcation. (Here I could just as easily have appealed to the cases discussed in chapter 2, especially One through Three; I want to make the no-self view's need for a principle of demarcation especially pointed: even if we provisionally accept an extended view of cognitive systems, the need for a principle of demarcation remains; and the systems-based view can meet this need, without contravening the no-self approach.)

What principle of demarcation might appeal to the fans of the no-self view? One likely candidate rests on the connectionist view of the human cognitive architecture (e.g., Dennett and Clark should be relatively friendly to this approach). A connectionist network runs through cycles of activation that produce intelligent behavior in a self-organized manner; such behavior emerges from competition between nodes that stimulate and inhibit each other in keeping with their pattern of connectivity, connection strengths, and so on (Rumelhart, McClelland, and the PDP Research Group 1986). Connectionist models of human cognition might be thought to ground the no-self view: in a connectionist network, there would seem to be no single self, no agent making decisions or controlling the transformation of activation vectors. Nevertheless, there is a clear distinction between the causal role of the connectionist network and the causal role of materials that are outside the connectionist network but that contribute causally to cognitive outcomes. The obvious way to demarcate cognition, then, is a version of the systems-based view: A process is cognitive if and only if it is the activity of part of the persisting connectionist network (the subject's cognitive architecture). Given the relative lack of extrabodily connectionist networks, as well as the lack of such networks integrated with neurally realized ones, this connectionist-inspired, no-self view supports the anti-extended conclusion of the Argument from Demarcation.

To claim that just any instance of information-carrying, computation, or dynamical flow constitutes a cognitive state or process trivializes the extended view. Doing so renders the extended view an exercise in relabeling of just the sort rejected in connection with the causal principle and the others considered in chapter 2. The extension-friendly proponent of the no-self view might have some further principle of demarcation in mind, but it is incumbent on her to present and argue for it.

Think now about empirical success. Regardless of which specific approach to cognitive modeling (and which kind of accompanying architecture) is embraced by the proponent of the no-self view, she must account for the successes of cognitive psychology and neuroscience—in connection with the study of language acquisition, theory of mind, perception, the understanding of narratives, visual neglect, etc. Many of these capacities have been fruitfully investigated, in ways that reveal robust effects, using methodology that presupposes the persistence of a relatively stable set of integrated cognitive capacities, abilities, and mechanisms. What is more, these processes have been investigated—both in relative isolation and in their more integrated operation—in ways that presuppose persisting properties of these mechanisms that operate across circumstances. Such investigation shows at least that, in some significant range of cases, a collection of capacities or mechanisms operates according to consistent principles that determine a behavioral outcome given an environmental circumstance. This work reveals important properties of the capacities or mechanisms involved, properties that govern subjects' responses. If the external materials involved were literally part of the cognitive system being investigated, one would expect instead a hash of results—given that different organismically bounded subjects interact with widely differing external materials across experimental contexts.

Laudably, the no-self view eliminates metaphysical excess: Central Meaners and the like. Nevertheless, the no-self view must account for this empirical success. The systems-based criterion, and the research programs consistent with it, offers to the no-self view a straightforward and nontrivial way to do so. Certain types of property-instances reappear in varying circumstances and work together according to consistent principles of interaction; and this explains regularities in the data. Furthermore, the persisting nature of physical bodies explains the reappearance, on token occasions, of similar clusters of types of property-instances. The integrated set of physical mechanisms underlying such continued reappearance constitutes a persisting instance of the human cognitive architecture. The activities of this integrated set explain the interaction with the environment in the standard experimental setups, as well as in the cases that are thought to extend cognition into the environment. On this approach, then, the Argument from Empirical Success and Methodology holds up.

To reinforce my point, consider learning. When I have an experience, it affects one cluster of reappearing instances of property-types (having to do with the flow of information or activation vectors or whatnot). In the standard case, this experience does not affect the patterns of reappearing property-instances produced by the workings of anyone else's body. One need not invoke a Central Meaner, Cartesian theater, or anything of the sort in order to account for such learning; but one must recognize a privileged cluster of types of property-instances that appear in connection with one continuing physical body, and this suffices to ground the Argument from Empirical Success and Methodology. A radical no-self view, according to which cognitivist explanation appeals to nothing more than token instances of cognition-related properties, might seem to account well enough for the production of token instances of cognitive behavior; but it cannot explain larger patterns in the data (e.g., learning).

Consider now a more general reformulation of a principle of demarcation friendly to the no-self view, a formulation not tied specifically to connectionist architectures. For a property-instance to be cognitive is for it to appear as part of an integrated cluster of co-instantiated properties that contribute distinctively and nontrivially to the production of cognitive phenomena. (Alternatively, for a property-instance to be cognitive is for it to be a state of a mechanism that constitutes a component of a persisting cognitive architecture.) What is it for a cluster of co-present property-instances to be integrated? It is for each of them to be instances of properties that, as types, make up a set to which causal-explanatory appeal is made when accounting for standard results and the instantiations of which appear together as the result of the workings of an integrated physical system. This does not beg the question against the extended view; for, at least in principle, it could turn out (or, perhaps more to the point, could have turned out) that experimental methodology produces a wide range of robust results only when the integrated physical system in question includes elements beyond the boundary of the human body.

3.5.3. Rejoinder and Response

In response, a proponent of the no-self view might claim that, as regards some robust forms of behavior, external cognitively relevant property-instantiations remain constant across circumstances. Thus, the external property-instantiations do occur consistently across experimental contexts. Therefore, these property-instantiations explain behavior in a way much like the internally instantiated properties do and should be considered part of the privileged collection.

Take the case of the false-belief task. The various stimuli used instantiate a common cognitively relevant property: the characters depicted or described all have false beliefs. So, perhaps if we were to focus on sufficiently abstract externally instantiated properties, we might find that these appear consistently and work together with internal properties in a consistent way. Thus, such external properties may be part of the consistently appearing suite of kinds of cognitively relevant properties responsible for the same kind of behavior across a wide range of cases, and thus part of the integrated cognitive system; these property-instantiations appear in specific contexts as part of the integrated, explanatorily privileged set of causal sources of behavior.

As a defense of extended cognition this rejoinder comes up short, for many of the reasons discussed in preceding sections. Consider the abstract nature of the externally instantiated properties at issue. Many of the examples that inspire the extended view involve a causal interleaving of fine-grained physical properties of the body and the environment (Clark 2006a, 2006b). This motivates the idea that the body becomes coupled to an environmental resource so as to form a single system causally responsible for the behavior of interest. In contrast, we are searching for the overarching explanation of the similarity in behavior across contexts where the external materials differ (in terms of their concrete properties). In these cases, it would be misguided to emphasize the fine details of the physical dovetailing between body and environment. The concrete physical properties vary greatly from case to case (from puppets to stories to cutouts to live people, in the case of false-belief task); thus, it is implausible that the similarity of behavior results from a similarity in the way in which the environment and the body become coupled, interwoven, or anything of that sort.

If the externally instantiated property supposed to become part of a cognitive system is highly abstract—say, the property of having a false belief—how does it make a consistent contribution to cognitive behavior? The standard story invokes mental representations. A plethora of concrete externally instantiated properties can, in various combinations, cause the tokening of the same internal mental representation (as, one might say, indicators of the external instantiation of that abstract property); the internally instantiated representation then controls behavior, for example, the subject's response that another person will look in the cupboard for his chocolate, even though the subject knows the chocolate is not there.

This undercuts the rejoinder under consideration. First, the representation-based account places the causally responsible, cognitively relevant property-instantiation within the organism: the mental representation we identify in terms of its content (e.g., as a representation of someone else's having a false belief). Compare this to the kind of case in which behavior emerges from an interleaving of concrete physical properties of the body and of the environment. In that kind of case, it is clear why the advocate for the extended view takes the external resource to make a direct and significant contribution to the causal production of the behavior. In the cases of interest, though, there appears to be no mechanism, other than the internal representation of the abstract externally instantiated property, by which that external property-instantiation can produce the behavior. In which case, the contribution of the external instantiation of the abstract property does not seem directly responsible for the behavior to be explained. There is no fine-grained meshing of body and world responsible for behavior, but rather a much more orthodox process of the body (including the brain, of course) representing the world and acting on the basis of that representation.

Second, and to reinforce the preceding point, consider the extent to which even *abstract* externally instantiated properties vary from case to case—particularly the variation in their presence or absence. In the case of the false-belief task, the common internal factor is a representation of a property that in many cases is not actually present in the environment. The subject represents that another person has a false belief, even though no appropriate person is present; instead, the representation is directed at a puppet, paper cutout, or picture. This seems fatal to the extended theorist's proposal. That proposal holds that, with respect to a given robust form of behavioral result, an externally instantiated property can count as part of the explanatorily privileged package of causally responsible, cognitively relevant property-instantiations—that is, it can count as part of the cognitive system—because its instantiations consistently contribute to the causal production of the behavior in question (and in doing so, cooperate in a principled way with internal, cognitively relevant property-instantiations). If, however, the abstract property is sometimes there in the external environment and sometimes not there, then it is simply false that this abstract property makes the kind of consistent contribution at issue.

This might seem like an artifact of the example being used, but the point is fairly general. Behavior is frequently caused by internal states, the behavior-controlling power of which is indifferent to whether the thing represented is actually present. If I token my representation *tiger-here-now* in just the way I would in the presence of a genuine tiger, even though in fact there is no tiger present, I will run just as fast as if there were a tiger present. (Do not think the antecedent describes a metaphysical impossibility: in the jungle at night, given the power of suggestion, I might run like mad were I to hear the wrong kind of rustling, which could be caused by a pig or another human; and I might do so precisely because I believe *tiger-here-now*.) If the internal representational state is responsible for behavior in the case when the external property of interest is not instantiated, then why think the external property contributes in a privileged way when it is present? The story that unifies cases most fully appeals to *internal* representational states across the board, and treats the externally instantiated property as a system-external causal factor even when it is present; as do many other things, it causally impinges on the cognitive system without becoming part of the explanatorily privileged package of cognitively relevant properties.

This discussion may bring to the reader's mind an important objection to the extended view: that externally instantiated properties are not genuinely representational (Segal 1997; Butler 1998; Adams and Aizawa 2001), whereas internal states are. This point does not alone refute the extended view, but it does create an embarrassment for it. The extended view would be much more compelling if it were supported by a theory of representation that allows the extended structures of interest genuinely to represent; after all, representing does seem to be a central feature of cognitive and mental states. The no-self view faces a special problem in trying to build a theory of representation without an integrated system. Consider, in contrast, what may be the most highly regarded naturalistic theory of representation, Fred Dretske's (1981, 1988). On Dretske's theory, full-blooded representations are likely to appear only within an integrated, persisting system.

Lastly, consider a more sweeping concern. Setting aside issues about representation, externally instantiated properties simply are not integrated with the various parts of the internally instantiated system in the way that those internal mechanisms are integrated with each other. With regard to some particular form of robust behavior, take the set of causally important, internally instantiated, and cognitively relevant properties. Token instantiations of these properties operate in overlapping subsets as well as in tandem with other kinds of internally instantiated properties to produce kinds of behavior other than the one at issue. To a great extent this is in what their integration consists. An abstract externally instantiated property of, for example, holding a false belief is not explanatorily implicated via membership in the same sort of integrated set. For these four reasons, I conclude that the externally instantiated abstract property is not part of the explanatorily privileged package of property-instantiations, even if instantiations of that property frequently contribute to the production of behavior. (And if the instantiation of the external property *always* contributes, the first, third, and fourth concerns still apply.)

The advocate of the no-self view begins with the claim that cognition is nothing more than a fluid, ongoing interaction of instantiations of cognitively relevant properties, all on a par. In response, I have argued both that there are privileged collections of such property-instantiations and that they appear entirely in the organism. The present shift in focus to external instantiations of abstract properties has not helped. Even here, perhaps especially here, internally instantiated cognitively relevant properties and externally instantiated ones exhibit theoretically important asymmetries. Thus, when we draw a line between a theoretically important package of property-instantiations and others that merely contribute causally to cognition, the former does not include externally instantiated cognitively relevant properties.

It appears, then, that my arguments against the extended approach go through on any plausible version of the no-self view. Cognitive behavior is primarily the behavior of organisms, albeit organisms together with varying bits of their environments. As a terminological stipulation, let us say that persons track bodies: sameness of body is tantamount to sameness of person. Persons conceived of in this way exhibit regular kinds of behavior—regular ways of interacting with the environment—across a variety of changing conditions. The regularities may be a function of, supervene on, or emerge from the distribution of instantiations of cognitively relevant properties each of which is seated in something smaller than a human organism. Nevertheless, the dispositions themselves play important causal-explanatorily roles. (They also serve as explananda in cognitive science; in exploring the underlying mechanisms producing cognitive behavior, cognitive science hopes to explain why persons-as-organisms have the relatively stable dispositions they have; cf. Block and Fodor [1972, point (1)] on functionalism and dispositional states.)

What do we assert when we say that persons learn language most efficiently while experiencing high levels of motivation with frequent exposure to new words and constructions (Bloom 2000)? Is this way of talking no more than shorthand for a long list of specific causal stories, or are we attributing a property to cognitive systems as wholes, perhaps a structural property or a property pertaining to the way the parts tend to interact? As noted above, many results in various areas of cognitive psychology and neuroscience of humans are robust. We can explain this robustness by positing cognitive capacities of the organismic system, even if construed only as properties of the interconnected structure of cognitive mechanisms. Doing so has been fruitful in many cases, giving rise to successful and diverse research programs. These claims, apparently about the dispositions of entire cognitive systems, should be taken at face value, at least until the advocate of the extended view produces a reduction of such explanatory claims to collections of claims about specific instantiations of cognitive properties. Doing so would be a heroic feat, however, given the history of failed attempts at reducing dispositions and their ilk to lists of effects (Swinburne 1980, 317–18; Martin 1997, 214–15). Better to set aside such attempts at reduction and, instead, to take the integrated cognitive system to be the distinctive theoretical construct of cognitive science.

4

Realization and Extended Cognition

4.1. The Argument from Empirical Success and Methodology, Restated

Chapter 3 argues for a systems-based principle of demarcation. It also argues against the extended view, by both the Argument from Demarcation and the Argument from Empirical Success and Methodology. The latter argument takes a certain pride of place, for it ties together much of the material from chapter 3, while motivating and giving shape to the remainder of part I and part II. Here, then, is a more detailed formulation of the argument:

ARGUMENT FROM EMPIRICAL SUCCESS AND METHODOLOGY, REDUX

Premise 1. A significant amount of successful research in cognitive psychology (and allied fields) presupposes the existence of human cognitive systems of temporal grain δt.

Premise 2. A causal principle of systems individuation yields systems of temporal grain smaller than δt.

Premise 3. Individuating cognitive systems such that their grain is smaller than δt compromises the research successes referred to in *Premise 1*.

Premise 4. The extended approach offers no distinctive and powerful results that outweigh the losses referred to in *Premise 3* (this claim rests on the availability of the systems-based view and will be more fully substantiated by part II's arguments that the systems-based view accommodates points made in support of the extended research program).

Premise 5.   Thus, the causal principle's individuation of cognitive systems is unacceptable.

Premise 6.   There is no alternative way to individuate cognitive systems that (a) accounts for the success of traditional research programs in cognitive psychology, (b) entails the extended view, when taken together with empirical data, and (c) avoids the now familiar objections based on conservatism, simplicity, and explanatory power. (The last condition holds partly because the systems-based approach naturally explains the phenomena that impress proponents of the extended view; full defense of this claim must also wait on part II.)

Conclusion.   The extended approach to systems individuation should be rejected.

A few caveats are in order. First, I do not claim to have considered all possible ways to individuate cognitive systems; as a result, *Premise 6* might be false. Nevertheless, I have presented my arguments many times to proponents of the extended view, and section 3.4 addresses the substantive suggestions made in response.

Second, I have not shown that consideration only of cognitive-systems individuation matters to the evaluation of the extended view. A principle of demarcation might have no particular application to systems, yet might explain the privileged role of persisting organismic resources while also extending cognition into the environment. This is a possibility, but chapter 1 gives fair hearing to the most obvious extant candidates. In addition, part II critically surveys arguments in favor of the extended view, partly in an effort to identify further principles of demarcation that serve as implicit premises in arguments for the extended view. No promising candidate is found, however.

Third, note the role of the systems-based view in the larger dialectic. Some of my concerns about the extended view might seem to constitute mere puzzles, were it not for the availability of a well-motivated alternative. Given the strength of the systems-based principle of demarcation, though, my arguments against the extended approach should seem more damning than puzzling.

My recasting of the Argument from Empirical Success and Methodology plays an introductory role relative to this chapter's primary purpose; for at least one influential view (Wilson 2004) embraces the fundamental vision of the systems-based approach, while developing a meaningful sense in which human cognition nevertheless extends into the environment. Let us move now to an evaluation of that view.

4.2. Extended Cognition and Realization

Robert Wilson (1999, 2001, 2004) accepts that cognitive states are states of the organism (or some portion of it); organisms are the individuals that have cognitive states. Wilson appeals to the theory of realization, however, to argue that cognitive processing is extended all the same. The physical substrate of cognition extends into the environment, Wilson claims, and this suffices to establish the extended view.

In criticizing Wilson's realization-based argument for extended cognition, I generally ignore the question of demarcation; for I agree with Wilson's basic thought, that anything that realizes a cognitive state or process is itself cognitive, at least in the sense in which cognition is physically located. Rather, I take exception to Wilson's general view of realization and how he applies it.

What, then, is it for one thing to realize another? Let us take things slowly. Materialism holds that our universe is entirely material (or physical). The history of scientific success provides a solid basis for materialism (Papineau 2001). Treated with prayers and incantations, disease does not respond; the application of physical substances, medicines, does a much better job. Examples can be multiplied ad nauseum.

There is a catch, however. Even though all *things* in the universe appear to be physical, many properties cannot be understood in any straightforwardly physical way, especially if we limit ourselves to the resources of fundamental physics. Mental states present the most obvious challenge. What is the physical nature of one's belief that England is in the United Kingdom or one's desire that judges reason objectively? Problem-cases extend, though, throughout the full range of what are sometimes called the 'special sciences' (Fodor 1974), including economics, anthropology, and perhaps even biology.

Many philosophers have hoped to resolve this tension by identifying a systematic relation that holds between physical properties and the so-called higher-level ones (e.g., mental properties), a relation that somehow preserves the priority of the physical while allowing a distinctive existence to the properties and kinds investigated by the special sciences. To invoke this relation would be particularly attractive if its obtaining were to help explain how distinctively higher-level states and properties arise from, and are ultimately constrained or constituted by, their physical bases (cf. Horgan [1993]). Enter the idea that physical properties *realize* nonphysical ones. On this view, one state (or property—let this be understood) realizes another if the realized state, on a particular occasion of its occurrence, takes the physical form of the realizing state. Mental states, for instance, can appear in a wholly material universe because each token mental state (i.e., each particular state that some particular mind enters into) takes the form of some physical state or other—a state of the brain, for instance.

Consider how this might bear on the extended view. Some proponents of extended cognition, Robert Wilson (2001, 2004), most prominently, appeal to the notion of realization to explain in what sense the extended view is true (see also Clark [2005, 3]). On Wilson's view, even if cognitive states are states of organismically bounded systems or individuals, or portions thereof, whatever realizes those states is cognitive; and since the realizers of cognitive states extend into the environment, cognition thus extends into the environment.[1] I discuss this view in greater detail below. Note first, though, that the standard examples of realized states place realizers firmly within the boundaries of the objects that are in the realized states.

Take the example of a mousetrap. There are many ways to catch a mouse, many different physical mechanisms that suffice. The property of being a mousetrap cannot literally be identical to any of the complex physical properties that constitute a specific form of mousetrap; else, by the logic of identity, two physically distinct forms would be identical to each other, which is absurd.[2] Nevertheless, in any given case, the compound physical state or property that realizes *being a mousetrap* does not extend beyond the boundary of the mousetrap. How could a mousetrap be realized by something at different location— even if only a partly different location—from the mousetrap itself? There is a deep metaphysical mystery involved in locating a state in one place and its realizer somewhere else, particularly when the realizer is meant to do the causal work of the property realized.

Faced with this mystery about realization, the proponent of the extended view might try a slightly different approach, which may merit a brief digression. Consider the possibility that a state's location and the location of the subject of that state can come apart, the former extending beyond the latter. If this were the case, it would be no mystery how the realizer could extend beyond the boundary of the subject and do the causal work of the state; for on this proposal, the cognitive state can also extend beyond the boundary of the subject, that is, beyond the boundary of the system in that state. (This suggestion could be recast in terms of property instantiations: the instantiation of the property could be located somewhere other than the thing in which the property is instantiated; cf. MacDonald [1990, 398–99].)

---

1. The appeal to realization can only do this work if we accept what Carl Gillett (2002, 2003) calls the 'dimensioned' view of realization. On the dimensioned view, the thing instantiating the realizer property can be something other than that which instantiates the realized property. In contrast, many influential discussions of realization presuppose what Gillett calls a 'flat' view, according to which the subjects of the realizer and realized properties are the same, in which case it cannot be that the cognitive state is a state of a system but the realizer is the state of something else.

2. Examples of this sort are thought to show that higher-level properties are multiply realizable, that is, they can be realized by different lower-level properties on different occasions (Putnam 1967; Fodor 1974). It is a matter of much recent debate whether such examples do, in fact, establish this (Wilson 1985; Bickle 1998; Bechtel and Mundale 1999; Batterman 2000; Shapiro 2000; Pereboom 2002; Gillett 2003). For present purposes, I can let this debate lie. I am trying only to explicate the idea of realization. That the thesis of multiple realization might have been oversold is beside the point.

I find this suggestion excessively obtuse, perhaps incoherent. Prima facie, a state is simply an object or entity's instantiation of a property; and for an object or entity to instantiate a property is just for *it*—the thing—to be the bearer of the property, to be the thing in which the property resides, or to be the thing in which the property instance inheres. The advocate for extended cognition might want to introduce new conceptions of states, properties, and property-instantiations, but one cannot simply assert the mysterious thesis under consideration without some alternative metaphysics. Moreover, it is not clear that accepting this suggestion would advance the case for extended cognition. Rather, it would seem to change the terms of the discussion without changing its substance. We could ask under what conditions a state can be partly located other than where its subject is, but this question would appear to raise the various difficulties discussed throughout part I, now under a different guise. Thus, I continue to focus on questions about realization.

Consider now the digital computer, an example that may seem more to the point than a mousetrap. When one reads an introduction to the theory of computing (Minsky 1967; Boolos, Burgess, and Jeffrey 2002), one learns much about the abstract structure of finite-state machines and the like, but, contrary to what might be suggested by the use of 'machines', one reads almost nothing about the physical constitution of any concrete device. A machine must somehow go through the appropriate series of abstractly described computational states in order to be a computing machine. Nevertheless, it is widely recognized that this can be done in a variety of ways. One might build the sort of Turing machine typically described, for heuristic purposes, in textbooks (with a tape and head that slides back and forth); however, it would be much more efficient to employ an architecture of the sort one finds in a contemporary desktop computer. Regardless, the realizations of the machine's computational states are *in* the machine, wherever it is.

Carl Gillett (2007) couches a similar concern in terms of causal powers. On Gillett's view, one of the metaphysical jobs of a realizer is to determine the causal powers of the state or property so realized. If the realizer appears spatially removed from what it realizes, by what mechanism could the latter derive its causal powers from the former?

4.3. Functionalism and the Causal Constraint on Realization

Discussions of realization played a central role in the development of one of the distinctive philosophical frameworks of the twentieth century: functionalism (Block 1980a; Shoemaker 1981). The general functionalist idea holds that many of the properties beyond fundamental physics should be understood in terms of their causal, or functional, roles; since various physical mechanisms can play the same causal role—say, the role of catching mice—such properties should not be identified with physical properties, even highly complex ones. Functionalism claimed instead that such properties are to be identified with their causal–functional roles, and that the realizer of a given functional state or property is the lower-level thing (e.g., state or property) filling the appropriate causal role on the occasion in question. On this view, if a lower-level state does not play the appropriate causal role, it is not the realizer of the functionally characterized mental or cognitive state of interest. This grounds a serious objection to the realization-based gloss of the extended view: in the standard, real-life examples adduced in support of the extended approach, the external materials do not play the right causal roles; their causal roles do not line up with those of the organismically bounded cognitive states in question.

Consider a standard functionalist account of realization, beginning with a functionalist account of mental states. On this view, a subject is in mental state M iff the subject is in some state or other that plays M's causal–functional role. The general idea is that to be in a given mental state is nothing more than to be in some (typically physical) state that bears the appropriate causal relations to inputs, outputs, and other mental states (or to their realizers): wanting apple juice *just is* whatever mental state combines with the belief that there is apple juice in the refrigerator and the perception of the refrigerator in a certain location to cause the appropriate output commands—the ones that will move the subject's body toward the refrigerator. This is a greatly simplified account of the desire for apple juice, and even so, it is schematic in certain respects. Nevertheless, the functionalist approach holds that if all of the relevant details were to be filled in, the state playing the causal role thereby characterized would in fact be the mental state of wanting apple juice. If one were to write out the entire set of causal relations into which a desire for apple juice enters, one would have captured what it is to be a desire for apple juice.

This idea can be expressed more formally using a variation on a method developed by Frank Ramsey and David Lewis (1970), the construction of what is often called a 'Ramsey sentence'. Begin with a theory of M, a property whose essence or nature is its causal–functional role; this amounts to a description of the causal or otherwise law-like relations M bears to other properties of interest. Formalize that theory, for instance, by representing it as a single compound statement in the predicate calculus. Now, allowing quantification over properties, existentially quantify over the position in which M appears in that formal statement. The result asserts that there exists a property related to others in such-and-such ways; this describes the causal role of M. If a property is not causally related in any theoretically important way to other functional-role properties, then the property in question can be characterized in a relatively simple way. Perhaps the theory of mouse killers is straightforward: something is a mouse killer if and only if it takes a live mouse as input and yields a dead mouse as output. In many domains, however, a number of functional-role properties are interrelated. In these cases, the construction of a Ramsey sentence requires quantifying over a number of interrelated causal–functional roles.

Assume, for example that all mental properties are functional-role properties; then, using the apparatus of second-order quantificational logic, a schematic formal characterization of a single mental property M looks like this:

$$(x)\{x \text{ is in } M \text{ iff} \exists F_1 \ldots \exists F_n[\mathbf{T}(F_1 \ldots F_n, I_1 \ldots I_m, O_1 \ldots O_l) \,\&\, F_i x]\}$$

The various I's and O's are antecedently understood predicates, that is, predicates that we do not include as part of our theory of mental-cum-functional-role properties. The I's and O's can be thought of as kinds of input and output (although the Ramsey–Lewis approach is more general than this suggests). In the case of psychology, the I's and O's are typically taken to represent kinds of sensory input and behavioral output. The middle portion of the Ramsey sentence, $\mathbf{T}(F_1 \ldots F_n, I_1 \ldots I_m, O_1 \ldots O_l)$, schematically represents the best theory of the constitutive causal relations that obtain between various mental properties and input- and output-properties. In the example given above, the Ramsey–Lewis method is used to characterize only a single state, M. Assuming, though, that $\mathbf{T}$ represents the best theory of mental properties (a completed scientific psychology or fully refined folk psychology, depending on one's brand of functionalism), $\mathbf{T}$ implicitly characterizes all of the other mental states as well—each corresponding to the value of a distinct F.

This characterization of mental states does not entail materialism, a fact that many take to be a shortcoming of the bare functionalist approach. Perhaps of greater concern is that the view allows for unacceptably flexible functionalist theorizing. As stated, only relations to input and output states constrain the attribution of mental states; given that innumerable structures of interrelated F's are consistent with the same observed pattern of input and output states, one should want some further constraint on the positing or attribution of functional states (Fodor 1981a, 12–14). A common solution requires that for $F_i x$ to be true, F_i and the other functionally characterized mental states must be realized in a corresponding network of x's nonmental states—physical states of x's brain, for instance. Put formally,

$$(x)\{F_i x \text{ iff} \exists P_1 \ldots \exists P_n[\mathbf{T}(P_1 \ldots P_t, I_1 \ldots I_m, O_1 \ldots O_l) \,\&\, P_i x]\}$$

where the right-hand side of the biconditional[3] results from the above characterization of M by systematic substitution of variables $P_1 \ldots P_n$ that range over physical properties for the property variables $F_1 \ldots F_n$, together with corresponding changes in quantifiers (cf. Shoemaker [2003]). In other words, to be

---

3. It would suffice for my purposes to state this in conditional, rather than biconditional, form; the latter, however, is the more familiar presentation.

in a given mental state, the subject must be in a range of physical states that are causally interrelated in ways that match structurally the range of ways in which the mental state in question is related to other mental states (and inputs and outputs). The subject can be in more kinds of physical state than can be paired with the mental states in the functionalist's original Ramsey sentence; and these can be interrelated in ways that have no analogue in psychological theory. No problem. Realization requires only that the physical states have at least as much structure in their causal interrelations as defined for the mental states, and that a portion of the structure of interrelations between the physical states be isomorphic to the structure expressed by the psychological theory in question.[4]

This approach to realization entails what I call the 'Causal-Structure Principle': the token realizer of a property M must enter into a network of causal relations a subset of which is isomorphic (in actual as well as in certain counterfactual cases) to the network of causal relations into which M itself enters. This principle has important implications regarding our proposed interpretation of the extended view. Before going on to discuss these, however, I should make clear the relation between my appeal to the Causal-Structure Principle and related issues in the debate over functionalism and the theory of realization.

Functionalism is often understood as a theory of the very nature of higher-level properties. The cognitive-scientific notion of realization, however, need not make this kind of metaphysical commitment. Realization requires that a subset of the causal powers of a token realizer match up with the causal powers of what is so realized on the occasion in question. Furthermore, as a way to understand the relation between properties in different scientific domains, this approach would seem to require that the causal relations into which a higher-level property enters—the causal powers expressed by the relevant Ramsey sentence— remain constant in the actual world. If we mean to characterize the law-like relations into which various higher-level properties enter, we might reasonably require also that the causal relations expressed by the higher-level Ramsey sentence hold across a certain range of counterfactual situations, the ones with the same laws of nature as the actual world. This falls short, though, of *identifying* the higher-level properties with the causal roles characterized by the higher-level Ramsey sentence. We can employ Ramsey sentences to characterize the causal roles of higher-level properties in the actual world (and possible situations a lot like the actual world), but our doing so does not entail that the higher-level, functionally characterized properties have these causal roles *essentially*. In other words, we need not be functionalists about the properties themselves; the

---

4. Nothing said in the text requires type–type reduction of mental states to physical states. It need not be the case that the same physical state play the role of, for example, P_2 in all subjects; so long as each subject is in some properly interrelated collection of physical states or other, the realization formula holds for each of those subjects, and at least on the functionalist view, each subject is in M_r.

Ramsey–Lewis technique can be employed merely as a way of mapping out the causal relations central to our working conception of the higher-level properties in question, and thereby the structure of causal relations into which their realizers must, in fact, enter. Think of this watered-down functionalism as a methodological guideline for studying the actual world, rather than as a metaphysical thesis concerning the nature of the properties involved.

The Ramsey–Lewis approach offers a perspicuous way to represent the matching of causal profiles asserted by the Causal-Structure Principle. Clarity is not its only virtue: in the special sciences, the Causal-Structure Principle is incredibly useful, perhaps, methodologically indispensable. Researchers in cognitive science treat something like the Causal-Structure Principle as a guide to the identification of realizers (although they may be more inclined to talk in other terms, say, of physical implementation). For example, David Marr (1982) proposed an abstract, mathematically characterized model of the computational process of edge-detection in human visual perception. To flesh out this proposal, Marr sought neural mechanisms—groups of on-center, off-surround and off-center, on-surround retinal and geniculate cells, it turns out (Marr 1982, 64–66)—possessing the same relevant causal profiles as the abstract units included in his computational model of the detection of zero-crossings (Polger 2004). John Anderson and his collaborators pursue a similar strategy in their attempt to apply the ACT-R framework to students' solution of algebra problems (Anderson, Douglass, and Qin 2005; for further examples of this kind of approach, see Anderson et al. [2004] and Anderson [2007]). It is one thing to posit cognitive processes of encoding, transformation, and retrieval (of, e.g., algebraic rules and problem-solving strategies); to confirm their psychological reality, though, one should attempt to find the realizers of the steps in the abstractly described cognitive process. Thus, Anderson and his associates use fMRI data to identify the regions of the brain active at various points in the hypothesized reasoning process; and by finding distinct, active areas that play the appropriately matching causal role, Anderson and associates provide weighty support for their model of the human solution of algebra problems.

Such examples might seem to confirm only that some working cognitive scientists implicitly endorse the Causal-Structure Principle. This would be small-minded, given the importance of the rationale driving their use of it. The Causal-Structure Principle provides a methodological constraint on work in cognitive science (and to the special sciences more broadly) that is necessary to the legitimacy of those science. It is the constraint from below, as we might say. To a significant extent, our confidence in the accuracy of a particular model or theory in a higher-level science should be grounded in our knowledge of the mechanisms that implement that model (cf. Fodor's account [1974] of the way in which, and the extent to which, the sciences are unified). Without such a constraint, theorizing in the special sciences tends to float freely. The potential problem, and the positive constraining power of the Causal-Structure

Principle, is particularly clear in the case of cognitive psychology. The black box of the mind takes inputs and issues outputs, but these alone are consistent with many incompatible models of cognitive states and processes. The Causal-Structure Principle constrains the choice of psychological theories. If two cognitive models are input–output equivalent, we can look, for example, to neuroimaging data for evidence favoring one model over the other (perhaps better still, to the prediction and control of higher-level states via the measuring and manipulation of one model's claimed neural realizers—see Rees [2007]). Finding such evidence consists in the discovery of a pattern of interaction among neural states that mirrors the pattern of causal interaction among the states proposed by one of the psychological models in question. The approach of Marr and Anderson illustrates the importance of this kind of cross-level integration in our theorizing.

Of course, in any particular case, one might try gerrymandering neural states so as to find some token realizer that satisfies one's favored model. Three further interrelated constraints work against such stratagems and should be considered supplements to the Causal-Structure Principle: first, there should be some significant degree of intrasubjective consistency in realizers; second, a realizer must be of a natural or independently explanatory kind from the standpoint of the lower-level discipline (e.g., neuroscience); and third, the causal relations between these lower-level kinds must be counterfactual supporting in the way alluded to above: at least in situations very much like the actual ones, the causal mirroring should hold.[5]

This approach to realization does not beg the question against extended cognition. The use of brain imaging to locate realizers is only one possibility. It is also possible that states entering into the causal relations necessary to realize a given range of cognitive states extend into the environment. It is possible, but in the next section, I appeal to the Causal-Structure Principle and facts about cognitive states to try to show that the external location of realizers is unlikely.

4.4. The Argument from Causal Interaction

4.4.1. Basic Statement of the Argument

In this section I argue that the *core* realizers of organismically local cognitive properties generally do not extend into the environment,[6] largely because such realizers would not satisfy the Causal-Structure Principle. What is a core

---

5. This helps to explain the epistemic facts about scientific practice, for example, that scientists act as if their theories should apply to hypothetical situations in worlds much like ours. It may also help functionalists to avoid the problem that Ramsey sentences can be satisfied too easily; this problem has arisen in many forms, probably the most widely known of which is due to Putnam (1988, appendix); see Chalmers (1996b) and Copeland (1996) for versions of the counterfactual solution.

6. Thus, my argument amounts to a rejection of what Wilson (2004, 116) calls 'radical wide realization', at least for the case of cognitive properties.

realizer? It is just the sort of realizer discussed above: the core realizer of any functionally characterized property Fn appearing in the relevant Ramsey sentence is the corresponding realizer property Pn in the Ramsified realization formula. In this section, when I discuss the possibility of extended core realizers, I have in mind core realizers that are partly internal and partly external. In later sections, I consider the view that *total* realizers extend into the environment, where a total realizer is simply *everything* sufficient to make the Ramsified realization formula true, that is, the entire set of core realizers and the relations between them (Shoemaker 1981, 97). A further view of interest posits entirely external core realizers of cognitive states of the organismically bounded system or its components. This view seems compelling only where there is no likely candidate for an internal realizer. Chapters 5 through 8 cover many of the cases that might be construed in this fashion. In those chapters, I argue that the organism offers satisfactory internal realizers, and thus that positing entirely external ones introduces a gratuitous metaphysical mystery.

Does any advocate for extended cognition truly wish to assert that the *core* realizers of cognitive states are partly internal, partly external? Wilson is sometimes tempted by this view (2004, 165, 196), although he is more confident of the case of social actions (2001, 13–14). Indirectly, the discussion also addresses proponents of extended cognition who appeal to dynamical systems theory (see chapter 7 for details); for they often take cognitive processes to be constituted by lower-level causal processes that involve the coupling of the organism with aspects of its environment even where the cognitive states in question are states of the individual organism (Hurley 1998).

A key distinction plays an important role in the argument to follow. I assume that single realizers can be compound from the standpoint of the realizing level science. This is the standard situation: the realizer of a heart, a single organ, is from the standpoint of cellular or molecular biology a compound entity. The Causal-Structure Principle requires only the compound lower-level state have the right causal profile as a single, possibly compound unit. Thus, assuming for the moment that there are partly extended realizers of cognitive states, such realizers have extended portions. In what follows, it is important to distinguish carefully between the extended portion of an extended realizer, on the one hand, and the entire extended realizer, as a single unit, on the other.

ARGUMENT FROM CAUSAL INTERACTION

Premise 1.   In the sorts of cases that motivate extended cognition, the causal profiles of the cognitive states in question require that those states interact with objects, states, or properties in the external environment. For example, when the subject sees a tree, reads a book, or swings a hammer, cognitive states of the organismically bounded subject (or cognitive system) causally interact with the tree, the book, or the hammer (or the states or properties of these objects that are causally efficacious in cognitively relevant interactions—I drop this qualification hereafter).

Premise 2. In these cases, the external object in question is also hypothesized to be an extended portion of the entire realizer of the very cognitive state in question.

Intermediate
conclusion 1. In the relevant cases, it is central to the causal profile of the organism's cognitive state that it interact with the external portion of its realizer. To illustrate, when the subject sees an object or reads a book, the subject's cognitive property or state causally interacts with some aspect of the object seen or the book read, and those latter things (or their realizers) are, by hypothesis, part of the relevant extended realizer.

Premise 3. The relevant extended realizers, as single units, do not enter into the causal relations described above. In a given case, there is causal interaction between two proper parts of the extended realizer, but the extended realizer as a whole—as a single core realizer of the subject's cognitive state—does not interact with, for example, the book, tree, or tool.

Intermediate
conclusion 2. Thus, in many cases meant to motivate extended cognition, the extended realizer does not enter into a causal relation included in the central causal profile of the cognitive state it is supposed to realize. The cognitive state interacts with an object with which the extended realizer, as a whole, does not interact.

Premise 4. The Causal-Structure Principle: State R realizes state P only if R's causal profile contains P's (central) causal profile as a subset.

Conclusion. Thus, in the cases in question, what is purported to be a partly extended core realizer is not.

The remainder of this section clarifies, defends, and elaborates on the argument.

4.4.2. Premise 1

A wide variety of activities that serve as explananda of cognitive science involve causal interaction between the organism and its environment. What is more, the cases used to motivate the extended view involve some such interaction, and in an essential way; the interaction itself provides the examples with their persuasive power.[7] Recall the cases cited in chapter 2: a robot's use of a lighted triangle on the wall of an arena to effect navigation (Wheeler 2005), the subtle interplay between organism and the object of perception (Hurley 2001; Beer 2003; Noë 2004), or a person engaged in the hitch-free use of a tool—a hammer, keyboard, or sketchpad, for instance (Clark 2003). The cases at issue would not motivate the extended view or any other thesis in cognitive science were the interactions in question not of genuine cognitive significance; as such they will appear as a central part of the causal profile of the cognitive states in question.

I do not claim that for any cognitive state whatever, it is essential to that state's cognitive profile that it interact with some environmental entities or other; perhaps the theoretical profile of some phenomenal states (e.g., the experience of a bitter taste) does not entail causal interaction with external objects or externally instantiated properties (Wilson 2001, 25–26). Such cognitive states are, however, dialectically irrelevant: they do not motivate the extended view. Instead, *Premise 1*, and the argument as a whole, aims only at the kind of interactive processing that might motivate the extended view.

4.4.3. Premise 2

In what are claimed to be cases of extended cognition, the external object, state, property, or process mentioned in connection with *Premise 1* is taken to be part of, or identical to, the extended portion of a realizer. At least, this is the version of the extended view currently under consideration: the organismically bounded person interacts intimately with some external object and this motivates the advocate of the extended view to count that external object as part of the realizer of the organismically instantiated cognitive state.

For whatever reason, one might eschew the strict identification of extended portion of a relevant realizer with an external object (property, or state—let this be understood) with which the organism's cognitive state interacts, holding instead that extended portion of the realizer in question merely realizes the object with which the organismically instantiated cognitive property causally interacts. This is a mere complication, however. It is easy enough to reformulate the requirement that a realizing state enter into a pattern of causal relations that includes the realized state's relevant causal relations: if it is part of the central causal profile of state P that it interact with an object O, then any state that realizes P must either interact with O or with the realizer of O. Take this option as read; it does not alter the argument in any substantive way.

4.4.4. Premise 3 and Beyond

Here we see the root of the problem most clearly. The partly extended realizer, as a single unit, does not interact with the external object with which the

7. Cases of what are supposed to be entirely external realizers provide an exception (see, e.g., Clark and Chalmers's discussion [1998] of Otto and his externalized nonoccurrent beliefs). I discuss such cases in chapter 5.

organismically instantiated cognitive state interacts; for the partly extended realizer, taken as a single whole, does not causally interact with a proper part of itself.

The preceding elements of the argument entail that the causal profile of the partly extended realizer, as a single unit, fails to include a causal relation central to the causal profile of the state it is supposed to realize. Together with a restatement of the Causal-Structure Principle, Intermediate Conclusion Two entails the final conclusion in a straightforward way. To summarize: the partly extended realizer is hypothesized to be the core realizer of a cognitive state, the subject of which is the organism or some system included in the organism. The Causal-Structure Principle requires that whatever realizes the cognitive state in question enter into whatever causal relations the realized state enters into (and which are important to the theoretical characterization of that cognitive state). The purported realizing unit does not, however, enter into one of those causal relations: the cognitive states interact with the extended portion of the purported realizer, but the partly extended realizer, as a single unit—the sort of thing that could be a core realizer—does not. Therefore, the partly extended, lower-level state is now shown not to be a realizer of the cognitive state in question.

4.4.5. A Rejoinder and a Rebuttal

In defense of extended realizers, one might try some fancy metaphysical foot-work. For instance, one might claim that an extended portion of a realizer can both cause continued existence of itself and, at the same time, bring into exis-tence the internal portion of the relevant partly extended realizer, as a single unit. On this view, there are two instances of the extended portion of the realizer. The first appears at time t_1, the second at time t_2. Also instantiated at t_2 is the internal portion of the realizer caused partly by the extended portion of the realizer at t_1. This framework seems to make room for an external object to be both cause of the cognitive state in question and, at a different time, a portion of that state's realizer, and thus seems untouched by the Argument from Causal Interaction.[8]

Can we find in this suggestion a candidate realizer that both satisfies the Causal-Structure Principle and motivates an extended view? There appear to be two possibilities worth considering. One involves a temporally extended real-izer: the extended portion of the realizer at t_1 together with the internal portion of the proposed realizer, which is instantiated at t_2. The second is the more natural candidate: the entire extended realizer instantiated at t_2 (the internal portion instantiated at t_2 together with the extended portion instantiated at t_2). Let us evaluate the candidates in order.

In the first case, the realizer is not caused by what should cause it. Being caused by what I am calling the extended portion of the realizer is central to

---

8. A response along these lines was suggested by Robert Wilson in personal communication.

the nomological profile of the cognitive state in question. (If, for instance, the cognitive state in question is the perceptual state of seeing a tree, then it is part of the state's functional profile that it be caused by a tree.) By hypothesis, the extended portion of the realizer at t_1 is part of the realizer, and it is not caused by any instance of the extended portion of the realizer property. (If it is caused by an earlier instantiation of the extended portion of the realizer property— extended portion of the realizer at t_0, for instance—then the case becomes essentially like the second, so let us defer that way of characterizing the causal story.) So, case one falls to the Causal-Structure Principle by the same sort of reasoning applied in the Argument from Causal Interaction.

In the second case, the realizer *is* caused by what it is supposed to be caused by, but in a strange way. We should like the entire core realizer of the cognitive state to be caused by the t_1-incarnation of the extended portion of the purported realizer. In this case, it is, but by two distinct causal processes: the t_1-incarnation of the extended portion of the realizer causes both the extended portion of the realizer at t_2 and, separately, the internal portion of partly extended realizer. Does, at t_1, what later becomes the extended portion of the t_2-realizer thereby cause the entire core realizer at t_2? Perhaps, but we should be skeptical, given the deviant manner in which it does so; independently causing distinct proper parts of a complex event is not the same as causing the event *simpliciter*.

This oddness directs our attention to a more serious problem. It is a mystery why the sort of interaction at issue motivates the extended view. These cases are meant to support the extended view by virtue of the intimacy of the causal interaction *between* organism and environment (Haugeland 1995). The intimacy is supposed to justify the thought that there is one, extended cognitive process or system. A process is a causally connected series of states, however, each of which is realized physically. It appears that we can have *either* intimacy of causal interaction or an extended core realizer, but not both. In the case currently under consideration, the extended realizer as a whole includes the extended portion of the realizer at t_2 but does not interact with the extended portion of the realizer at t_2, intimately or otherwise. As a single core realizer, the extended realizer interacts with extended portion of the realizer at t_1, but why should that make the extended portion of the realizer at t_2 part of realizer? After all, the extended portion of the realizer at t_1 causally contributes to many events or states other than the immediately following instantiation of a property of the same type as the extended portion of the realizer at t_1, and we are not at all inclined to include any of those events at parts of the realizer of the cognitive state in question. We should not be seduced by the fact that the extended portion of the realizer at t_1 and the extended portion of the realizer at t_2 instantiate the same kind of property (they are both trees, for instance). The extended portion of the realizer at t_1 is intimately causally related to the internal portion of the relevant partly extended realizer, let us concede, but its connection to the extended portion of the realizer at t_2 is accidental, relative to cognition. The extended portion of the realizer at *t2* could just as well never appear, or be something other than the content of the cognitive state realized (which it likely will be in the case of perceiving a tree), and the network of intimate causal relations would remain the same. Given that the extended portion of the realizer at *t1* and the extended portion of the realizer at *t2* are typically the same thing (i.e., the extended portion of the realizer does not change after it has causally affected the organism), it is tempting to shift unwittingly between the two in our thinking about these cases. That, however, is a temptation we must avoid if we are to evaluate correctly the rejoinder on offer.

At this point, the defender of the extended view might hold that the Causal-Structure Principle is too demanding, that the central conception of a cognitive state requires something less restrictive of its realizers: perhaps the realizer of the state of seeing a tree need bear only *some* close causal relation to the tree. This might allow that one proper part of the realizer of *seeing a tree* (i.e., the tree) causes another proper part of the realizer (i.e., a brain state); in which case the Argument from Causal Interaction collapses. This tactic leads to trouble, however. Not only does it reject the clearest notion of realization on offer,[9] it does so gratuitously. It undermines the theory of realization by rejecting a precise and methodologically valuable approach, putting in its place only a loose relation of no apparent value in the cognitive-scientific enterprise.

A better version of this response would substitute a different, but still precise, plausible, and independently motivated, criterion of realization. Wilson (2001) expresses general hostility toward the Ramsey-sentence approach, but the only precise alternative he seems to have in mind is a necessary-condition approach similar to the view criticized in chapter 2. The essential idea of the necessary-condition view holds that *S* is the core realizer of *M* if and only if *S* is a necessary condition for *M*'s obtaining, bracketing background or boundary conditions.

This approach faces serious objections, though. First, consider how background conditions are to be separated from the necessary conditions that count as part of the realizer. For Wilson, the distinction rests on a prior identification of the coherent *system* in play (Wilson 2001, 9, 14). Background conditions for the obtaining of state *M* are the necessary conditions for *M* that hold beyond the boundary of the system in question, the system of which *M* is a state. This way of identifying realizers speaks in favor of the nonextended view, however. The human cognitive system does not typically extend beyond the boundary of the organism; thus, none of the necessary conditions beyond the boundary of the organism are parts of the realizers of human cognitive states; thus, there are no extended core realizers of human cognitive states.

---

9. Gillett's approach to realization is arguably as clear and rigorous as the Ramsey-sentence approach, but its application does not advance the extended cause (see Gillett [2007]).

Second, this account of realization would seem to be of no use to cognitive science.[10] Too many things are part of the necessary conditions for the occurrence of a given cognitive state: Aristotle must exist in order for me to be reasoning about Aristotle, but Aristotle is not part of the realizer of any of my cognitive states. Of course, we could stipulate a notion of core realizers such that Aristotle is part of the core realizer of one of my cognitive states; but in doing so, we would stipulate into existence realizers of no use in the scientific study of human cognition. This objection may not move those who, unlike Wilson, think content-laden states have no special role to play in cognitive science (as ultimate *explanans*—more discussion of this distinction below). It should, however, be of concern to Wilson. Moreover, keep in mind the objections raised in chapter 2, in connection with the discussion of metaphysical principles of demarcation. Those objections did not appeal to the aboutness relation or the contents of subjects' thoughts.

In contrast, a satisfactory alternative is on the table. Assume, as we have been, that the proposed extended realizer has distinct proper parts, at least one of which is within the body of the organism. This assumption yields a plausible candidate for the core realizer, one that plays the role demanded by the Causal-Structure Principle. Furthermore, as we shall see in later chapters, the very models of intimate causal interaction with the environment that motivate the extended view can also help us to locate organismic realizers; these models typically offer a detailed story about the interaction between two different kinds of state: the ones internal to the organism and the external ones with which the organism causally interacts. Thus, to extend core realizers by altering our theory of realization appears pointless; rather, we should identify the internal states included in interactionist models of cognition as the realizers of the cognitive states in question. Behind this point stands a general thought: other things being equal, if a local realizer—one within the boundaries of the individual the state of which is being realized—is available, it is to be preferred over a nonlocal realizer; for a local realizer stands in much better position to play the causal role we take realizers to play.

To summarize: Realizers must play a causal role structurally analogous to the causal role of whatever they realize, at least with respect to the theoretically important causal relations into which the realized property or state enters. The organism's cognitive states of interest interact with the environment in distinctive ways. These states' realizers must be in a position to share

---

10. This is not to say that cognitive scientists do not sometimes invoke necessary conditions to argue for the extended view. After describing the extended view approvingly, Spivey, Richardson, and Fitneva (2004) offer what appears to be a necessary-conditions-based argument: "...and thus certain crucial bits of information that are necessary for complex behavior are provided not by neural-based memory representations but by the environment itself..." (Spirey et al. 2004, 166).

that causal profile. The only plausible such position is within the boundary of the organism.[11]

4.5. Wide Realization, Total Realization, and Causal Powers

4.5.1. Wilson on Realization

In this subsection, I address the possibility that the total realizers of some cognitive states are wide and that this grounds a kind of extended cognition. A total realizer is everything sufficient to make the Ramsified realization formula true, that is, the entire set of core realizers and the relations between them (Shoemaker 1981, 97). When Wilson talks about cognition and mental states, he seems most often to have this sort of view in mind (2001, 12–14). Thus, I will frame the problem in the way Wilson does, coming at the issue via his objections to the standard philosophical notion of realization and its connection to total realization.

The conjunction of two widely accepted theses concerning realization cannot, given the empirical facts, both be true, according to Wilson. The first thesis—Constitutivity—asserts that the "realizers of states and properties are exhaustively physically constituted by the intrinsic, physical states of the individual whose states or properties they are" (Wilson 2001, 5). The second—Sufficiency—asserts that "realizers are metaphysically sufficient for the properties or states they realize" (ibid., 4). Consider, though, the commonly held view that the instantiation of certain psychological properties requires cooperation of the external environment (cf. McGinn [1989, 104–5]). In many cases, the intrinsic physical states of an organism are consistent with variations beyond the boundary of the organism, variations that are thought to alter organismically instantiated cognitive properties (content-properties—Burge 1979). Thus, the standard view of realization faces trouble. If Sufficiency is true, it follows that the realizer is spread into the world: only when we include the environmental conditions in the realizer do we get a sufficient determinative base for the subject's cognitive states; in which case Constitutivity must be abandoned. In contrast, if we hold onto Constitutivity, limiting the realizer to the intrinsic physical properties of the organism, then it must be admitted that the realizer does not suffice for the instantiation of the psychological property in question: the internal physical properties in question could be instantiated without the cooperation of the external world, and thus without the instantiation of the cognitive property in question. Given that some

---

11. Perhaps cognitive states are *constituted* partly by organismically external elements, rather than realized by them. An argument analogous to the Argument from Causal Interaction speaks against the constitution-based view, however. The constituting basis of cognitive state *P* must enter into the causal relations into which *P* enters. The extended constitution-base of *P*—for example, the seeing of a tree—does not enter into one of the causal relations that is a central characteristic of *P*: the extended constitution base does not, as a whole, causally interact with the tree; it includes the tree. What use is this notion of constitution if it does not accord with an appropriately adjusted Causal-Structure Principle?

external conditions help to determine which mental states the subject is in, Sufficiency and Constitutivity cannot both be true of the actual world.

Wilson rejects Constitutivity, embracing Sufficiency—modulo background conditions—and from this view can be wrought a version of the extended view. As Wilson sees things, cognitive states are states of individual organisms (Wilson 2004, 142), but their total realizers are wide (ibid., 208): they extend beyond the boundary of the individual organism, for in many cases it would appear that only an extended collection of physical properties or states suffices to determine the cognitive properties in question, even after the contribution of background conditions has been bracketed.

4.5.2. Semantic Externalism and Total Realization

Consider the connection between Sufficiency and semantic externalism (or content-externalism—Putnam 1975; Kripke 1980), hinted at above. Semantic externalism holds that factors beyond the boundary of the organism partly determine the contents of our thoughts (or words, as the view was originally developed by Putnam and Kripke; for externalist theories of mental content, see Burge [1979], Dretske [1981, 1988], Millikan [1984], and Fodor [1987, 1990]). In this context, Wilson's argument is straightforward. Sufficiency requires that the realizer of a cognitive state suffice for its instantiation. Assume that sameness of content is a necessary condition for the sameness of cognitive state. Then two cognitive states that are indistinguishable with respect to the intrinsic properties of the organisms involved, yet which have different external content, constitute different cognitive states. In which case, the organismically internal facts simply do not suffice for the realization of the cognitive state in question: that same internal arrangement could realize one of a number of cognitive states depending on the environmental factors to which those internal states are related (cf. McGinn [1989, 105]).

According to the diagnosis offered by many philosophers of mind, Putnam's fictional Oscar (1975) serves as an illustration: Standard Earth-dweller Oscar is in the mental state of thinking about H_2O, even though his physical duplicate on Twin-Earth is thinking about what is to both Oscar and his twin an indistinguishable, but distinct substance, XYZ (which this Twin-Earth has in place of H_2O). The only difference between Oscar and Twin-Oscar is their causal interaction with two distinct external substances, which play the same respective role in their lives (of quenching thirst, cleansing dirt, etc.). This confers different contents upon their physically identical mental states. Oscar thinks about H_2O; Twin-Oscar thinks about XYZ. Thus, if Sufficiency and semantic externalism are combined, wide realization follows.[12]

12. The contents of cognitive states directed at abstract entities (e.g., numbers) would not seem to appear in the physical order of causes and effects; thus, including them as part of the physical realizer of the relevant cognitive states seems misguided, perhaps incoherent (see McGinn's discussion of weak externalism; also see Block [1986, n7]; Burge [2003, 293]). This should make us question Wilson's application of Sufficiency.

Why, though, should we accept Sufficiency? Wilson's argument shows that *if* Sufficiency and semantic externalism are true, realizers are wide, and thus Constitutivity false. Nevertheless, even someone committed to semantic externalism might hold that Sufficiency misrepresents the realization-relation, at least insofar as it is of any use to cognitive science. This, I think, is the correct response. If Sufficiency (together with uncontested premises) entails wide realization of the sort one gets from semantic externalism, then either Sufficiency is false or Sufficiency is moot (true of a kind of realization that plays no role in cognitive science).[13] Thoughts can be about all sorts of *things* that themselves play no role in cognitive processing—they can be about my late grandmother, about the 1968 World Series, about *pi*—and including these as literal, physical constituents of cognitive processes offers no payoff to cognitive science (Fodor 1980). The semantic properties of a thought often depend on the existence of some distant or abstract external thing, but we should not thereby infer extended realizers, not if realization is meant to be part of a naturalistic investigation of the person and her cognitive capacities.[14]

4.5.3. *The Role of Relational Properties in Cognitive Science*

When we correctly attribute externalist semantic properties to subjects— for example, Oscar's believing that water is wet—we pick out nothing more than certain relations between subjects and their environments (Armstrong 1978; for discussion of some complications, see Fodor [1990], chapter 6 and Rupert [2008]). The subjects do not instantiate some further natural property (Lewis 1983), a relational property, in addition to their entering into the relations in question. Although cognitive scientists are interested in various relations subjects bear to their environments, they are primarily interested in these *as explananda* (cf. Papineau [1993, 89–90]). Believing that water is wet is a relational state, holding between the organism and H_2O. Cognitive scientists should want to know what it is about the organism that allows it to come into this relation; and they should want to know how the organismic *relatum* accounts for various forms of the organism's behavior, which are often themselves described relationally. There is nothing in the practice of successful cognitive science, though, that commits us to relational properties that inhere

13. Wilson recognizes that "cognitive scientists themselves would likely opt for the constitutivity over the sufficiency thesis" (2004, 118). Nevertheless, he thinks doing so requires some significant revisions to physicalism, to which many philosophers and, presumably, cognitive scientists are deeply committed. Presently, it will become clear why the rejection of Sufficiency has no such consequences.

14. Note the extent to which I depart from Lawrence Shapiro's view (2004, 39), according to which we should bracket methodological considerations in favor of attention to our *concept* of realization. The present project is in the philosophy of cognitive science, so methodological considerations are far from being mere "biases or commitments of individuals" (Shapiro 2004, 39). Rather, they take center stage: methodological practices of successful research programs provide the central data, and in many cases the conceptual tools, driving a satisfactory philosophical gloss of those programs.

in the subject and confer causal powers over above those entailed by the mere relational state (the state comprised of the organism, the external stuff, and the relation between the two). The attempt to elevate these relational properties to properties of the subject, that somehow have their own causal roles to be studied in their own right, causes the metaphysical mischief driving Wilson's view. By thinking that the subject has a distinctive relational property, we are seduced into thinking that there is something specifically about the subject that somehow can be essentially or constitutively grounded in (or realized by) material beyond her body.

Thus, it is either trivial or misleading to describe beliefs in the standard way, as having their externalist contents essentially. If the relational state is our concern, then the externalist content of a belief is essential to the state; the externalist content—the H_2O being thought about, for example—is one of the *relata*. If we are instead concerned with the causally efficacious psychological state, externalist content is not essential to that state. It is perfectly natural to have the externalist intuition concerning Putnam's Oscar, to think *he* instantiates an essentially relational psychological state; for he instantiates an organismic state that is importantly related to H_2O. Furthermore, given the way our world works, anyone in the same internal psychological state is related to H_2O in the way Oscar is. In other words, much talk about beliefs as relational states rests on a natural mistake, an equivocation born of our convenient situation, that of living in a world where Oscar's being in his local psychological state is almost perfectly correlated with that state's also being one *relatum* of the representing-relation, the other of which is H_2O (cf. [Fodor 1994]). What is more, as I see things, this correlation is no accident. It results from the normal developmental conditions under which content is fixed and under which the local psychological state becomes functional (for details, see Rupert [1996, 1998, 1999, 2001]—cf. Dretske [1988]).

Wilson (personal communication) suggests that the property of evolutionary fitness is a scientifically legitimate relational property that can serve as a model for cognitive properties with wide realizers. I doubt that this suggestion has any bearing, however, on the view of semantic properties I have articulated. No organism (or species) possesses a degree of fitness *simpliciter*. An organism (or species) is fit to degree n only in relation to a particular environment. This case does not differ in any substantive way from standard relations, such as being-taller-than. Admittedly, one can change the fitness of an individual by changing the environment, which might suggest that the degree of fitness of the individual somehow includes the environment. To the contrary, this shows only that the individual, or some of her properties, can enter into various relations; depending on what is around for her to be related to, she might enter into one relation rather than another. Change the external relatum, the environment, and you have changed the relation as a whole. Such changes are interesting because differences in the environment, in combination with the intrinsic properties of the individual, tend to lead to different reproductive outcomes. These different outcomes result from different relations, however—that is, different relational complexes—not from differences in the relational properties had distinctively by the individual organism (or the average member of a species at a given time).

Returning, now, to the case of externalist semantics, I am not claiming that external semantic values are completely irrelevant in cognitive science, quite the contrary. First, consider the widely held view that mental and cognitive states have truth-conditions (or conditions of warranted tokening or some other form of correctness or satisfaction-conditions), regardless of whether such truth-conditions constitute or directly determine any of the causal powers of the states investigated by cognitive psychology (cf. Fodor [1991/1995, 207]). We recognize this as an intuitive datum, and the work on causal theories of reference and mental content gives us some idea what relations our organismic states stand in, such that they have the truth-conditions they do. Having truth-conditions is, however, a matter of coming into certain relations to things in the environment, not a matter of coming to have relational properties in need of further explanation, that is, beyond the explanation of how the relations themselves come to obtain.

Second, the intuitive data concerning truth-conditions is not likely to be entirely overruled by cognitive science. Any epistemically serious cognitive theorist must recognize that her own project presupposes the existence of cognitive states with truth-conditions (or satisfaction-conditions, or conditions of accuracy, etc.); it presupposes her own states. Cognitive science aims to formulate correct theories of human cognition; and the philosophy of cognitive science aims to formulate correct theoretical claims about cognitive science itself. These enterprises presuppose that mental states or cognitive states—the theorist's own mental or cognitive states—stand in relations of some importance to properties and kinds in the environment. Cognitive states must enter into wide semantic relations in order that cognitive states express theories *of* anything. For example, anyone who holds that, for example, cognition is nothing more than the transformation of vectors in the brain's state space owes us an account of how *that* sort of cognition grounds her own assertions that cognition is nothing more than the transformation of vectors. It is not out of the question that a revisionary cognitive theorist will produce such an account in the future, but we are owed something more than a mere sketch (cf. Churchland [1981]). This is a meta-constraint, not part of cognitive science itself, but an important constraint nevertheless.

Third, and perhaps most importantly, the capacities, state, and abilities that cognitive scientists investigate are capacities construed in relation to the external world. This is what sets cognitive science in motion: relationally characterized capacities are, for the most part, what we care about. Humans are capable of language use; they can produce and react to certain external objects:

acoustical patterns in the air beyond the boundary of the organism. It is a striking feature about humans that they interact in this way with the world. This holds as well for off-line cognition, when the subject is not actively engaged with the world. We want to know which of a subject's states participate in relations that, as a whole, consist of the organism, the relation (of aboutness), and the external stuff—relations the holding of which *just is* the organism's thinking about the relevant portion of the world. We would like to know how states of the organism facilitate the person's coming into the relevant relations to environmental states and properties and how various of these organismic states cause a subject to come into further relations to external objects (e.g., by behaving in certain ways). Cognitive scientists account for these relationally characterized *explananda* in terms of the organism's local properties, which entail a range of tendencies and capacities that the subject has to interact with various things in the external world. Of course, a full accounting of the relations in question requires mentioning *relata* in the environment. This does not, however, entail that the explanatory properties hypothesized by cognitive science and attributed to organismic subjects are essentially relational; nor does it entail any commitment to the causal efficacy of distinctively relational properties attributed to the organismic subject.

Moreover, it is no surprise that cognitive scientists characterize some of their explananda and theoretical constructs relationally. How can we characterize the forms of behavior to be explained except by reference to external objects with which the organism enters into causal relations? In many cases, we can tell that an organism has a certain capacity—that is, stands in a certain relation to the world—only by (or most easily by) watching that capacity in action when it has been triggered by the relevant external condition. Lacking any other name for the capacity, we identify it as the capacity to interact with that kind of external thing. Thus, both the behavior and the capacity producing that behavior are conveniently labeled by referring to external *relata*. As noted above, there are very few real-life XYZ–H_2O cases, so it is almost never the case that psychologists have to make explicit whether transportation to Twin-Earth would change the way they describe their data or the capacities hypothesized.[15]

I end this section by raising a pair of concerns of special interest to philosophers of mind who have followed the debate about externalism (other readers might wish to skip ahead to section 4.6). Given what I have said about external content and cognitive science, one might wonder whether two physically identical people—Putnam's Oscar and Twin-Oscar, for instance—have different beliefs when a difference in environmental context is the only difference between them. If we think of each belief as a relation between the organism

---

15. Twin-Earth cases typically involve semantic values determined by nonsocial, causal interaction with the environmental. In contrast, Tyler Burge (1979) focuses on socially determined content. For an argument against the appeal to socially determined content in at least some developmental research, see Patterson (1991). For an impressive and staunchly individualistic account of linguistic meaning, see Landauer, Foltz, and Laham (1998).

and the belief's externalist semantic content, then clearly the two organisms—
Oscar and Twin-Oscar—have different beliefs, simply in virtue of being parts
of different relational states. If one clarifies the question differently, so as to ask
a question only about local *relata*, then they are in the same states.

What about the causal powers of twins' states? Oscar's and Twin-Oscar's
beliefs seem to have distinct causal powers. This seems to show that beliefs, as
relational properties of the believers, are something over and above mere relations. Twin-Oscar's thirst typically causes a search for XYZ, whereas Oscar's
thirst typically causes a search for H_2O. That kind of fact can, however, be captured completely in terms of the relations involved, without attaching additional causal powers to relational properties. There is a single intrinsic state
that serves as organismically local relatum in each case (Oscar's and Twin-
Oscar's); this single state exhibits a range of causal powers. The intrinsic properties of the organism's various states confer upon the organism the capacity to
come into a semantic relation to XYZ, in one set of circumstances, and H_2O, in
another. In this sense, the two beliefs have the same causal powers. They cause
different relationally characterized behavior in prevailing circumstances, however, because the circumstances are different. Of course, if the beliefs are taken
to be the entire relations—which I do not recommend doing if our discussion
is of beliefs as treated by cognitive science—then the two beliefs have different
causal powers. They are different relational complexes and thus can affect the
world differently.

4.6. Cleaning Up

4.6.1. *Socially Embedded Properties and Wide Core Realization*

According to Wilson, the best examples of wide *core* realizers are socially
embedded actions. For many actions, even the smallest portion of space-time
that we could plausibly count as their realizers extends beyond the boundary
of the organism. Wilson offers the example of signing a slip of paper to withdraw money from the bank (Wilson 2004, 116). One cannot sign a withdrawal
slip without a piece of paper's being there, a piece of paper external to the
organism. Furthermore, the signing of a withdrawal slip represents a wealth of
cases. Many, perhaps most, behavioral properties are individuated by reference
to external objects and entities: climbing steps, dialing the phone, mailing a
letter.

The relation-based framework described above handles these cases naturally enough. The local realizer confers certain causal powers on the organism.
These can be described broadly, but this description is a shorthand specifica-
tion of the organismically instantiated cognitive state and the complex law-gov-
erned relations into which the local state enters. Organismically instantiated
cognitive states confer a certain complex of causal powers on the organism; and

as with most properties, their effects vary with circumstance (with the other properties also instantiated). The subject signed the slip, but there is a clear sense in which had he done the *same thing* to a different piece of paper, he would have committed fraud—if, say, that piece of paper had been a counterfeit check he printed and made out to himself. The organismically local property is, intrinsically, neither the ability to sign a withdrawal slip nor the ability to sign a phony check. It is the ability to move one's body in a certain way—as we would normally say, the ability to sign one's name. This is a cognitive-motor capacity that allows one to come into a variety of relations to a variety of things. Cognitive scientists should want to explain the subject's capacity to come into the signing-relation to all of these different things, but in doing so, the cognitive scientist does not commit herself to the existence of irreducibly relational capacities; rather, the intrinsic properties of the system allow it to enter into a range of causal relations to external things.

Talk of conditional causal powers provides a nice way of making sense of these cases, while also jibing with the methodology of cognitive psychology. The data of a psychological experiment may sometimes be categorized in terms of the external relations of the behavior, for example, the subject labeled the toy monkey 'animate'; but behavior is compared across conditions, and two instances are treated as the same behavior even when the external stimulus differs. The experimenter asks, for example, "Did the subject give the *same response* to the toy monkey as she did to the real monkey?" hoping to discover how the same range of cognitive capacities manifests itself given different conditions (and thus indirectly to probe the nature of those capacities). Of course, experiments often include an operational characterization of the capacities they are meant to probe. This is misleading, however. It is one thing to operationalize one's particular experimental arrangement, to say very precisely, for instance, what counts as success on the part of a subject in a certain condition; this is common place, in fact, required of legitimate experimental work. It is quite another thing to operationalize the cognitive capacities themselves. This sort of operationalization has an ignoble history, and for obvious reasons; it entails one cognitive capacity for attributing false beliefs where puppets are involved, a different cognitive capacity where storyboards are involved, and on down the line. To individuate actions with respect to the actual objects with which the subject interacts—as Wilson's view suggests—courts this second, highly implausible sort of operationalism (cf. Kelly [2001, 97]). The action of signing a withdrawal slip puts the subject into a relation to things in the world. Cognitive science should explain how that subject comes into that relation by adverting to the organism's local persisting cognitive capacities that can manifest themselves in a variety of ways in a variety of circumstances.

Some would dismiss this approach as knee-jerk reductionism. Consider Wilson's alternative, however, that the core realizer of the action includes the piece of paper signed. To distinguish total realizers from background conditions, Wilson relies on the objective boundaries of systems. This seems like good sense. Notice, however, that the combination of a subject's body and some particular piece of paper is not a system of scientific interest on a par with the circulatory system (Wilson 2004, 142). Thus, the piece of paper is not part of the total realizer of the signing; and something that is not part of the total realization of the signing cannot be part of the core realization of it, for the core realizer has to be part of the total realizer.[16] Wilson's view creates a conundrum that the relation-based view avoids altogether.

4.6.2. The Single-Neuron Argument

Wilson considers views similar to the one I have been pressing (e.g., Denis Walsh's attempt [1998] to shunt external factors off to context—see Wilson [2004, 133–37]; cf. Wilson and Clark [2009]). In general terms, Wilson objects to these moves on the grounds that they involve an ad hoc, rather than a principled, identification of realizers. If one is allowed to make such distinctions ad hoc, absurd results follow; for one could just as easily make the ad hoc move of treating a single-neuron as the total realizer of a mental state. If the supposed extended portion of a realizer can be treated as background conditions, then why not think that, for the purpose of identifying the realizers of cognitive states, all of the human body except a single-neuron can be treated as background conditions?

Wilson's concern misses the mark. Consider first why we are not inclined to count single neurons as *core* realizers. Typically, no individual neuron has the causal profile necessary to be the core realizer of any particular cognitive state. This cannot be ruled out, however; recall the hypothesis of grandmother cells (Barlow 1972; Lettvin 1995). If there were good evidence of grandmother cells, we should be perfectly happy to accept that single neurons serve as core realizers of some cognitive states; perhaps recent reports of Jennifer Aniston and Halle Berry cells will hold up (Quiroga, Reddy, Kreiman, Koch, and Fried 2005). Of course, in that case, there would be nothing absurd about saying that individual neurons can be core realizers.[17]

Now consider total realizers, the actual target of Wilson's reductio. As in the case of core realizers, it is largely an empirical matter whether single neurons are the total realizers of cognitive states; but when it comes to total realizers, we can be more confident of the matter's resolution. First, if core realizers encompass more than individual neurons, then no individual neuron is a total

---

16. This point bears on the earlier discussion of extended core realizers of cognitive states. If, for example, the tree seen is not part of the objective system that provides the subject of the pertinent perceptual state, then the tree cannot, on Wilson's view, be part of the total realizer of that state, and thus it cannot be part of the state's core realizer.

17. Empirical considerations drive this response. I am not relying on an a priori principle of smallism, that is, the blind privileging of smaller units over larger ones (Wilson 2004, 121–22).

realizer; for the total realizer of a given state M must include M's core real-izer as a part. If the core realizer is larger than a single neuron, then, perforce the total realizer is as well. If, in the end, the empirical research goes against grandmother cells (and Aniston cells, etc.), we should reject the hypothesis that single cells serve as total realizers of cognitive states simply because those cells are not plausibly core realizers of cognitive states.

Second, independent of the question about core realizers, no one should be at all tempted to count single cells as total realizers. The total realizer of a given cognitive state contains the core realizer of that state *together with* all of the core realizers of the properties to which that state is importantly related, *together with* the conditions of the relevant system that guarantee that the appropriate causal relations hold among those core realizers. This is an amazing amount of structure to find in one neuron. We cannot simply decide to banish certain central features of a cognitive state from its theoretical description (e.g., we cannot say that being typically caused by a tree is not part of the theoretical profile of seeing a tree). Rather, all of the theoretically important relations into which a cognitive state enters must be accounted for by that state's total real-izer. Because the typical cognitive state enters into numerous and fairly specific patterns of theoretically important causal interactions, it is highly unlikely that any single neuron possesses the requisite structure to be a total realizer of a cognitive state or system; for it is highly unlikely that the neuron has the right number of parts, one for each core realizer, related to each other and to inputs and outputs in just the right ways. This follows directly from the application of the Causal-Structure Principle. Furthermore, collection of fMRI data during subjects' performance of cognitive tasks reveals groups of neurons interacting in roughly the ways core realizers do. Given the fruitfulness of such methods, the hypothesis of a single neuron as the sole total realizer of the entire cognitive system seems questionable on empirical grounds.

Thus is rebutted the charge of ad hocery and the attempted *reductio ad absurdum*. Given the current state of the evidence, we should not dismiss the hypothesis that single neurons sometimes serve as core realizers of cognitive states. It is, however, hardly a live hypothesis that a single neuron is a *total* realizer of any cognitive state or, what would seem to follow, is a realizer of an entire cognitive system. The independently motivated Causal-Structure Prin-ciple, together with the empirical facts about the structure of neurons, rules this out.

4.6.3. Additional Support

To close this chapter, I run briefly through a pair of additional supporting considerations. First, locating realizers somewhere other than the location of what they realize creates practical problems. Cognitive psychology aims to be an experimental science; cognitive psychologists would like to explain behavior and related cognitive capacities by manipulating cognitive states and recording the results. This requires that cognitive psychologists be able to manipulate the entities the powers of which they are investigating; however, this would seem difficult if realizers spread throughout the environment. The most successful sciences take the far-flung environment as fixed and manipulate local entities to discover their causal powers. In doing so, however, they are investigating the causal powers of the local entities; and there the realizer should be, at least the portion of the realizer that has any relevance to experimental practice.

Second, given their extended nature, it is not clear how the extended portions of realizers can enter into the required causal interactions with other mental states. Say that an extended state realizes a particular mental state $M1$ that causes a further mental state $M2$. If the extended portions of the realizers of $M1$ and $M2$ are spatially separated, this would seem to prevent them from playing a role in the theoretically important causal interaction between $M1$ and $M2$. In the absence of a single integrated cognitive system, grounded in an integrated physical system, it is a challenge to identify the channels by which the various extended portions of the realizers have their requisite influence on each other. Of course, there is a principled solution: the various causal processes all run through the individual organism, coming together via the interaction of the internal portions of the supposedly extended realizers. This, however, favors the embedded view over the extended one.

The view I have encouraged also has the weight of conservatism on its side. Rather than trying to find a new theory of realization, a new account of psychological method, and an account of causation at a distance, why not stick to the existing framework and work out its kinks? If it is coherent and fruitful, if a bit boring, why switch? The literature on situated cognition contains no dearth of answers to this question. In part II, I address a wide variety of proposals, including the claim that some core realizers are *entirely* external.

Arguments for the Extended View

5

Functionalism and Natural Kinds

In making a case for an organismically bounded view of cognition, part I criticized various arguments used to support the extended approach. Part II examines—in an explicit and sustained way—further arguments for the extended view. In each case, I conclude either that the argument fails independently of the considerations of part I or that the considerations of part I undermine whatever appeal the argument in question might have.

The present chapter focuses on arguments that might appropriately be called 'similarity' arguments. Such arguments hold that some extended states are genuinely cognitive because they resemble, in all relevant respects, unquestionably cognitive, internal states. The reader should not attach too much significance to this grouping or the very general description I have given of similarity reasoning. The individual arguments must ultimately be evaluated on their merits.

5.1. The Functionalist Argument

In chapter 2, I discussed the Parity Principle at some length. There I was particularly interested in its potential as a principle of demarcation. As Clark and Chalmers sometimes seem to conceive of it, however, the Parity Principle does not itself play a foundational role; rather, it is meant to direct our attention to what are the foundational considerations: a consideration of functional role. Clark and Chalmers seem to have functionalist considerations in mind at various points (see, e.g., Clark and Chalmers [1998, 8, 13] for talk of external processes and externally encoded information serving a function). Furthermore, Clark (2003, 69) has since taken a more explicitly functionalist position, and Chalmers (2008) also expresses sympathy with a weakly functionalist reading of the Parity Principle. There is a straightforward connection between functionalism and the Parity Principle: The *location* of a state does not matter, according to the functionalist view, so long as the state in question plays the appropriate causal–functional role (see chapter 4 for a more detailed discussion of functionalism in philosophy of mind); and on one way of reading the Parity Principle, it directs us to ignore location when evaluating something's cognitive status.

Here is a functionalist argument put partly in terms of physical realizers, which makes explicit the connection between functionalist considerations and the physical location of the states involved:

FUNCTIONALIST ARGUMENT

Premise 1.   A mental or cognitive state of kind F is realized by whatever physical state plays the functional role that is individuative of F.

Premise 2.   Some realizers of mental or cognitive states have physical parts external to the human organism (or are entirely external).

Premise 3.   A mental or cognitive state is located wherever its realizer is located.

Conclusion.   Therefore, some mental or cognitive states are located at least partly beyond the boundaries of the human organism.

On the functionalist view, having a certain causal–functional profile is simply what it is to be a state of a given kind. The mind is as the mind does, and "matter matters only because of what matter can do" (Dennett 2005, 17); thus, if an externally realized state does what is definitive of a given mental or cognitive state-type, it is an extended mental or cognitive state.

Recall Clark and Chalmers's case (1998) of Otto, the Alzheimer's patient. As Clark and Chalmers see things, Otto has nonoccurrent beliefs with the same contents as the scribblings in his pad. Why? Because the information stored in the pad functions in the same belief-related ways as information stored in the average person's brain. In both Otto's case and the standard subject's case, "The information is reliably there when needed, available to consciousness and available to guide action, in just the way that we expect a belief to be" (Clark and Chalmers 1998, 13).

Given our interest in locating a fruitful theoretical framework in which to set cognitive scientific research, Otto's case might seem too speculative. Even if there are some cases like Otto's, they seem too rare to drive a paradigm shift in cognitive science. The existence of a few outliers such as Otto should not change the fundamental methods or presuppositions of, for example, developmental psychology, psycholinguistics, or the theory of vision.

A second concern sounds a more philosophical note: one might wonder what reason we have to think functionalism itself is true. Given the checkered history of functionalist theorizing, why should we accept *Premise 1*? Philosophers have leveled numerous, powerful objections against functionalism (Block and Fodor 1972; Block 1978, 1980a, 1990; Kim 1998; Rupert 2006a), and many of those who advocate some limited form of it have their qualms—pertaining, for example, to conscious experience. Objections duly noted; there is no denying that functionalism remains a leading contender as a theory of cognitive states. Thus, we should give the Functionalist Argument our careful attention.

Statement of my third concern requires some setup. Functionalism takes a variety of forms, and thus, applications of functionalist theory must begin in clarification. It would lead us too far afield to canvass all variants of functionalism. One broad distinction will, however, be useful: the contrast between analytical functionalism and psychofunctionalism. Analytical functionalism holds that the individuating functional role of mental (or cognitive) state F is entailed by our very concept of F, the concept expressed by the term 'F'. On this view, an analysis of commonsense concepts of mental state-types, which proceeds partly by reflection on our use of terms referring to those state-types, determines the Ramsey sentence that both captures the meaning of mental state-terms and expresses the essential causal role of mental state-types. In contrast, psychofunctionalism holds that scientific psychology delivers distinctive causal roles of cognitive state-types. The psychofunctionalist holds that cognitive states are the general kind of thing the subtypes of which are (at least nomologically) individuated by the distinctive causal roles their instantiations play in the actual world. The psychofunctionalist might or might not accept this on a priori grounds; for she might think that functionalism itself is an empirical hypothesis (one on which she places her empirical bets). Regardless, according to the psychofunctionalist, we must do empirical work to discover the individuating roles of the particular subtypes, for example, *working memory*.

Neither analytical functionalism nor psychofunctionalism effectively grounds the Functionalist Argument. Consider first the analytical approach, taking the case of memory as an example. Our everyday conception of memory entails that a memory is caused by interaction with a certain state of affairs (which we might normally describe as what the memory is a memory *of*) and, under certain conditions, causes the subject to have a belief with the same content as the memory. Applied in a straightforward way, this analytic approach does not serve the extended view well, for common sense rules strongly against external portions of memories (and likewise for nonoccurrent beliefs). The commonsense conception of memory precludes its being *seen* by its possessor (i.e., precludes its being a cause of a perceptual, as opposed to an imaginative, state). A standard method of analyzing commonsense concepts tests our reactions to sentences containing terms supposed to express those concepts. Try the two following sentences: "Yesterday I saw my memory of last week's trip to the beach, and I threw it across the room," and "I left my memory of your phone number on the bus with some chocolate smeared on it." These sentences exude semantic deviance, at least if one keeps clearly in mind that the sentences are meant literally, not metaphorically. Insofar as these examples share a common thread, it is the reference to memories in physically external locations. Similarly, the commonsense functional characterization of belief precludes the encoding of Otto's belief-states in his notebook, for according to the commonsense conception of belief that an analytical functionalist theory must capture, a subject cannot literally see portions of her belief-states. The Ramsey sentence expressing folk psychological theory will not assert a causal (or even merely conditional) relation between belief-states and perceptual states, where the latter is a visual perception of a portion of the former; if any statement regarding such a connection makes its way into the Ramsification of commonsense psychology, it will be an explicit denial of the connection.[1]

My worry might not trouble the extended theorist. A solid functionalist analysis results only from careful reflection on a variety of examples and considerations, she might claim; only then can we separate the wheat from the chaff in the folk understanding of the relevant concepts. Thus, the proponent of the extended view might continue, we should cast a skeptical eye on the folk's rejection of extended states and instead formulate our functionalist analysis via a more refined method. Compare Clark and Chalmers's discussion (1998, 16) of a proposed disanalogy between the normal person's belief that MoMA is on 53rd street and Otto's alleged belief: Otto perceives his notebook, but the average person does not perceive the location at which her beliefs are stored. Clark and Chalmers respond, in essence, by recommending revision: once we properly conceive of Otto and his notebook as a single cognitive system, we no longer take his visual interaction with the notebook to be a relevant point of disanalogy.

What, though, could motivate such revision? Given that the extended view is typically offered as a thesis in the philosophical foundations of cognitive science—that, at least, is the primary angle of interest here—empirical considerations seem to provide the only plausible source. Notice, however, the oddness of such a result, even if it were to favor the extended view. If successful empirical work were to deliver extension-friendly descriptions of psychological kinds and properties—so as to revise folk intuitions in the relevant ways—its doing so would render the analytical version of the Functionalist Argument

---

1. Perhaps common sense does not so obviously deliver such proscriptions when it comes to realizers. After all, folk concepts do not restrict what can play the causal role of a given mental state. Folk concepts do, however, demand that a realizer bear the right causal relations to other realizers; if the mental states are to do so, then their realizers must also. This demand suffices to ground the argument given in the main text, at least if folk concepts make any allowance at all for realizers and physically located mental states.

an afterthought; we would have reason to accept the revised conceptual analysis only because we already have in hand a well-supported psychofunctionalist account of cognitive states, in particular, one that supports the extended view. The folk intuitions would be most convincingly revised by a highly successful scientific research program that establishes the extended view; but upon the flourishing of such a program, the Functionalist Argument makes no dialectically important contribution. Thus, the analytical version of the Functionalist Argument is vindicated only by considerations that render it moot.

Compare a similarly quixotic strategy: We would like to convince the folk that they can see the realizers of their beliefs when given a mirror during neurosurgery (under local anesthetic). To do so, we must have in hand a convincing neuroscientific theory of belief-realization; otherwise, the folk will have no reason to think that they are seeing the realizers of their beliefs (as opposed to some brain-goo having little directly to do with belief-realization). It would be hopeless to try to use the folk intuitions tutored by a neuroscientific theory of belief-realization to show that belief-states are, in fact, realized by neural states. The first portion of the strategy presupposes we already have in hand a convincing neuroscience of belief-realization, so from the standpoint of someone arguing that beliefs can be neurally realized, it is moot to appeal to folk intuitions revised on the basis of neuroscience; the relevant argument appeals directly to the neuroscience.

Some proponents of the extended view might nevertheless insist on a purely analytic method. Thought-experiments alone, they might claim, can tutor folk intuitions about mental states, so as to deliver a convincing version of the Functionalist Argument. To the contrary, once it is made clear how removed this method is from empirical work, it appears irrelevant. Why should cognitive science care much about the details of the way in which the average folk apply mental or cognitive concepts, particularly to hypothetical cases? Everyday use might provide cognitive scientists with some general direction or an initial categorization of certain forms of behavior as intelligent, but everyday use is normally dispensed with, or at least heavily revised, as science advances. Consider the important theoretical constructs in cognitive science, from the idea of a connectionist cognitive architecture to that of a goal-stack to that of an emulator circuit. Nonspecialists simply do not possess the relevant concepts. Moreover, in cases in which the folk do have concepts roughly in the vicinity of the scientific ones, cognitive science is not beholden to those concepts. If the average person associates much of anything with the word 'computation', there is no reason to think such associations provide a notion of much use in the scientific modeling of cognitive processes. Thus, when it comes to many, perhaps most, cognitive states and processes, analytical functionalism offers no guidance at all, and more importantly, no support for the extended view. Either there is no folk concept to be analyzed or the concept is not, from the standpoint of cognitive science, worth analyzing.

Consider a last-ditch defense of the analytic interpretation of the Function-alist Argument. Perhaps the argument can be saved if we stress the distinction between the mental and the cognitive. When we are focused on the extended *mind*, in contrast to the case of extended cognitive states, the concepts at issue *are* folk concepts, it might be claimed. Even with regard to the *mind*, we should doubt that the analysis of folk concepts is of much importance. Assume that the folk analysis of belief does, in the end, vindicate the status of certain extended states as human beliefs. Assume also that cognitive science does its work, and the closest thing to belief characterized by cognitive science is wholly nonex-tended in the human case. Here we are to imagine a successful, complete cog-nitive science that refers to nothing precisely described by the folk concept of a belief but describes states much like belief in many respects, virtually none of which extend into the environment (in the human case). Where are beliefs, then, *really*? If one accepts the naturalistic approach—endorsed by most of the cognitive science community interested in situated cognition—then the cogni-tive-scientific results trump the folk concept. We can describe such an outcome in two ways: (1) there are beliefs but they are not extended in the way the folk concept (together with empirical facts) entails; or (2) there are *no beliefs* at all, but there are beliefs*, very close in nature to beliefs, but which are not extended. Nei-ther result should console the theorist who holds would like to derive extended minds from the situated revolution in cognitive science; for by hypothesis that revolution gives us only nonextended states—however they be labeled.

Thus, the force of the Functionalist Argument derives entirely from psy-chofunctionalist considerations. Assume that cognitive science does its work, yielding functional-role descriptions of cognitive state-types. If, in a sufficient number and range of cases, extended material fills such roles, the Functionalist Argument is sound and important.

Two kinds of problem arise for this approach in practice, however. The psychofunctionalist version of the Functionalist Argument succeeds only if cognitive science has yielded descriptions of cognitive states such that some external material fills the roles individuative of those states. The most straight-forward way in which working cognitive science might yield such role-descrip-tions is, as we might say, bottom-up. That is, cognitive science might construct models of the relevant processes and then generalize over them to formulate descriptions of the roles in question. If this procedure is to yield descriptions of the functional roles of cognitive states, however, a prior decision must be made regarding which aspects of the models involve *cognitive* states and which involve merely important elements with which the cognitive states causally interact. A model of reading should certainly have something to say about the role printed text plays in the process of reading; it requires further argument, though, to establish that anything playing the role of the text counts as a cogni-tive state. Thus, even a sound psychofunctionalist version of the Functionalist Argument threatens to be obsolete, being rounded out only after the debate about extended cognition is settled—because, for example, it has been settled on independent grounds that text is a genuinely cognitive part of the process of reading. Absent some independent argument telling us what to count as the genuinely cognitive states, then, we cannot be sure that the various causal roles included in psychological models of cognitive processes are all cognitive roles.

A more general fact about psychofunctionalism underlies this objection: psychofunctionalist characterization of the functional role of mental or cognitive states is, to a great extent, a summary of successful experimental and theoretical work in the relevant sciences. As a result, one must look to the relevant sciences to provide accurate descriptions of cognition, and of which systems exhibit cognitive processing, before issuing the psychofunctionalist summary—the summary of only the genuinely cognitive functions, setting aside the noncognitive ones (which play the role, say, of inputs in the functional characterization of cognitive kinds). Think of the problem in terms of the formulation of a Ramsey sentence of a completed psychology. In order to formulate the Ramsey sentence, one must choose what to treat as input and output; if such choices are taken to mark the boundaries of the cognitive system, then it is a prior condition on the formulation of the Ramsey sentence that one have, already in hand, sound empirical reason to delineate cognitive systems in a particular way.[2]

This is not an insoluble puzzle. In the absence of the identification of the relevant psychofunctional roles, the success of certain kinds of empirical practice can ground a principle of demarcation. As argued in chapter 3, the systems-based criterion has just such status. Thus, the systems-based criterion can tell us what is cognitive and what is not. A psychofunctionalist can then proceed to characterize in functional terms the cognitive contributors to cognitive phenomena, and can do the same for noncognitive contributors—as, say, causes of inputs—if the latter are best understood in functionalist terms.

In response, I think the best the proponent of the extended approach can hope for is favorable future developments: let cognitive science proceed, business as usual, keeping in mind the possibility that, in the end, a compelling vision of extended cognitive processing will emerge. Perhaps in a completed cognitive science, some roles will be uncontroversially cognitive, and these might turn out to have external realizers.

Thus, we arrive at the second problem for psychofunctionalist version of the Functionalist Argument. I contend that, although in principle, cognitive science could serve up extension-friendly psychofunctionalist roles, thus far it has not. The most interesting and useful profiles of psychological states and

2. Similar remarks apply to Clark's appeal (2007, 171) to local mechanistic supervenience bases: surely cognition is wherever its mechanistic supervenience base is; but to know where the latter is, we must first determine which processes are cognitive and which are only causally related to cognitive processes. Knowing the location of the mechanistic supervenience base of processes merely causally related to cognition does not tell us where cognition is located.

properties detail causal roles that external materials are not likely to fill (Adams and Aizawa 2001, 2007; Rupert 2004; Weiskopf 2008a); the empirical study of memory, for instance, reveals many fine-grained properties that external resources—notebooks, for example—do not, for the most part, exhibit.

Below I delve more deeply into the empirical issues, paying special attention to Clark's examples (2007) of empirical results meant to support the extended view. First, however, I introduce another powerful similarity argument; when the time comes, discussion of the empirical work can do double-duty, as part of the critical evaluation of both the Functionalist Argument and what I will call the 'Natural-Kinds Argument'.

5.2. The Natural-Kinds Argument

By endorsing the Functionalist Argument, a proponent of extended cognition might take on more theoretical baggage than she needs. What are the alternatives? One might appeal instead to the idea of natural (or causal-explanatory, or scientific) kinds. Generally speaking, scientific theories group things together when doing so generates causal-explanatory and predictive power. When such theorizing is successful, we should take seriously the categories in terms of which these theories are cast.[3] This way of thinking inspires the following argument for the extended view:

NATURAL-KINDS ARGUMENT

Premise 1.   A taxonomy that characterizes cognitive kinds in such a way that they include extended states provides the most powerful theoretical framework for research in cognitive science.
Premise 2.   Our most successful empirical theories are likely to reflect the genuine nature of reality.
Conclusion.   The extended view is likely to be true.[4]

Compare Clark and Chalmers:

We do not intend to debate what is standard usage [of 'belief']; our broader point is that the notion of belief *ought* to be used so that

---

3. Natural kinds and properties are those that play an important role in successful scientific practice: reference to such kinds grounds successful induction or plays a role in satisfying causal explanation; alternatively, natural kinds and properties are those that appear in our most highly confirmed statements of the laws of nature or causal-explanatory generalizations (Quine 1969; Fodor 1974; Kitcher 1984).

4. Although the Natural-Kinds Argument is cast in starkly realist terms—in terms of the true nature of reality—this is not essential to the debate; we would like to know how best to describe cognition, but that best way can be interpreted as either an accurate description of ultimate reality or simply the way that coheres best with accepted standards of scientific practice.

Otto qualifies as having the belief in question ... By using the 'belief' notion in a wider way, it picks out something more akin to a natural kind. The notion becomes deeper and more unified, and is more useful in explanation. (1998, 14) (cf. Rowlands [1999, 121])

In a similar vein, Clark and Chalmers remark that "one could always try to explain my action in terms of internal processes and a long series of 'inputs' and 'actions', but this explanation would be needlessly complex" (1998, 10).

The argument's central thread is this: When we understand cognitive kinds in such a way that, as a matter of contingent fact, individual kinds have both internal and external instances, we avail ourselves of simpler and more elegant explanations of cognitive phenomena. The extended view, but not its competitors, offers the philosophical underpinnings for this simpler and more elegant framework, and this unique power validates the extended view.

The reader may now see a common thread running through the Functionalist Argument and the Natural-Kinds Argument. Each argument depends, for its cogency, on a certain kind of cognitive-scientific result: our best cognitive science groups internal and (at least partly) external states together—most likely by identifying a relevant range of similarities among internal and (at least partly) external states that justify these groupings. In contrast, if our most successful cognitive science is especially interested in causal-explanatory traits not exhibited by extended states, or if the best interpretation of our most successful cognitive science allows that traits of external states are causally interesting yet not cognitive, then both arguments fail: the Functionalist Argument fails because psychofunctionalism does not yield role-descriptions of cognitive states that are filled by extended realizers, and the Natural-Kinds Argument fails because there do not exist the useful cognitive kinds of the sort Clark and Chalmers envision.

Elsewhere (Rupert 2004), I have argued at length that, in the case of one important natural kind, *memory*, cognitive psychology has uncovered theoretically interesting properties not likely to be shared by the external materials normally proposed as candidate components of extended cognitive processing. This creates a dilemma for the extended theorist.[5] As regards the dimensions typically of interest in cognitive psychology's study of human memory, external materials do not normally play the same functional role as the internal ones; neither do they exhibit the same theoretically important properties, and thus they are not of the same natural kind as the relevant internal states. Therefore, if there is any hope for the Natural-Kinds Argument, it would seem to be via the invocation of 'generic' cognitive kinds (Rupert 2004, 418–21); for instance, generic memory is the property of *being information that the subject has some kind of access*

---

5. Although the argument focuses specifically on memory, it is meant to illustrate a dilemma that the Functionalist and Natural-Kinds Arguments face with regard to a wide range of empirical investigations of human cognition.

to. Such kinds are not, however, likely to play an important causal-explanatory role in cognitive psychology. We have prior reason to posit internally instantiated cognitive systems that allow access to externally encoded information; to the extent that the general flow of information plays an interesting role, an orthodox or embedded model accommodates that role. The appeal to generic cognitive kinds thus involves the needless introduction of new labels or gratuitous kinds.

This worry about the second horn of my dilemma may seem familiar enough. Let me say a bit more about the first horn, having to do with fine-grained properties, before moving on. Interference in paired-associates experiments provides one kind of empirical result that seems to differentiate internal memory from the typical candidates—notebooks, sticky notes, computer files—for extended status. In paired-associates experiments, subjects learn assigned associations between pairs of stimulus items, with subjects' recall of these associations tested in various ways and at various time intervals (Anderson 2000, 239–43; Bower 2000, 9–14). Negative transfer, a particular form of interference effect, appears when past learning detrimentally affects subjects' capacity to learn and remember new associations; it is observed in the following experimental paradigm, among others: experimenters direct subjects to memorize associations between pairs of words on a list—these might be names of men, as stimuli, and names of their female spouses, as the target responses. Call this first list of pairs the 'A–B' list, A-words being those used as stimuli at the recall stage, B-words those that must be recalled upon exposure to A-words. The subjects learn the intended associations to criterion. In the next stage, experimenters shuffle the pairings, telling subjects, for example, that the couples in question have all divorced and remarried. Subjects are asked to learn the new pairs, on what is called the 'A-C' list, and they do so significantly more slowly than they learned the A–B associations (or than they learn associations on a list made up of entirely new names). There is, it is said, negative transfer, an interference of the old associations with the learning of the new. The problem seems to be that if, for instance, John was married to Sally according to the A–B list, subjects have a hard time blocking out this association and forming a new association between 'John' and, say, 'Mary', with which 'John' is now paired on the A-C list.

There is no reason to expect negative transfer in the learning of paired associates when a subject relies on an external store. The experimenter dictates the A–B list to the subject, and she records it in her notepad. After using the written list to answer the experimenter's questions, the subject sets it aside. Later, the experimenter dictates the pairs on the A-C list to the subject, and she writes them down. Why would the items on the first list interfere with the accuracy of the data she enters on the second? The subject listens to the experimenter; she says, "John, Mary"; her words rebound through the subject's auditory working memory; the subject writes down the pair. Period. No problem, no interference. Similarly with recall: after the subject has recorded the A-C list, she sets it on the table for immediate access. When the experimenter provides only an A-word as stimulus, looking to the subject for the pair's completion, the subject simply consults her handwritten A-C list; presumably, she gets the right answer the first time, right away, with no negative transfer from related pairs on the A–B list. In fact, not only is there no interference; there is lacking entirely any typical learning curve for paired associates, under conditions that create interference or otherwise: assuming the subjects can take dictation and read their own handwriting, lists of pairs are "learned" immediately, on the first try, contrary to observations made under a wide variety of experimental conditions where subjects are allowed to use internal resources only. Granted, someone might lose her written list of paired associates, but there is no reason to think that, in general, "list-losing curves" will even approximate the forgetting curves found in paired-associates experiments.

The preceding example is one of very many (Adams and Aizawa 2001, 2007; Rupert 2004; Weiskopf 2008a). Thus, the Natural-Kinds Argument, as well as its functionalist cousin, founders on a dilemma: characterize the relevant causal-explanatory kinds in terms of the fine-grained similarities, the study of which has proven to be theoretically fruitful or, instead, opt for a coarse-grained (or generic) conceptions. Neither alternative offers. both (a) extended kinds (i.e., kinds that singly subsume both internally and externally realized states in a substantial number of cases) and (b) a resulting causal-explanatory advantage; the fine-grained approach is not likely to yield extended natural kinds at all, and the coarse-grained approach yields extended kinds unlikely to do substantive causal-explanatory work.[6] Thus, both arguments fall to false or unsubstantiated premises: in the case of the Functionalist Argument, it is the premise claiming that some cognitive states have external realizers; in the case of the Natural-Kinds Argument, it is the premise claiming that an extension-friendly taxonomy provides a more powerful theoretical framework for cognitive psychology.

5.3. The Empirical Response

5.3.1. Short-Term External Memory?

Can friends of the extended view return serve? How might the Functionalist or the Natural-Kinds Argument be strengthened? Most impressive would be the identification of extension-supporting empirical results. In this regard,

6. In Rupert (2004), I explicitly attacked the Natural-Kinds Argument (or the causal-explanatory kinds argument, as I called it—Rupert [2004, n30]) in just this way, posing the dilemma described in the main text (Rupert 2004, 407). The discussion there has frequently been misinterpreted (Menary 2006; Clark 2007; Bartlett 2008) as a direct criticism of the extended view or being as somehow based on a misinterpretation of the Parity Principle. A criticism of an argument for P, however, is not itself an argument against P; and as should be clear, the criticism of the Natural-Kinds Argument has nothing particularly to do with the Parity Principle.

consider the work of Dana Ballard and colleagues (Ballard et al. 1997). They ran a series of experiments in which subjects appear to show preference for the use of external resources during problem-solving. One experiment requires subjects to copy a structure made from colored blocks, in a computer simulation (and similar results have been achieved in experiments with real blocks—ibid., 732). Subjects were given a pool of colored blocks—the resource pool—and a distinct workspace in which to replicate the target structure. One might expect subjects in a given experimental trial to memorize the target structure, then to devote their further attention to the resource pool and workspace. In fact, subjects make less extensive use of internal memory. By tracking subjects' eye movements, Ballard et al. measure how often subjects return to the target structure for information. Subjects do so surprisingly frequently: with respect to an individual block, subjects often work in two steps, first copying the color of the target block into memory, then going to the resource area to find a block of that color, then looking back at the target pattern to store the target block's location, then back to the workspace to place the block. On the basis of such results, Ballard et al. suggest that humans employ "minimal memory strategies" (ibid., 732), using external storage even when it would be more efficient to commit more information about the model to internal memory. This, in turn, might lead proponents of extended cognition to claim a victory: Ballard et al. demonstrate the role of the external world as working memory.

I do not think we should be moved by the extension-friendly interpretation of the results. Visual pointers can act like demonstratives. The organism may, for instance, utilize a context-dependent representation, REACH THERE,[7] where THERE is simply wherever attention is focused (i.e., whatever position in space is represented by a specially active symbol) (cf. Ballard et al. [1997, 725]). Perhaps the context-dependent nature of such representations obscures the line between the external environment as a source of information and, in contrast, as something that actively guides cognition. This role for pointers can, however, be easily understood in terms of an embedded model and a theory of the content of demonstratives that assigns an external object, location, or property to a pointer. On this approach, the pointer (or if the pointer calls information from an internal register, the internal state constructed from that information) actively guides behavior. No doubt, in some circumstances we refer to the pointer in terms of its content, so as to explain the subject's behavior in relation to the external thing the pointer (or the accessed contents of the register) indicates in the environment; but this is a standard reason for referring to the external content of a cognitive state.

---

7. I adopt the following orthographic conventions: terms referring to properties or kinds, in the abstract, as well as terms that refer to mental contents, are set in italics; concepts, considered as mental particulars, are set in capital letters, where a given concept's label (HORSE, for instance) derives from the content we assume to be carried by that mental particular.

In the case at hand, Ballard's visual pointers serve an important function: they help the visual system to make active the information it needs—say, a block's color—which it then collects from the world and represents internally. The subject cannot pick up a block the same color as *that* one without representing the specific color (impressive though it may be that the subject need not represent much else at that step in the process). It appears that the information in question can guide behavior only by being physically encoded in the organism, however fleetingly. It is one thing to say that subjects acquire information from the environment much more frequently and in much smaller bits than was previously thought; it is quite another to say that the external world becomes part of the active cognitive system because subjects consult it so frequently.

We understand well enough the idea of a cognitive system as distinct from the information that it might come across or have access to in a given situation. This suggests an embedded interpretation of Ballard's results. Moreover, Ballard et al.'s results nicely model a way to flesh out the embedded account. Causal interaction between the organismically limited cognitive system produces explicit (if short-lived and not very rich), internal representations that guide the behavior of the organism. The embedded interpretation offers a coherent story of how an integrated set of cognitive capacities produce a given behavior especially well within a particular kind of environment—a hallmark of embedded modeling. The mere availability of an extended parsing of the system does not overcome the various weaknesses of that parsing; the worries about simplicity, conservatism, and the mere-semantics objection speak in favor of the embedded approach.

Compare this to an example discussed by Richardson, Dale, and Spivey (2007). They describe results in which subjects who are listening to a narrative use eye movements to mark the locations described in the narrative. For instance, the subject might hear, "You're looking at a forty story building. Joe is on the fire escape on the tenth floor. Some workers are on the roof performing maintenance." Although subjects sit in front of a blank screen while processing the story, they fixate visually on a series of locations the relative positions of which reflect the structure of the locations in the story: they fixate on a significantly lower point when hearing about the tenth-floor fire escape than when they hear about work being done on the roof. Richardson et al. comment that "storing in working memory the relation *above (x, y)* may not be necessary if the eye movements, and their allocation of spatial indices, have embodied and externalized that spatial relationship in the environment already" (ibid., 13). The spatial indices are, however, encoded in parietal cortex (ibid., 10), and thus, there is a relatively straightforward internalist story about the activities of an organismically bound cognitive system: parietal cortex encodes a spatial relation, even if only in the form of links to relative eye positions, that can then affect cognitive processing (e.g., in the disambiguation of the narrative or the drawing of inferences from the narrative). Motor commands to eye movements can be bound to parietally represented locations. Admittedly, it is sometimes useful to think in terms of the semantic content of the related pointers (either eye-movement commands or neural structures in parietal cortex): the relation they bear to each other is the relation that two pointers normally bear to each other when they refer to two locations, one above the other, in the immediate environment; and they normally have effects on cognitive process that coheres with this content. Nevertheless, it is superfluous to say also that locations on the blank screen actively control cognition.

5.3.2. Cognitive Impartiality

In a recent paper, Clark (2007) claims that the work of Wayne Gray and his colleagues (Gray and Fu 2004; Gray, Sims, Fu, and Schoelles 2006) supports the extended view. One series of experiments (Gray et al. 2006) employs a variation on Ballard et al.'s pattern-copying task. Administered on computers, Gray et al. can control subjects' access to the resource, workspace, and target (or model) areas. All areas are occluded by a gray patch on the screen. Workspace and resource areas can be accessed simply by running the cursor over the boundary of the occluding screen. The experimental manipulation concerns access conditions for the target area. One experiment includes three different conditions for gaining access to information behind a gray screen: (a) press and hold the control key for immediate removal of the gray screen, (b) run the cursor over the boundary for immediate removal of the gray screen, or (c) run the cursor over the boundary with a one-second lockout period before disappearance of the gray screen. Another experiment employed a radio button, which had to be depressed in order for the occluding screen to disappear. To test the effect of requiring different investments of time (via the indirect measure of differing amounts of effort), the size of the radio button varied among conditions: 260 × 260 pixels (easy condition), 60 × 60 pixels (medium condition), and 8 × 8 (difficult condition). A third experiment varied the lockout time, using six different delays ranging from 0.0 to 3.2 seconds.

Results of pattern-copying tasks are analyzed along three dimensions: (a) mean number of target-window access-events over the course of a complete trial, (b) duration of the subject's first look at the target in a given trial, and (c) the number of blocks correctly placed after the subject's first look in a given trial. A consistent pattern emerges across all three experiments. Increasing difficulty in access to the target window—measured in terms of time—leads to fewer target-window access-events, longer first-looks, and a greater number of blocks placed correctly after the first look. A model of cognitive processing sensitive only to the time-cost of encoding and accessing information (whether via internal memory or a perceptuo-motor process) fits the data naturally and accurately. It looks, then, as if the cognitive system is indifferent to the resources used; time-costs are all that matter. This grounds Gray et al.'s argument (2006, 478) for the extended view. The cognitive system itself treats the locations, internal or external, as equivalent. Thus, internal and external locations are on cognitive par. Assuming the uncontested—that the internal locations are part of the cognitive system—the extended view follows.

To my mind Gray's results show something very different: that when there is no great cost in terms of time, the cognitive system will use resources beyond its boundary. The contrasting argument for extended cognition seems to rest on the following premise: a system that uses resources beyond its boundary must (or at least is very likely to) treat the external nature of the location of those resources as intrinsically relevant to the decision whether to use those resources. I take this premise to be exceptionally implausible, a matter to which I shall return presently.

Before developing this concern, consider a pair of preliminary points. First, we should not be misled by Gray and Veksler's characterization of their model: "The central controller makes no functional distinction between knowledge in-the-head versus in-the-world" (quoted in Clark [2007, 172]). This is an over-statement. Gray et al.'s full model *must* draw a functional distinction between the use of internal stores and external stores. The use of the latter requires the application of perceptuo-motor routines not required for the use of the former. For the two kinds of location to be treated differently—one accessed via perceptuo-motor routines, the other not—there must, by definition, be a functional difference between the role of the two locations. More accurately, then, the central controller does not treat the external store's being external as *in itself relevant* to the calculation concerning which resources to use.

The preceding observation suggests a second, reminiscent of my comments on the work of Ballard et al. and Richardson et al. When we consider what *is* relevant in the calculation, our attention is directed to the mechanisms by which the cognitive system gains access to internal and external information; for which mechanisms are used helps to determine the time-cost of such access. Use of the internal store need not involve the running of online perceptuo-motor routines, whereas external stores are accessed only via such routines. Perhaps the process of accessing external stores draws on the system's implicit knowledge of reliable sensorimotor contingencies: motor-command p is followed by a sensory experience that should be treated as the answer to a given query. Represented this way, though, there is no question of a competition between internal and external memory stores. Rather, there is a competition between the use of one internal store and the use of a distinct internal store. The computational process "chooses" between the retrieval of information from various internal registers: memory register A—part of, say, short-term, declarative memory; and register B—a visual buffer. When "deciding" between the use of A and B, the central controller "cares" only about the cost of using one register over the other; but both A and B are inside the organism.

Conceived of in this way, the process of choosing between the registers has no bearing on extended cognition, except perhaps a negative one: by showing how the internal system chooses between two internal stores (standard memory versus information held in sensory buffers), the work of Gray and his colleagues shows how the embedded, organismically bounded cognitive system manages its interaction with, and exploitation of, environmental structures.

Perhaps the preceding point rests too heavily on a certain view of sensory input, one that proponents of extended cognition will likely challenge. Set aside, then, questions about the internal sensory register, and let us return to my primary objection, to do with the ambiguity of Gray et al.'s results; for this worry persists even when we take at face value the externalist characterization of the location of information accessed via sensorimotor routines. Assume that the abstract representation of the computational process fails to assign, in terms of absolute privilege or specially strong weighting, a unique status to the internal resources, and thus is impartial. Nevertheless, this kind of impartiality is also to be expected in cases where we contrast the use of internal and genuinely external storage (where, by 'genuinely external', I mean 'external to the organism *and* external to the cognitive system, in case the latter is extended'). Take a cognitive system that sometimes uses resources external to it, where, again, 'external' simply means beyond its boundaries, wherever they happen to be. Now assume the system uses some decision-procedure for selecting those resources. Why should we expect the system to mark the difference between external and internal resources, assigning internal resources privilege simply in virtue of their status as internal? If there is no reason to expect this, then Gray's results alone provide no reason to prefer one of the two following descriptions of the human decision-making process: as involving (1) a choice between two systemically internal locations or (2) a choice between the system's internal resources and some external resources to which it can also gain access.

Take seriously the idea that the extended view is false. Now assume someone wants to hide a written piece of information. She might be just as inclined to memorize the information, then eat the paper, as she is, say, to hide the paper in a hollow log. She might care only about how easily the information will be found by others. The fact that she treats both locations solely in terms of costs and benefits that have nothing intrinsically to do with the organismic boundary (how quickly can I hide information? how likely is it to be found?) does not show our initial supposition to be incoherent or strange. Wherever the boundaries of the cognitive system are, it should be possible that the system sometimes uses resources beyond its boundary without the choice to do so having been driven by a direct consideration of the external–internal boundary.

Thus, I see no reason to think that if there are two resources, one internal and another genuinely external to a given system, then if that system chooses between the use of these two resources, the system must (or is at least very likely to) treat the differential status of the locations as intrinsically relevant.

Without this premise, however, Gray's results provide no support for extended cognition. Gray et al.'s demonstration is neutral in respect of two kinds of system—an extended system and one that is internal but sometimes chooses to use external resources—because both systems would be modeled in the same way: with a range of locations that are, in the abstract, treated on a par, as two possible locations the choice between which is determined by further considerations. In both cases, the representation of the relevant algorithm will, if it contains a representation of the external location at all (as opposed to a sensory register), not mark it as intrinsically second-rate: the various locations of information will simply be marked with subscripts or the like, so that they can be treated as distinct options when the decision-making computation is carried out. Thus, the sort of impartiality discovered by Gray et al.—even if it is understood in terms of a choice between organismically internal and external locations—does not increase the likelihood of the extended, relative to the nonextended, hypothesis. Each hypothesis predicts that aspects of human cognition can be effectively modeled using an impartial algorithm. Thus, independent considerations must be brought into play. Such considerations, in the form of the arguments of part I, support the nonextended conclusion.

5.4. The Pragmatic Turn

It is sometimes suggested that, even if the existing research does not provide much of a case for the extended view, it would be of pragmatic value—*vis-à-vis* empirical research, in particular—to adopt the extended view (cf. Clark and Chalmers [1998, 10]; Clark [2008b]). By accepting the extended view, we free ourselves of biases that impede progress in cognitive science. The progress facilitated by the adoption of a scientific hypothesis determines its value. If adopting the extended view can lead, or in fact has led, to significant advances in cognitive science, this speaks in favor of its adoption.

Fair enough, but we should distinguish between (a) an outlook verified by the successes that it, in some very general way, helps to cause and (b) a theoretical perspective that, together with reasonable ancillary assumptions, uniquely (among existing competitors) entails, predicts, or explains a range of successful results. The pragmatic argument is much stronger if the successes in question come via route (b); yet, my general argument for the embedded view over the extended view suggests that, if adopting the extended view yields benefits at all, it is via route (a).

Even with regard to the question of motivation and researchers' psychology, the extended view does not have anything special to offer. The embedded outlook does just as much to motivate the sort of work that has most impressed advocates of the extended view (cf. Vera and Simon [1993]). In fact, much of the empirical research that inspires advocates of the view is not driven distinctively by the extended view. This research is driven by a general interest in the environment's effect on human cognitive processing, but that does not distinguish between the extended view and the embedded view.

The work of Gray and associates seems to reinforce this diagnosis. In a recent paper, Fu and Gray (2006) describe their results in terms of the embedded view rather than the extended view (see, e.g., their section titled "Information seeking as the interface between cognition and the environment," (ibid., 196). Why, then, do Gray et al. (2006, 478) explicitly endore the extended view? Here is one plausible way to understand the big picture: Gray and associates can draw various morals from their work and they can cast their results in various terms *for the very reason that* the extended perspective is doing no particular motivational work, either theoretically or psychologically. The work is motivated by a general interest in the role of the environment and as such can just as well be cast in terms of the embedded view as it can be in terms of the extended view. Consider also the way in which Ballard et al. (1997, 723) describe their approach: "Our central thesis is that intelligence has to relate to interactions with the physical world, meaning that the particular form of the human body is a vital constraint in delimiting many aspects of intelligent behavior." This thesis neither uniquely entails nor uniquely gives voice to the embedded or the extended view.[8]

For much of the nineties, advocates of the extended view and related positions were unclear as to which position they were advocating at what point and by which arguments. To my mind, this casts further doubt on the claim that trailblazing researchers from the nineties, whose work inspires the extended view, were motivated specifically by the extended view. Interesting though much of this work is, all that seemed required of researchers was the vague conviction that interaction with the environment significantly affects cognitive processing, and that differences in the structure of the environment can affect the structure of that processing. Thus, neither from a psychological nor theoretical standpoint does the extended view make a unique contribution; when it comes to what matters—the emphasis on interactive processing—the embedded, systems-based view does just as well.

Lastly, it should be noted that pragmatic considerations present a double-edged sword. Adopting the extended view may well have negative consequences, enough perhaps to outweigh whatever positive ones it has. For example, too forceful an insistence on the extended view may distract researchers' attention from the asymmetric relations between the persisting organismic portion of the purportedly extended cognitive system and the system's external portions. Much of the theoretically important action occurs at the interface between

---

8. See the discussion in Rupert (2004, 393–94, n9) of the ambiguity of message in Kevin O'Regan's work on vision.

organism and environment, for example, in the ways the organism extracts, stores, and uses information that it picks up from the environment. Adoption of the extended view may well cause researchers to give short shrift to the asymmetries involved in this process. In contrast, acceptance of the embedded alternative encourages researchers to keep clearly in mind the important asymmetries (e.g., that certain forms of motivation rest distinctively in the organism) while in no way encouraging them to neglect the interface with or heavy dependence on the environment.

6

Developmental Systems Theory and the Scaffolding of Language

In this chapter, I consider two kinds of argument for the extended view. The first invokes nontrivial causal spread (Wheeler and Clark 1999, 110; Wheeler 2004, 703), an idea encountered in the discussion of the causal principle of demarcation in chapter 2: external causes are responsible, in a nontrivial way, for the behavioral phenomena that cognitive science sets out to explain, and thus, such causes are themselves cognitive. The second argument appeals to the complementary or transformational role external resources can play (Clark 2003, 22, 110). These resources supplement the organismic package to such an extent that they transform humans' cognitive resources. The entire extended package exhibits cognition-related properties of a wholly different kind from those displayed by the organism alone; therefore, that extended package is a cognitive system in its own right.

As a general form of argument, neither carries much force. Nevertheless, when given concrete shape, these arguments can seem quite compelling. Thus, after a brief section criticizing the general forms of argument, this chapter elaborates upon and responds to detailed versions of them. These detailed versions concern biological systems, in the case of nontrivial causal spread, and human language, in the case of transformational power.

6.1. Causal Spread and Complementary Role

6.1.1. Nontrivial Causal Spread

According to the argument from nontrivial causal spread (Wheeler 2005, especially chapter 9), environmental factors are causally responsible for the distinctive characteristics of cognitive processes, and they are responsible to such an extent that they become a literal part of human cognition. This might be put in terms of patterns of co-variation or counterfactual dependence. Systematic variation in the external resources is accompanied by corresponding changes in human performance. Were the external factors in question not present, human performance would fall off dramatically; and were the external factors reintroduced, performance would improve.

A covering premise provides an essential piece of the argument: "Whenever A causally contributes in a nontrivial way to effect B, A becomes part of a distinctively B-producing system (or A takes on properties distinctive of B-producing systems)." Call this covering premise the 'General Causal Principle'. Perhaps advocates for extended cognition do not have this premise in mind. Nevertheless, the following argument is invalid: "External materials are nontrivially causally responsible for cognitive-scientific explananda; therefore, the extended view is true." Some premise must be added to connect the observation concerning nontrivial causal responsibility to the extended view.

Now, the advocate of nontrivial causal spread might wish to replace the General Causal Principle with a cognition-specific covering premise, for example, "If external factors contribute causally and nontrivially to the production of the *explananda* of cognitive science, then the extended view is true." This begs the question, though, given that—as I argue presently—analogous claims do not hold in other domains. Perhaps this difficulty partly explains why discussions of nontrivial causal spread often focus at length on the empirical details of causal control, without having much to say about the covering premise. It may be that the empirical details line up; nevertheless, we should insist on an answer to the further question, "Why do those details support the extended view?"

Consider my phenotypic trait of having brown eyes, which, let us assume, has a genetic explanation. Certainly my parents' genes contributed nontrivially to the development of this trait in me. What does this entail about the biological system that has brown eyes? Are the brown eyes a feature of a single, discrete biological system composed of me and my parents? If one is inclined to think so, why stop there? My parents' parents possession of the relevant genes nontrivially causally explains my having brown eyes. So, if my parents and I make up a single, theoretically important biological system, then so also, it would seem, does the collection consisting of my parents, their parents, and me. This strikes me as intuitively absurd; much more to the point, its not at all clear what biology gains by such a taxonomy of biological systems. One might try to lessen the absurdity by excluding my grandparents from the biological system in question, perhaps by claiming that my parents' contribution "screens off" the contribution of my grandparents, rendering the latter taxonomically irrelevant. Then, however, one wonders why the contribution of my own genes does not screen off the contribution of my parents, rendering them taxonomically irrelevant. And if this kind of argument is legitimate here, then why not in cognitive science? If screening off is taxonomically relevant, then we should say that, because the states of proximal stimulation (e.g., sensory states) screen off the contribution of the environment in cognitive processing, the extended view is false. I hope the point of this example is clear enough: if applied in the biological realm, General Causal Principle yields unacceptable results. If so, General Causal Principle is false, and cannot be appealed to in an argument for the extended view.

Is there a nonarbitrary way to tailor General Causal Principle to cognitive science? One might appeal here to local success—that is, success in cognitive science—to support a cognition-specific version of General Causal Principle. This strategy, however, seems to collide with the arguments laid out in the preceding chapters. Given the success of organismic individuation, together with standard methodological canons, we should want to explain the results at issue in terms of organismically bounded systems: cases in which the environment contributes nontrivially should be understood as cases in which the organismically bounded cognitive system has the capacity to use certain resources in the environment in certain ways. It has the ability to use hammers to build houses, for example. Thus, we should not be surprised that if the hammers are missing, human nail-driving performance degrades dramatically—particularly when there is nothing else around the human can use efficiently in place of the hammer.

A second rejoinder involves narrowing the kind of causal contribution at issue: nontrivial causal contribution is relevant to systems individuation only when the contribution explains the distinctive aspects of the behavior (or other effect) involved. This, however, does not carry the argument for the extended view very far. Flexibility is one of the most distinctive aspects of cognition, and an organism-based view accounts for this more naturally than an extended view (see chapter 3). Notice, too, that an appropriately altered General Causal Principle faces problems similar to the more permissive version considered above. Both my parents' and grandparents' genes contributed nontrivially to the distinctive aspect of the phenomenon in question—the very brown-*ness* of my eyes. This does not, however, make it any more plausible to say that there is a single biological individual consisting of me, my parents, and my parents' parents (and so on) possessing these brown eyes. Arguments from conservatism and simplicity suggest that we commit ourselves only to biological individuals, existing during different time periods, that have causally interacted in theoretically important ways.[1]

---

1. Perhaps some cases are special because of the short time-scale on which the environment contributes; this idea will be explored more fully in the chapter 7, in the discussion of dynamical systems theory.

6.1.2. *Environment as Complement*

As an isolated cognitive machine, the human organism is less powerful than frequently supposed. Even the brilliant individualist needs her tools. This seemingly quotidian observation turns grave in the hands of the extended view's proponents. It is only by greatly augmenting our biological capacities with those of the environment that we can perform the feats we take to be distinctive of human cognition; this is especially clear as regards our most impressive technological achievements, which typically require the use of sophisticated mathematics that cannot be done without external aids. It appears, then, that the use of external tools provides humans with abilities of an entirely new kind. Thus, the entire extended system must have the cognitive capacity in question, according to the argument from complementarity.

The most sweeping case of transformation involves the human use of language, to be discussed in detail below. First, though, consider the general principle underlying the transformation-based argument. Even if language transforms the cognitive capacities associated with human organisms, why should that entail an extended cognitive system? By what principle do we make the inference? A Generalized Transformation Principle might do the job: "If the use of A transforms the capacities normally associated with distinct system B, then there is a single system, the A–B system, which has the capacities pretheoretically attributed to (or displayed by) B." Few arguments explicitly invoke this principle, or any principle in its vicinity. Nevertheless, a complete transformation-based argument must include something along these lines.

Is transformational power taxonomically relevant in the way Generalized Transformation Principle claims? In general, it would seem not. Practically speaking, it is impossible for me to fix a hole in my roof without a ladder or similar external device. The roof is high, and if I shinny up the gutter, I will have no tools or shingles to work with upon reaching the top. Nevertheless, this provides little reason to introduce a new entity into our scientific ontology, the human-ladder system. I am tempted by this gloss instead: the human organism can fix the roof because it has the capacity to use a ladder. There are distinct items: humans, roofs, and ladders. The capacities of first and second to interact in distinctive ways are explained by the capacity of the first and third to interact in a distinctive way (and these facts are determined entirely by the three items' intrinsic, physical properties and the laws of nature governing the interactions of these properties). Here the introduction of new kinds of systems is gratuitous. Why should the cognitive case be any different? Admittedly, there is something special about language, which explains why the topic merits extended discussion. Ladders have a fairly specific use in the pursuit of such practical crafts as roof-repair; in contrast, language-use lies at the root of very many of our cognitive skills. Nonetheless, even here skepticism should be the default position, or so I argue below.

6.2. A Case of Nontrivial Causal Spread: Developmental Systems Theory

Developmental systems theory is often seen as an antidote to twentieth-century biology's over-emphasis on the gene. For many years, textbook presentations characterized genes as the codes for, and the determinants of, phenotypic traits of living things; these encodings were selected for because they determined the presence of phenotypical traits conferring reproductive advantage on their bearers. In contrast, the advocates of Developmental Systems Theory point to the wide range of contextual factors affecting gene expression and, more generally, the development of phenotypic traits. The most uncontroversial of these contextual factors reside in the organism itself. Developmental systems theorists go one further, however, arguing that determination involves the entire host of factors shaping the phenotype—the entire host of factors that create a life cycle—which, in many cases, includes factors in the environment beyond the organism's boundary (Griffiths and Gray 1994, 2004).

Developmental systems theory emphasizes the ways in which organismic resources contribute to the shaping of environments (e.g., in niche construction) that confer reproductive advantage on the very organismic resources that help to create those environments. As a result of such selection, those environments are more likely to be recreated or maintained. Thus, environmental factors can themselves participate in the dynamics of selection as they are thought to operate on genetic resources: the environmental resources exhibit traits that, given the context (including the presence of certain organisms), increase the environmental structure's own likelihood of being replicated. Because reproduction of the two systems—of organismic resources and external ones—rely on each other, selection is for the composite package of resources, internal and external: the entire developmental system, organism-and-environment, is selected for.

Developmental systems theory thus appears to support the extended view in a fairly straightforward way. According to Developmental Systems Theory, evolutionary forces often operate on transorganismic, or extended, biological systems. Assuming that cognitive traits were selected for, it is no surprise that such traits should be exhibited by transorganismic systems. The extended theorist simply takes the systems instantiating cognitive properties to be, or to at least be similar in scope to, the systems of fundamental importance in respect of the biological processes that give rise to cognitive phenomena (cf. Griffiths and Stotz [2000]).

What is more, the argument from Developmental Systems Theory to the extended view suggests an instance of nontrivial causal spread. It is largely because environmental factors make a nontrivial causal contribution to the life cycle—to the kind of maintenance and reproduction that are distinctive of biological systems—that environmental factors partly compose the biological system, according to the advocate of Developmental Systems Theory. On Developmental Systems Theory, evolutionary processes select for traits determined by more than the organism itself. Cognitive systems mirror the grain of biological systems and do so because the environment contributes to the maintenance of the cognitive skills that lead to the continued reproduction of creatures with those skills.

Closer examination reveals a different picture, however. One of the primary problems currently faced by Developmental Systems Theory is the problem of systems individuation in the theory of selection (Griffiths and Gray 2004, 423–24). Advocates of Developmental Systems Theory have made a strong case that external resources contribute significantly to the traits on which selection operates. Nevertheless, this does not settle the issue of what are, properly speaking, biological individuals; if we were to accept that just anything causally relevant to the development of a trait becomes part of a biological individual, we would saddle ourselves with a profligate and unmanageable metaphysics for biology. There are alternatives, however.

If one focuses on selection for individual traits, one can, in many cases, interpret the selection process either of two ways: as the selection for extended biological systems or as the selection for traits of individual organisms that occurs within a particular environment (which might, e.g., include the presence of other organisms with the same or a complementary trait; Sterelny and Griffiths [1999, 166–72]). To distinguish cases, Sterelny and Griffiths propose a common-fate criterion (1999, 161, 172–77). Say that we encounter what appears to be an extended system, one that includes something more than a single organism. We can ask to what degree the various components of that system are subject to the same selection pressure, that is, to what extent the reproductive fate of the components is shared. In the extreme case, every part of a system reproduces together or not at all; there is no independent reproduction or survival of parts.[2] In such cases, a trait exhibited by the entire system is possessed by that system as a biological individual.

In other cases, though, the organism interacts with its environment in reproduction-enhancing ways, without shared fate. In these cases, traits are selected for because of their bearers' interactions with components of some larger system. It is only in the context of those interactions that the trait confers its selectional advantage. Still, the bearers in question can and sometimes do go it alone: they can survive and reproduce in the absence of the other components on which the utility of some of their own individual traits depends. In such cases, although an extended system might seem to

---

2. The form of independence I have in mind is not full-blown probabilistic independence but rather the more intuitive idea of there being a non-negligible probability of one thing's reproducing successfully when the other does not.

exhibit a single trait, the components of that system are reproductively independent; and thus the traits on which selectional forces operate are traits of distinct biological individuals, not of a single biological individual. In these cases, component-based explanation—that is, explanation given in terms of selection pressures operating on the traits of the separate components as biological individuals—is to be preferred. In this way, we avoid profligate metaphysics. Many selection-based explanations depend on distinguishing parts of the system. Once such smaller individuals have been admitted into our ontology, there is no reason to add an extended system; analysis in terms of the smaller individuals situated in their environments suffices to explain whatever effects the trait in question has, including effects that change how selectional forces operate on the trait.

This point might be articulated in terms of trait groups. A trait group in respect of trait F is a collection of individuals such that instantiation of F by some sufficient number of the individuals enhances the fitness of each of the individuals in the group. (The idea is that sometimes the presence of a trait enhances the fitness of an individual, even where that individual does not possess the trait in question but rather benefits from other individuals' possession of it.) A given individual, however, can be a member of many trait groups the members of which vary significantly. Thus, to avoid a Byzantine network of partially overlapping, composite biological individuals (and to ensure that our account of composite, biological individual tracks only the theoretically important individuals—see Griffiths and Gray [2004, 423]), we might lay down the following necessary condition: for two individuals to be members of the same composite biological organism, both should be members of all, or nearly all, of the same trait groups. A given person's brain and heart, for instance, are part of the same composite biological individual because the brain's and the heart's probabilities of contributing to the appearance of others of their own kind are enhanced by the same (or very nearly same) group of traits. The token brain and heart are components of the same biological individual because they are members of the same range of trait groups. Any composite biological individual satisfying this criterion is such that its component individuals have a very high probability of a shared fate; they almost certainly will not reproduce independently of each other.

Thus, although Developmental Systems Theory might lay firm biological ground for some extended cognitive systems, significant limitations apply: extended systems exist only where the parts of the extended system share a common fate; only in those cases might facts about extended trait selection bear on cognitive-systems individuation, because only in those cases do facts about extended trait selection bear on the individuation of biological systems. Problem is, most of the systems of interest to extended theorists do not satisfy the shared-fate criterion; these systems exhibit significant asymmetries among their components, analogous to asymmetries resulting in reproductive independence in the biological context. In lieu of some more compelling criterion for the individuation of biological systems, these asymmetries undermine Developmental Systems Theory's case for the extended view.

Consider the genesis of what are alleged to be extended cognitive systems. The volition of the organism, its intention to take up tools, and its capacities to do so are asymmetrically responsible for the creation of the external resources included in these systems (cf. 'locus of control' arguments for the privilege of the organismic system—Butler 1998, 180–81, 212; Wilson 2004, 197–98). For example, an organism with no need to solve complex mathematical problems does not create a system of written numerals the manipulation of which facilitates the solving of mathematical problems; an organism with such needs does. In contrast, it does not happen that a system of numerals exists without a user, then, because the system of numerals has needs or goals that could be served by having a biological user, the system of numerals creates one.

Recall the example of an artist using a sketch pad to create drawings via a feedback loop (Clark 2003, 76–77). The artist begins a sketch by making preliminary figures. The results of these early strokes impinge on the organism, causing her to see the artistic possibilities a new light and thus to make different, often more sophisticated sets of new strokes; the cycle repeats, with the final art-object taking a form that the artist would not have envisioned without the use of the sketch pad as a tool. This is a striking case of embedded cognition at the least. Nevertheless, if the organismic subject had not been interested in drawing, the organism would not have taken up a sketch pad, that is, the extended system in question would never have come into existence. Asymmetrically, the sketch pad's interests, goals, or other internal processes provide little impetus for the creation of the system in question. (An artist might describe her sketch pad as calling to her, but she would, I take it, be speaking figuratively.)

Admittedly, there is some bare counterfactual sense in which the sketchbook causes the existence of the extended system: in the nearest possible world in which the sketch pad does not exist, the particular extended system in question does not come into existence (Lewis 1973). Despite this causal contribution on the part of the sketch pad, the asymmetry is genuine. Consider what happens if a particular sketch pad or a particular artist is deleted from history. The human, wishing to draw, is likely to find or make a different sketch pad if the particular one she would otherwise have used is destroyed. The sketch pad seems less likely to find or make a different human if her user has been removed. This is partly a contingent statistical factor: given prevailing material conditions, I would guess that the proportion of artists who want to sketch who find sketch pads is much greater than the proportion of sketch pads ready for use that in fact get used. Behind this mere contingency, however, lies the point about impetus made above: the human who wants to sketch will go out of her way to find or make a sketch pad; the sketch pad instantiates no internal processes that home in on or actively create users.

Type-level obliteration represents a slightly different kind of counterfactual variation. Wipe the sketch pads from history and human organisms still exist. Wipe the humans from history, and there will be no sketch pads (at least not on Earth!). So, there appears to be a deeply asymmetrical relation between the organismic portion of the allegedly extended system and the external portions.

Compare Clark's sustained argument (2003) that humans are, by their nature, tool users. Clark may well be correct about human nature, and there is at least a clear sense to his claim. It is a bit difficult to understand the converse claim, that it is the nature of external resources that they be used by humans; insofar as it does have clear meaning, it seems obviously false: it is not the nature of iron ore that it be wrought by humans into automobile parts or anything else. Given the asymmetric contribution of human organisms to the formation of such systems, I take Clark's argument to support the embedded view rather than the extended one.[3]

Return now to the question of whether Developmental Systems Theory, qualified by the shared-fate criterion, supports the extended view. Given the asymmetries discussed above, it seems clear that the human organism is reproductively independent of the sketch pad and thus that the composite system of sketch-pad-plus-human does not satisfy the shared-fate criterion. Does this concern carry over to other examples of what are supposed to be extended cognitive systems? It would appear that the standard examples of extended systems—those involving external language, mathematics, external memory storage, and nautical artifacts—manifest the asymmetries discussed above. Although the development of these tools surely affected humans' rate of reproduction, human organisms are reproductively independent of all such resources; humans reproduced without them for millennia, and if a ban on the use of such resources were suddenly instituted, humans would find ways to solve problems and reproduce.

In the end, then, two systems-based concerns threaten the marriage of Developmental Systems Theory and the extended view. First, a plausible Developmental Systems Theory validates only a narrow range of genuinely extended biological individuals; the shared-fate criterion severely limits the number of such extended systems. Second, no matter how things turn out in respect of biology, we cannot ignore the potential for mismatch between the extended individuals established by Developmental Systems Theory and those systems claimed by the extended view to be extended cognitive systems. Clearly these two worries operate together: given the broad range of what are thought to be extended cognitive systems, the narrowness of the range of extended biological systems dims the prospects for cross-disciplinary fit. It may well be that natural forces sometimes select for extended systems, but such systems might not be the ones of interest to psychology (Wilson 1999, 363; Rupert 2004, n22).

3. Sterelny (2004) argues for other substantial asymmetries, both epistemic and representational.

Consider that extended selection requires a stable environmental contribution, yet cognitive science is interested in abilities that can be exercised flexibly
across a wide range of environments; here danger of mismatch looms large.
These concerns about mismatch, as well as criticisms of the general form of
argument being used, suggest that the proponent of the extended view try a
different tack: she should appeal to psychological, rather than biological, standards of systems individuation. As argued in part I, however, this road holds
little promise.

6.3. The Most Powerful Transformation: Language-Learning

Language is, among other things, a system of extraorganismic marks and
sounds with extraordinary transformational power. Via our interaction with it,
we know history, construct buildings, formulate complex philosophical ideas,
inculcate values—the list goes on and on. Because language-use transforms
our cognitive capacities to such a great extent, advocates of the extended view
frequently treat language as a central device of cognitive extension (Dennett
1991, 1996; Clark 1997, 1998); call this kind of reasoning the 'language-based
inference'. This section examines a number of ways in which such extension
might occur, concluding that there is no compelling reason to think language-
use extends the cognitive system. Language profoundly influences our thoughts
and greatly affects the development of the human cognitive system. Nonetheless, these observations provide no reason to rethink the conclusions of part I;
to the contrary, a detailed discussion of the ways in which language affects the
cognitive system reinforces those conclusions, by clarifying the shape a satisfactory embedded approach is likely to take.

6.3.1. Linguistic Content and Thought Content

There is widespread, though not unanimous (Keijzer 1998), agreement that
some notion of representation and representational content continue to be
of use in the study of cognition. Parties to this prevailing view include many
philosophers and cognitive scientists who at least sometimes work outside
the orthodox tradition in cognitive science (Clark and Toribio 1994; Elman
1995, 221–22; Grush 1997, 2003; Churchland 1998, 31; Wheeler and Clark
1999; Wheeler 2001, 2005; Clark 2004, 719; Rowlands 2006). This suggests
a version of the language-based inference pertaining specifically to the content of cognitive structures. On this approach, the content of organismically
internal representations depends in some specially strong way on the content
(or perhaps content-related structure) of external, linguistic materials. Language transforms our cognitive capacities by giving us the very content of our
thoughts.

In what follows, I examine three appeals to content-dependence: (1) it might be that, in an important range of cases, we off-load the contents of our thoughts onto external representations; or (2) it could be that, in some cases, internal cognitive structures inherit their content from external representations after which those internal structures are patterned; or (3) it might be that thought content is determined by the structure of internal cognitive processes, where the structure in question is shaped by the causal or temporal structure of external linguistic resources (even though content is not directly inherited from external, linguistic structures).

Consider case (1). Persons frequently make lists, write down ideas in personal journals and academic papers, and so on. In such cases, one might think that the content-bearing external resources play a sufficiently integral role in the subject's cognitive life as to warrant the language-based inference: the external resources seem to be part of the realization of the subject's thought; and since a thought is wherever its realization is, and a mind is at least partly wherever its thoughts are, we might conclude that the subject's mind is extended to the external matter that carries her thought's content (Houghton 1997).

At this point, it is natural to ask about the source of externally represented content. In virtue of what do the external markings (or auditory forms) have content? In many cases, the content clearly originates within the subject of the mental states in question (Segal 1997, 153; Adams and Aizawa 2001): the subject first thinks that he needs some milk, then writes it on his shopping list. In such cases the subject's thought content is prior to the content of the relevant external linguistic tokens; thus, these cases do not seem to implicate language, in any particularly strong way, in the determination of thought content.

Perhaps, though, once content is off-loaded, that is, encoded in external linguistic tokens, the content takes on a life of its own. The subject no longer tokens any persisting, internal representation carrying the content of the state, but instantiates only a memory that there is, say, a shopping list (even this might be missing in some cases; the subject might not remember the list until he sees it lying on the table). In this case, the subject has the relevant thought, but the only physical structure carrying the thought's content is an external inscription. Does this suffice to extend cognition?

We should not be too quick to externalize subjects' thoughts in these cases, given availability of the embedded alternative. If an individual has the relevant belief (say, that he needs milk) at a given time, yet not because he tokens persisting internal representations carrying the content of that belief, it is most likely in virtue of the appearance of internal representations that take fleeting values relative to the task being performed (Ballard et al. 1997); such pointers can carry the contents represented on the list by deferring to the content of what appears on the list, which, in turn, has its content in virtue of the subject's past investment. In which case, although the subject's internal demonstrative-like representations have whatever content the external structures have, the content is attached to organismically internal structures—to the pointers them-selves. This picture seems especially compelling when we consider the causal efficacy of the mental states in question. The external resources have the kind of causal efficacy we expect a subject's thoughts to have only insofar as the external resources have intervening effects on the subject, which effects are then causes of further actions.

Now consider a different way of understanding (1): the content of thought has its source not in the subject but in the external linguistic units themselves. The idea here is that the linguistic content appears in the linguistic token prior to the subject's use of it or internalization of it. If it could be added that the subject's thought content is somehow constituted by the content of the linguis-tic tokens, this would support the language-based inference. How might this work? Here is a possibility. The subject proceeds absent a thought with the content P. The subject comes upon external linguistic units having the content P; she picks up a book, for example. She then "docks up" to those external resources, coupling to them in a way that creates an occurrent mental state in the subject, for example, a belief that P, without there being an internal vehicle with the content that P (Hurley 1998); in which case the content of the external resources seems to constitute the content of the subject's mental state.

This kind of case does not fit neatly into the mold of a transformation-based argument, but, insofar as the external linguistic units affect behavior, the cases do seem to exhibit nontrivial causal spread. The central point, however, is this: the content of the external resources seems to constitute the content of the subject's mental or cognitive state; and that alone grounds the language-based inference, regardless of whether it is a transformational argument or a version of nontrivial causal spread.

Two considerations recommend against this version of the language-based inference. First, we should bear in mind methodological and empirical consid-erations concerning systems individuation discussed in earlier chapters. These considerations speak in favor of a general understanding of the human cogni-tive system as organismically bounded. If reading, for instance, constitutes an unusual case, one in which we are not sure whether to posit internal represen-tations that carry thought contents, then it might well be considered spoils to the victor, that is, a borderline case to be decided in favor of whichever theory is better supported by independent considerations.

Second, return to my earlier worry about mental causation. What is caused by the mental states of a subject who is reading? One possibility, commonly explored in research on reading comprehension, is that these states cause the subject to give particular answers to questions asked after the reading mate-rial has been put away. Such comprehension studies employ both measures of literal memory for details and also inferences drawn from them (Gathercole and Baddeley 1993, 228). Differences in performance on such tasks is best explained by differences in various subjects' construction and maintenance of internal representations, for the reading material has been taken from the subjects at the time the capacities are tested. This, however, presupposes that the subject, at some point prior to questioning, formed internal representations (whatever form these take) of the text or its meanings. Presumably, this occurred during reading. Therefore, we have independent reason to think that when a subject engages with text, she forms internal representations that carry the content of the text being read. Docking-up to text does not create an extended system that has mental or cognitive states the content of which is in the text; rather, to the extent that the cognitive system enters into new states, they may inherit their content from the text, but they do so via the construction of organismically internal representations with such content. Thus, although the view in question occupies its own bit of logical space, it can claim little empirical support.

This brings us to (2), according to which there are internal, mental representations active in the relevant cases, but those representations inherit their content from the content of external linguistic units. A significant amount of thought is, on this view, the use of internalized language (that is, the manipulation of mental representations of linguistic units). This picture obviates concern about systems-identification by claiming a privileged role for linguistic content *vis-à-vis* thought content, without requiring that external linguistic resources be present at the time the subject employs the relevant internal resources; instead, the linguistically generated resources can be used off-line (Wheeler 2004). Here we find a transformational argument for the extended view: we become thinkers by internalizing external language, and thus, the contributing linguistic structures are themselves cognitive.

This argument invokes an empirical claim that may be worth spelling out a bit. How is thought content derived from the content of external linguistic structures? Here is one fairly plausible story. Assume that neural or syntactic facts determine whether the same mental representation is active on two different occasions—modulo, perhaps, some architectural facts that help to determine which units are active. Assume also, that, as a matter of causal history, some mental representations, neurally individuated, have taken on a role in cognition as an effect of the subject's interaction with external language: successful responses to the external units caused the strengthening of connections between the neurons that together realize the mental representations in question (Rupert 2001). The proponent of content-dependence might add that via this causal process, the content of internal units is copied, in a straightforward way, from the content of the linguistic units that caused the formation of coherent, internal ones. Later, when off-line processing takes place, the cognitive system manipulates the same internal structures that are active when a subject is affected by external linguistic resources. If correct, this picture appears to support the language-based inference, by identifying a robust sense in which thought is an aping use of external linguistic resources; in keeping with the transformational argument, those external resources provide the cognitive system with the power to have thoughts possessing the relevant contents.

As the argument stands, it is weak. Exposure to language might be a nomologically necessary condition for having certain thoughts (Carruthers and Boucher 1998a, 2, 10; Carruthers 2002, 659), but we should not conclude on this basis that external language is literally part of the resulting system (recall the arguments of section 2.2.3). As Carruthers (2002, 660) notes, the relation here is merely diachronic. These concerns would hold even if a fairly strong version of the Sapir-Whorf hypothesis were correct:[4] even if the range of thoughts available to a subject are limited to those expressible in her natural language and even if she cannot think those thoughts until she has had sufficient interaction with that language, thought proceeds absent actual tokens of that language (visual images and subjectively heard sounds are *not* part of any external natural language).

Furthermore, (2) does not jibe very well with our best accounts of language learning (Bloom 2000). If one takes the internal representations to have the same content as the external units, and thinks this is so *because* the internal units were patterned after or caused by the external units, one has excluded from the picture the mental content necessary for the child to learn language. For example, it appears that the child uses pragmatic hypotheses, including suppositions about what other people are likely to do, in order to learn the names of things. The child can frame such hypotheses only if she has at her disposal a significant conceptual repertoire—with content fixed, not inherited from language.

Lastly, even if we allow that some mental representations acquire their content by a principle of deference, whereby they inherit their content from independently content-laden linguistic units, the associated language-based inference seems perilous. The dependence-reasoning in question would seem to support equally the inclusion of many other minds in the subject's mind (or cognitive system). Insofar as the external units possess independent content, it is in virtue of the content of the mental states of ancestors, elders, and current-day speakers other than the subject. Language does not suddenly appear in the world, its content in place. If our subject's mind extends into the world because the content of her thoughts derives from the content of the external units that caused the development of some of her internal resources, then our subject's mind should also encompass the minds of those ancestors and the like, the mental states in whom are responsible for the current external units' having the content they have. However exactly the dependence-reasoning is supposed

---

4. There is good reason to reject the Sapir-Whorf hypothesis in its stronger forms (Goldin-Meadow and Zheng 1998, Bloom 2000, Carruthers 2002), but many important questions about the relation between thought and language remain open (see Majid, Bowerman, Kita, Haun, and Levinson [2004], and the essays in Carruthers and Boucher [1998b] and Gentner and Goldin-Meadow [2003]).

to proceed, it seems unprincipled to include external linguistic resources as part of the extended mind, while excluding the minds that give rise to the content of those external linguistic resources; in both cases—moving from current subject to linguistic units and from linguistic units to other subjects—content-dependence is the issue.[5] Yet, to include all of these other speakers (or their minds) in the current subject's cognitive system is a reductio of the extended view; cognitive science has no use for cognitive systems that include the dead and decomposed.

Alternative (3) offers a more roundabout route to content-dependence, then to the extended view. According to (3), internal units are structured or processed in certain ways, and they, or their governing processes, take on that structure as an effect of interacting with external linguistic resources; and it is on account of this structure that the internal units possess the content they do.

Part of what it is to acquire concept C is to come to have a mental representation with the content c. Now assume that coming to have a mental representation with c is largely a matter of coming into the right causal relation to the property or individual c. A mental representation's coming to stand in such a relation may require, at least for the typical human, much mediation (Fodor 1987, 121–22). It might be that, in some cases, the structure of external linguistic resources provides a model of some sort, say a model of which inferences can be used to detect Cs. Internal processing might be patterned after such linguistically provided structure, eventuating in the acquisition of the concept in question—not, however, because the inferential model gives the content of the mental representation, but rather because, for practical purposes, subjects must use such models to get into the causal relation to Cs that is (at least partly) constitutive of having the concept C.

This offers us a way to make sense of Carruthers's and Boucher's remark that language is obviously a prerequisite for the acquisition of such concepts as ELECTRON (1998a, 2). Furthermore, the view makes sense even on the assumption that the mental representation ELECTRON is atomic (i.e., not a structured representation that has further mental representations as components). For even if it is atomic, it is very likely that, closely connected to it, are complex mental representations of sentences containing the word 'electron' (in the case of English speakers). To acquire a mental representation that has the content *electron*, the mental representation ELECTRON must come into the right causal (or other content-making) relation to the property of being an electron; but until the subject reads about electrons or has a model of the atom explained, it is very unlikely that she has any mental representation appropriately causally sensitive to electrons. On this view, external linguistic units

---

5. A counterfactual test does not help to isolate language from users other than the subject; there are no nearby worlds where external words have their content but that content does not derive from minds.

catalyze the acquisition of such concepts as ELECTRON, by creating causal dependences within the subject (among her various internal representations) as well as between the subject and the extraorganismic world. Understood in the preceding fashion, (3) takes us no further toward the extended view, for it merely asserts a causal or historical dependence of the content of certain mental representations on the presence of external linguistic structures.

In response, the proponent of the extended view might invoke a more robust aspect of linguistic structure as the ground of (3). For example, it is plausible that mathematical language provides processing guidelines that indirectly fix the content of those mental representations disciplined to follow these linguistically given guidelines (Bloom 2000, chapter 9). Perhaps this is because mathematical concepts (and maybe logical terms as well; Fodor 1990, 110–11) are subject to an inferential-role semantics (Block 1986); in contrast to the cases discussed in the preceding paragraph, it is plausible the content of a mathematical concept is fully determined by the inferences in which the concept participates. Part of what one learns when learning mathematics is how to proceed, in counting, adding, and solving various other sorts of problems, and one learns this by internalizing certain relations that hold among external linguistic structures (e.g., patterns of recursive combination). If the patterns of relations holding among bits of language cause certain internal processes to be far more likely to occur in the subject, and these processes determine the content of the subject's relevant mental representations, then language plays a central role in the determination of mental content, in at least some important cases.

This interpretation of (3) still amounts to little more than a causal or historical dependence claim; if there is anything more to the position, it pertains to the content of the external structures: that the external structures have the same content as the internal ones. The basis for the attribution of such content, however, seems to be the contribution of other minds in creating linguistic structures with the right patterns. If no one intended to use the structures in this way, they would not now exist. Thus, either the present interpretation of (3) asserts that linguistic structure has caused the subject's brain to process internal units in a way that confers on those units particular contents—a straightforward claim of causal–historical dependence that in no way advances the language-based inference—or the present interpretation of (3) asserts a kind of content-inheritance. On the latter view, the content-dependence extends equally to the minds of those who first began using mathematical language in a way that gives it its content, thus inviting the charge of a gratuitous bloat in cognitive systems.

6.3.2. Structural Effects

Cognition, though, consists of more than the activation of mental representations. For a cognitive process to occur, such representations must be combined and transformed. Cognitive science hopes to map out the causal processes leading from one content-laden state to another (in, say, belief-revision upon the receipt of new evidence), from one set of capacities to a new set (in development), and from a task-situation to the responses given in that situation (in, e.g., solving a problem such as the Tower of Hanoi). In explaining how these internal cognitive processes come to take the relevant forms, we might advert to subjects' interaction with external linguistic resources; and this interaction might be so transformative that the external linguistic resources in question constitute parts of human cognitive systems.

Building on suggestions made by Dennett, Clark has done the most to develop this line of thinking (Clark 1997, 1998, 2004, 2006a). In what follows, I consider three kinds of argument Clark has used: one emphasizing the internalization of dynamical structure, one on the role of external language as an active control structure, and the last on the way in which language facilitates higher-order thought.

A subject's experiences of external, linguistic structures can have lasting effects on the way in which she solves problems. For instance, when introducing rules of inference, some logic instructors use as examples particular natural-language applications of the rules, to which these instructors then refer repeatedly in the weeks that follow. These natural language instances might—if they do their job—stick in a student's head to the extent that, when the student has to work a proof on her own, she replays internal representations of the sound-forms produced by the instructor or visual images of the sentences constituting the instructor's example. In some cases, such mental processing might follow an internalized causal dynamics; in the cases at hand, the process is more likely to be merely temporal. The student replays the sound of the instructor's voice, order intact, and her reasoning follows the structure provided by the mental representation of the instructor's voice.

Although the preceding story, and many more of its ilk, seems psychologically realistic, it lends no support to the language-based inference. Insofar as the language-based inference gains any traction here, it results from an equivocation. There is external language and there are mental representations of external language, and it is tempting run the two together. It is sometimes difficult, especially in the case of spoken language, to separate clearly the external linguistic objects from mental representations of them; in first-person experiences of spoken language, the words and the hearing of the words seem indistinguishable. Distinct they are, though. Thus, complex, ordered mental representations of words may become part of the persisting cognitive system, but this gives us no reason to treat the causal instigators of this process—the utterances or inscriptions themselves—as part of the cognitive system. To the contrary, the focus on mental representations renders salient the embedded alternative.

There is a further reason for skepticism here. In many cases of language-dependent skill acquisition, the subject learns a generalization, something that applies beyond the training cases. The best logic students understand the idea behind, for example, hypothetical syllogism (these are the students who do not have to ask whether it matters in which order two premises of a hypothetical syllogism appear in a natural deduction proof). The nature of generalization is, of course, poorly understood. Nevertheless, flexible intelligence does not exist without the capacity to generalize. In the cases at hand, it involves knowledge of what in general to look for when comparing a proposed solution to a new problem with the remembered auditory or visual representation of the instructor's examples. Bear in mind that in the typical case, the observed problem has little in common—linguistically speaking—with the instance originally given by the lecturer. The stored mental representation of the instructor's examples would thus seem to act more as trigger, allowing the student access to the mental representation of a general rule, than as a template that guides processing. Thus, the problem-solving process is even further removed from concrete external resources than it might at first appear.

Dennett suggests that experience with language transforms the architecture of the cognitive system, by causing the formation of virtual machines in the connectionist wetware of the human brain; the structure of external language itself causes some of a language-user's thought processes to take the form of serial operations on discrete units (Dennett 1991, 224–25). If Dennett is right about the effects of language on language-users, this a testament to the transformative power of language-use, but not an argument for including language in the physical system that realizes the cognitive system. Many factors have profound and lasting effects on children's development—parents' political attitudes, for example. But, if one takes seriously the idea that the cognitive system *has* a location (perhaps because one thinks cognitive science should respect science's general materialist scruples), this transformative effect does not support the extended view. The physical part of the parent's brain that carried her political attitudes has not literally become part of the physical system that is the child's cognitive system (the parent may, regrettably, have passed away).

Turn now to the second of Clark's three arguments mentioned above. Sometimes Clark emphasizes the role that external linguistic resources play as active control structures (1997, 195–96, 1998, 173, 181). Such a control structure might be produced by the subject herself—talking herself through a problem, for example—or it might be a list of written instructions given to the subject. Regardless of the source, one might think that when an external structure controls cognitive processing, there exists a single system with the external part playing the role of a command in working memory; the external linguistic units play the guiding role of a program in a standard computational system.

We now face the same sort of situation encountered in the discussion of content-dependence, version (1). For the external code to do its business, surely it must have effects on the organism. Even if very little of the code is explicitly represented in the organism at any given time, it is only that small portion explicitly represented by the organism that plays a causal role, working together with whatever traces or other effects remain from earlier bits of explicit representation in the organism. Thus, we have available an embedded model of the process, one that involves the organism's use of internal representations of external instructions.

Two further critical points are worthy of mention. First, in some of the parade cases of external linguistic control—children talking themselves through complex tasks, for instance—there is an independent argument for the internal representation of the instructions: the child must have these internally encoded else she would not be able to produce the external linguistic instructions, her own spoken words. This makes it all the more plausible that vocalization merely strengthens the role of an internally represented code, giving *it*, the internal code, control over the computational process. At the very least, this observation counteracts a tendency to think that the external linguistic units exhaust or nearly exhaust the representational resources at work (cf. Rowlands [1999]).

Second, note that many advocates of the extended view are sympathetic to connectionist models (and not merely as models of the implementation of classical theories of cognition—see Fodor and Pylyshyn [1988]). If, however, this is the correct account of the human organism's cognitive architecture, the language-based inference faces further difficulty. Connectionist views claim that the cognitive system consists of simple interconnected units, their connection strengths, and various rules for the activation of those units and for the alteration of the connections holding between them (there are many variations, but this is the general picture—see Rumelhart et al. [1986]). Distinctive of such models is the inseparability of data and process. There are no encoded instructions stored at memory addresses, waiting to be called up for execution. To the extent that they are present in a connectionist system, such things as concepts, programs, and data structures are implicit in the system's processes, built into patterns of connectivity, connection strengths, and activation profiles. In contrast, external linguistic units are discrete, repeatable and have local causal efficacy (Clark 2004, 723), functioning, qua control structures, in the fashion of explicitly encoded instructions. For connectionists, this marks a theoretically important distinction between the organismic cognitive system and external linguistic units; an explanation of how these two different forms of architecture interact encourages an embedded view.

Clark's third processing-related version of the language-based inference appeals to the way in which external language facilitates higher-order thought. This approach itself comes in two flavors: one internalist, the other externalist.

The internalist approach claims that external language provides the subject with augmented computing power and new cognitive strategies by causing the subject to form internal units that serve as stand-ins for her own thoughts, units which can then be the object of further reflection and manipulation. External language contributes discrete orthographic and auditory units, after which internal representations are patterned by straightforward causation. Because those bits of external language express prior thoughts of the subject, and because the internal copies inherit that content, it becomes manageable for the subject to think *about* the thoughts expressed by the sentences internally copied (Clark 2003, 70–71; cf. Gentner [2003]).

Many of the objections raised earlier apply equally to this proposal. The ability to think about our own thoughts substantially transforms the human cognitive system—of this there is little doubt—and surely language-use helps humans to develop the capacity for higher-order reflection. Such observations do not, however, constitute responses to our concerns about systems individuation, about the causal responsibility of organismically internal resources, and about the general form of reasoning involved in the language-based inference. The last of these problems is cut and dried. The people who fit new parts into an existing aircraft can, if all goes well, substantially transform the craft's powers. This fitting may transform the craft from a low-altitude flier to a craft that moves with ease in the upper atmosphere. This, however, provides no reason at all to think that the mechanics involved have become literally part of the aircraft. In the cases at issue, language plays the role of the mechanics, and the inference from causal transformation to systems-constitution is equally deficient.

This leaves only the externalist option. Clark emphasizes the extent to which our cognitive achievements are rooted in iterated interaction with external resources. Consider, for example, the function of external bits of language in the production of an academic paper (Clark 1997, 206–7). This is partly a matter of external storage, but of greater interest in the present context is the extent to which we actively engage with the external linguistic units that codify our previous thought processes. Here I think Clark blends the pursuit of multiple goals. He wants partly to dispel the hubris of those who think they do it all themselves. Dispelling this hubris hardly entails that the mind is extended, however. More importantly, Clark is moved by the extent of dependence, the thought being that our cognitive lives and achievements depend on the scaffolding of language in such a deep way that the connection becomes essential or constitutive. The sheer number of times one interacts with bits of language when, say, writing a substantive paper boggles the mind. Do not the external bits of language thereby become part of the cognitive system writing the paper? Is there not something about the cumulative and complex nature of the case that outweighs the weakness of dependence reasoning?

It seems to me that there is not. Take one instance of a paper writer's use of her notes. The previous thoughts she recorded in those notes were her thoughts just prior to the time she wrote them; they were, apparently, not thoughts of an extended system. Reviewing her notes now reminds her of those prior thoughts and helps her to hold in mind a complicated structure of mental representations, even if only a complicated structure of pointers that make more readily accessible material held in long-term memory (Ericsson and Kintsch 1995). Why should this make the external reminders part of her mind, though, especially when the explanation of the relevant phenomenon—the formulation of a new or additional thought—factors readily into the subject's prior contribution of nonextended content and the current causal contribution of the external symbols? Furthermore, why should the nature of the explanation change simply because the process recurs, say, 200 times, rather than occurring only once? The subject contributed the content to the notes she made initially, when she set out to write her paper; apparently she can have *those* thoughts without notes. If she can make further notes of the thoughts catalyzed by the first-stage notes, then clearly she can have those second-stage thoughts independently of the second-stage notes she uses to write down those thoughts. In fact, she can have those second-stage thoughts independently of the first-stage notes; it is not as if she must stay in constant contact with the first set of notes in order to have the ideas that are then expressed in the second set. Reiteration introduces no extended aspect into the explanation, nothing beyond content-dependence and causal interaction.

Driving the language-based inference in such cases might be an inference from "the final paper consists of the (nonextended) author's thoughts" to "there was a single time when the author had, clearly in mind, all of the thoughts expressed in the paper," taken together with the view that the author simply could not have had the entire structure of the paper in mind at once. This would be a mistake, though. First off, the inference is bad. The attribution of written work to a nonextended author does not entail that the author ever had the entire work in mind at a single time. (Jack built a house, but he did not build it all at once.) Second, much of the work reviewed in Ericsson and Kintsch (1995) suggests that human memory is really quite impressive. This is especially clear in cases of expertise, which is the sort of case we are addressing when we talk about professionals writing papers and books. Note, too, that impressive memory capacity is not a freak show trick mastered only by a few (contrary to what some of Clark's remarks [2003, 74] suggest); the experimental work reveals such skill among everyday people operating in their own domains of expertise, for example, servers in restaurants (Ericsson and Kintsch 1995, 233).

To close the chapter, let us briefly consider two somewhat different approaches to the language-based inference, one historical and the other rooted in the ubiquity of language in the human environment. Merlin Donald (1991) argues that language has a historical role in the shaping of human cognition. He describes large-scale changes in the form of external code, taking place over thousands of years, changes that have significantly affected the form of human thought and culture. Donald's discussion is fascinating, but an extended inter-pretation of it faces familiar sorts of objections: interacting with different exter-nal structures has different effects on cognitive systems, whether or not those external structures were the product of the activities of previous cognitive sys-tems. Thus, the historical record can be more economically explained by the embedded view than by the extended view. In fact, Donald's work makes more pointed the contrast between cognitive systems as they have been fruitfully studied and the unwieldy nature of the cognitive systems that would result from including, in a single cognitive system, the organism together with every-thing that has had a significant impact on the shape of the organism's abilities; for in some of the cases Donald discusses, the relevant causal antecedents go back centuries.

Consider now the ubiquity of language in the human environment. Lan-guage permeates the cognitive lives of contemporary humans. We would be very different without language. Be that as it may, we should be careful when characterizing the kind of ubiquity at issue. It is one thing to say that some bits or other of language are frequently in the subject's environment; it is another to say that there is some particular subset of external linguistic resources that is constant in the subject's environment, enough so to become part of her cogni-tive system. Language is frequently in the air, as it were, but it is not that any particular bit of language is ubiquitous in the typical subject's environment. What is ubiquitous is the subject's persisting ability to engage with language, whatever bits of language happen to turn up in her environment (with some limitations, of course; she might know only one language): this is an organis-mically instantiated capacity resulting partly from past interaction between the organism and the environment the outcome of which was partly determined by the capacities the organism instantiated at the time of that interaction.

As general styles of argument, both the argument from nontrivial causal spread and the transformational argument are weak. Both depend for their validity on overarching premises that yield patently unacceptable conclusions when applied across the board. The advocate of the extended view might sug-gest formulating more specific versions of these premises, driven by biological and linguistic considerations. This strategy faces difficulty as well. The specific claims made about cognition do not appear to underpin a case for the extended view. To the contrary, objections have proven legion and the embedded view a less problematic alternative.

7

Dynamical Systems Theory

Chapter 6 broached an important topic in the literature on extended cognition: the role of densely interactive processes, those in which the organism and the environment affect each other in an ongoing way. Emphasis on this issue is nowhere stronger than in discussions of dynamical systems theory and its relation to cognitive science. Accordingly, the current chapter is devoted to these topics. After a brief introduction to dynamical systems theory, I consider its connection to the extended view. Ultimately, I argue that, although dynamical-systems-based models of cognition could, in principle, provide strong support for the extended approach, extant dynamical-systems-based models are not of the right sort. Rather, they can be naturally accommodated by an embedded approach to cognitive science.

In the final section, I address a further argument in support of the extended view that has appeared in the dynamical-systems-based literature and beyond. On this view, cognition is tailored to its environment, largely under the pressure of evolutionary forces. This argument conflates questions about epistemically useful information, to which cognitive scientists should attend, and questions about the metaphysical status of cognitive systems.

7.1. Dynamical Systems Theory and Cognitive Science

A dynamical system can be thought of as any system that changes over time. In fact, the tools of dynamical systems theory can be applied to any system, even a simple and eternally unchanging one. Nevertheless, these tools apply in a fruitful and interesting way only to systems that occupy distinct states at different times. When I speak of dynamical systems in what follows, I have such systems in mind.[1]

Take a deterministic system that can occupy a range of states. This range of possible states constitutes the system's *state space*. The state space of a typical system can vary along more than one dimension, and thus, its state space consists of the possible combinations of values along these dimensions. Given deterministic laws of nature, a closed system (i.e., one with no perturbation or input from beyond its boundaries) will, from any given state, immediately evolve into only one other state. Any initial state of the system will thus be followed by only one possible series of states. For many purposes, it is useful to think about a variety of such series, in particular, about their similarities and differences. Such information is contained in the system's *phase space*. This is an *n*-dimensional mathematical space, where *n* equals the number of free parameters (i.e., dimensions of possible variation) in the system. Points in the phase space correspond to those in the system's state space, but the phase space carries additional information. Each point in the system's phase space lies on a path (a 'trajectory', as these paths are often called), a line showing the evolution of the system through the phase space. A graphical representation of the various paths the system can take constitutes the system's *phase portrait*.[2] The phase portrait shows the relevant clusterings and divergences of the system's possible paths and shows, by comparison, how differences in initial state affect the system's evolution; along these lines, it is frequently illuminating to compare overall phase portraits for systems that are highly similar but not qualitatively identical (they might, e.g., be made of slightly different materials).

Physical systems frequently evolve according to continuous dynamics, expressed by sets of differential equations, and the dynamical-systems-based framework may seem to apply most naturally in such a context. Nevertheless, movement from one state to another might come in discrete steps (or might be idealized to do so), and a system's state space and phase space can easily (and often more tractably) be cast in discrete terms; in which case, difference equations describe the evolution of the system.

The dynamical-systems-based program in cognitive science holds that the mathematical framework of dynamical systems theory provides the most fruitful approach to cognitive modeling. Its analytical tools provide for the most illuminating conceptual framework, the application of which reveals the true sources of behavioral patterns—often obscured, it is claimed, by computational

---

1. See Wheeler (2005, 100–11) for detailed discussion of the merits of various definitions of dynamical systems.

2. This papers over an important distinction, which will become important in part III. A phase space is a purely mathematical construction; only if it accurately models a given physical system does the phase space carry information about the system's patterns of evolution.

modeling. Extended theorists have been especially interested in the dynamical-systems-based idea of *coupled systems* (van Gelder 1995; Clark 1997; Wheeler 2005), two (or more) systems that can be treated independently but that influence each other in an ongoing way. If two subsystems exhibit ongoing mutual causal influence, these two coupled systems can be fruitfully thought of as a single larger system. When the coupled system is made up of parts of the organism and the environment, and it produces intelligent behavior, the coupled system is sometimes claimed to be an extended cognitive system.

Let me make the idea of coupled systems more precise. When two systems are coupled, the overall state of one subsystem (or of some subportion of it) acts as a control parameter of the other, and vice versa. Typically, equations describing the behavior of a dynamical system include terms the values of which influence the behavior of the system without being changed by that behavior; these are control parameters. Part of the point here is that once control parameters are fixed—say, as a function of the physical substance of which the system in question is made—that fixed value contributes consistently to the evolution of the system: the shape of the phase space is determined partly by the fixed value of that control parameter. In contrast, values of other terms track the changing aspects of the system and thus vary with the position of the system in its state space. Of greatest theoretical interest are quantities that track some composite state of the system (often with some dimensions suppressed); these are called 'order parameters' or 'collective variables'. As noted, a change in the value of a control parameter can significantly change a system's phase portrait. The temperature of a system, for example, might serve as a control parameter: differences in its values can change drastically the way the system moves through its state space from an initial state, and thus the way the values of the system's order parameters evolve. When two systems are coupled, an order parameter of one subsystem acts as a control parameter of the other, and vice versa; as a result, one subsystem's evolution can change the very character of the evolution of the other.

In cognitive science, the dynamical-systems-based approach made a splash in the nineteen nineties, largely as the result of the work of Esther Thelen and Linda Smith (1994; also see Thelen, Schöner, Scheier, and Smith [2001]; Schöner and Thelen [2006]), Scott Kelso (1995), and Randall Beer (1995) (see Port and van Gelder [1995] for an influential collection of papers). In one series of experiments, Thelen and Smith showed that the infant's ability to walk depends on much more than the maturation of a pattern generator in the central nervous system. Instead, walking is something more like an emergent behavior of a larger physical system best analyzed as a dynamical system (Thelen and Smith 1994, chapters 1 and 4). For instance, when, by the use of a treadmill, the right amount of tension is created in the four-month-old's leg muscles, the trailing leg naturally springs back forward in a walking motion (ibid., 111–12). Also, the stepping patterns of the infant's leg can be altered by putting the child in water, thereby changing the relative contribution of the child's mass to the larger dynamical system (ibid., 12). These more encompassing systems (e.g., infant-plus-treadmill) cause the behavior of walking and do so when the child is, as we might normally put it, too young to walk.

It is important to note that neither of these cases involves truly coupled subsystems; for the child's movement does not act as a control parameter for the external surfaces or substances involved (at least not in any way that is relevant to the explanation of walking). Nevertheless, there is one-way dependence: in each case, external pressure acts as a control variable for the infant's musculoskeletal system. One-way dependence has alone inspired talk of extended cognition, for it appears that the entire system is responsible for the walking behavior. The walking behavior is the output of an extended apparatus that is, as it is sometimes described, soft-assembled and self-organizing. The capacity to walk is the capacity of an extended system pieced together from components placed in just the right proximity to each other, under just the right conditions.

Thelen and Smith's treatment of walking commanded attention not only because of the novelty of its approach but also because of the breadth of Thelen and Smith's accompanying theoretical gloss: antinativist, anticomputational, and antirepresentational. For present purposes, I bracket these grander theoretical claims. In part III, I consider in more detail the relation between the embedded approach and dynamical-systems-based research, and there I address more directly some of the questions dynamical-systems-based cognitive science raises about the role of representation and computation in human thought. For now, consider only one critical point, which anticipates some of the concerns to be developed below. Learning to walk is hardly a paradigmatic *explanandum* of cognitive science (and neither is Scott Kelso's parade example [1995, 46–53] of waggling one's fingers back and forth). To be fair, further studies in Thelen and Smith's book, as well as elsewhere, have attempted to extend this approach to what are clearly cognitive phenomena; and some of these studies are discussed below. It would appear, though, that the closer we get to dynamical-systems-based models of genuinely cognitive phenomena, the less support such dynamical-systems-based models provide to the extended view. To the contrary, they nicely illustrate what I have in mind when I claim that the organism instantiates persisting cognitive capacities to engage with the world.

7.2. Dynamical Systems and Extended Cognition: General Patterns of Argument

As the preceding discussion suggests, some arguments from dynamical-systems-based research to the extended view are versions of the argument from nontrivial causal spread. Whether the organism is genuinely coupled to some portion of the environment or there is merely a one-way dependence of the shape of the organism's phase space on some aspect of the environment (as in the case of walking), the external environment contributes causally and distinctively to the production of the relevant behavior. As a general form of argument, however, nontrivial causal spread is glaringly deficient: it is not the case that, as a general rule, when two things make a significant causal contribution to a given outcome, there is, ipso facto, a single system of interest to the relevant science. Earlier chapters present numerous examples to the contrary. Can the proponent of the extended view extract something more useful from dynamical-systems-based models?

Emphasis is frequently placed on behavior's exceptionally strong and ongoing dependence on the environment. The organism's reliance on the environment at every step in the production of behavior shows how deeply dependent the organism is on the environment. What, however, is the strength of this dependence? I think the strongest it could be—that is, the strongest that empirically confirmed dynamical-systems-based models can offer—is nomological necessity given a context. For example, given the context *being on Earth in the year 1926* A.D., it might be that the only way for a given human to calculate compound interest is to use pencil and paper. There is no other physically possible way for her to solve the problem.

This form of dependence should sound familiar; chapters 2 and 6 criticized arguments appealing to it. In principle, the current case differs little from those discussed earlier. Prior to creation of electric light, the human ability to see (in the absence of fire) depended on light from the sun or other stars. That is, in the context of Earth 10,000 B.C. where no fires are lit, the presence of stars was nomologically necessary for humans to see. No one should be tempted, however, to say that sun, or more distant stars, thereby becomes part of an extended cognitive system.

The advocate for extended cognition might respond that it is not the stars, but the ambient light that becomes part of the cognitive system; the stars themselves are not actually needed for the human to see. Why, however, should we draw the line between the stars and the local light arriving from them? So long as the retinal cells are stimulated properly, the human will see. Following the logic of the rejoinder, we should include the retinal cells, but not the ambient light, in the cognitive system. It may be that, given the context, there is no nomologically possible way to stimulate properly retinal cells absent ambient starlight (and fire); we can concede this to the extended theorist. But equally, there is no nomologically possible way to introduce starlight into the environment without there being or having been stars. To be consistent, then, if one—ambient starlight—becomes part of the cognitive system on account of degree of nomological dependence, then the other—the star itself—must also become part of cognitive system. (Do not say, "ah, but any old star would do, relative to a given occasion of seeing," for again, the same is true of the particular ambient light—it is not as if *those very photons* were nomologically necessary given the context. Others would have stimulated the retinal cells just as well.)

Perhaps coupling is the key. On this approach, it is not the mere degree of dependence that extends the cognitive system; rather, it is degree of *interdependence*. Recall, though, that stringent requirements must be met in order that two systems become genuinely coupled; merely having mutual, ongoing effects does not suffice. Instead, the control parameters and order parameters must be mutually intertwined. In consequence, this is a dangerous gamble for the extended theorist. By demanding coupling, she forfeits some of the parade dynamical-systems-based examples. In many, perhaps even most, cases where the organism causally interacts with the environment, the organism's effect on the environment does not alter the phase portrait of the external object; when the subject rotates an object—or a zoid (Kirsh and Maglio 1994), for that matter—so as better to see the opportunities provided by that object, the fundamental dynamics of the external object are not changed: its evolution in state space from any given point remains the same as it was before the rotation. Conversely, the state of the external system (the value of its order parameter) often does not act as a control variable for the internal system. Rather, the external system is better understood as causing variation along a small number of dimensions (e.g., input units) of the organismic system. Even if these changes in these values cause phase shift, it would appear that values of the input units, rather than the state of an external subsystem, act as control parameters.[3]

Moreover, we should doubt that, when coupling does occur, its existence supports the extended view. Change perspectives for moment, and consider an external object for which the state of an organism acts as control parameter. Take a basketball. As the human acts on the basketball, the human deforms the ball, which changes the shape of the ball's phase space (which also changes the way in which the human system reacts to the ball—thus, the suggestion of coupling). A basketball has many of its important properties in virtue of its providing a sealed, fairly elastic container for gases. If we had begun by studying basketballs, we would not, I submit, have come to the conclusion that, when dribbling a basketball, the human becomes part of a single system having the distinctive properties of an elastic orb that encases gas. Thus, we should not make a parallel inference when we begin with the human organism and look to its interaction with the world. By treating the cases differently, the advocate for extended cognition makes an un-argued-for assumption: that the study of cognition gets special systems-expanding treatment that does not apply to other objects or domains.

---

3. See Kelso (1995) on the possibility that the value along one of a system's dimensions can act as control parameter for the system as a whole.

Consider a final general strategy, which appeals to the maintenance-related effects of coupling. It might be that the organism's repeated coupling with the environment helps to maintain (Hurley forthcoming) what I have been calling the organism's cognitive capacities. On this view, each time the organism interacts with the world in a certain way, the activity itself hones or helps to maintain the ability to interact with the world in that, or a closely related, way. The interactive experience causes the organismic system to retain the relevant phase portrait, perhaps by resetting internal control parameters that are drifting. The analogy here is to the maintenance of motor skills that occurs each time one plays a given sport.

The extent to which such maintenance effects result from coupling is an empirical question. Nevertheless, even if they are widespread, I wonder about their relevance. Apply the concept of maintenance in another domain: a crew of mechanics might continually maintain an engine, but that hardly makes the crew part of the engine or gives the members engine-related properties (they do not exhibit piston-driven internal combustion or have rpm's). Advocates of the maintenance argument might point out that cognitive maintenance differs in the following way: the engine is not maintained *during* normal performance, yet the relevant cognitive capacities are. Why, though, is that a relevant difference? Return to the analogy with motor skills. My ability to take corner kicks in soccer may be maintained by my act of taking many corner kicks. Why should that make the ball, the pitch, or the goalposts part of my capacity? To the contrary, the capacity honed by my ongoing play is a capacity to interact with these other things: I can kick the ball over the pitch inside the far post—on a very good day, anyway. This natural way of describing things does not suggest that the ball develops athletic skill or acquires the capacity to take corner kicks. To the contrary: the ball does not take on the properties normally attributed to the organism qua athletic agent.

7.3. Six Kinds of Dynamical-Systems-Based Model

The description of coupled systems suggests a certain deflationary (orthodox, mundane) reading of dynamical-systems-based models. The terms in the relevant equations are interdependent, yet the terms themselves track changes in quantities in separable systems—one or more terms tracking the changing values of quantities in the organism, one or more terms tracking the changing values of quantities beyond the boundary of the organism. Why not the following gloss, then? The human organism has psychological or cognitive capacities to interact with its environment in various ways, by coupling with it; part of the human organism couples to a part of the environment, and in doing so, the organismically bounded cognitive system carries out its cognitive work by interacting with external materials. On this view, the human is sensitive to changing values in inputs and can modulate its outputs accordingly, so as to complete some task. This, however, is an orthodox view of the organism–world relation. External objects stimulate receptors, and cognitive processing takes place in the organism.

Even if this deflationary treatment of dynamical-systems-based models is correct, cognitive psychology stands to gain much from dynamical-systems-based theory. Cognitive psychology hopes to explain the abilities of cognitive systems to interact with their environment. Cognitive psychologists would like to know how the organism acquires such abilities and how these abilities are manifest in different ways in different circumstances, and a dynamical-systems-based approach may provide the best route to such knowledge. This, however, is a science of nonextended systems interacting in complex ways with their environments. It is embedded and embodied, perhaps, but not extended.

Thus the dialectic is framed. We now face the question, "Which treatment of dynamical-systems-based models is correct, the extended gloss or this more modest view?" Because dynamical-systems-based models come in various forms, though, we must instead address the more subtle questions, "What kind of dynamical-systems-based model would, if accurate, support the extended view over the more mundane approach?" and "Have such models been developed?" Below I survey six different forms a dynamical-systems-based model might take, arguing that in most of these cases, a successful model of the sort described would not support the extended view in any direct way. In the end, I locate one kind of dynamical-systems-based model that would strongly support the extended view, but find a dearth of successful models of this kind.

Of practical necessity, my conclusions are tentative. There are many dynamical-systems-based models in the field and the interpretation of them is not always straightforward; in fact, to my mind, one of the most difficult aspects of the literature is the mismatch between empirical work and the theoretical gloss laid over it.

7.3.1. Model-Type One: Historical Grounding

The first kind of model emphasizes the generative effects of environmental coupling (or one-way environmental control—take this as read for the remainder of this subsection). For instance, motor interaction with the environment creates structural patterns in the organismic agent's phase space, including what are known as attractors: areas in the phase space that the system is especially likely to enter into or move through. These can serve as the basis for grammatical categories, such as *agent, patient,* and the various forms of relation expressed by prepositions (Petitot 1995). This is a historical process. Partly for this reason, those who emphasize models of type one can easily acknowledge the importance of off-line processing. Simultaneously, however, an extension-friendly argument might be made: that where prior online coupling provides the ultimate explanatory ground for cognitive processing, cognition—even off-line cognition—is extended.

This is a fascinating and in some ways promising proposal concerning the causal genesis of our mental representations (Rupert 1998). Yet, the off-line nature of so much cognition suggests an obvious nonextended interpretation of the coupled system's contribution. Coupling helps causally to generate representational units (i.e., the vehicles that carry conceptual or representational content) and perhaps "programs" rules into the cognitive system, and does so in a way that is explanatorily important; but this does not extend later cognitive processing into the environment. A human might design a computer, then drop dead. No one, I hope, would be tempted to say that, because of her explanatorily important causal contribution to the computer's later processing, the designer's corpse partly constitutes that machine's computational processes. Why should it be any different when cognition is understood as a dynamical process of type one?

Notice, too, that, on this approach, prior coupling must somehow affect later, off-line cognitive processing. The route of such influence would seem to run through the organism; how else could the interaction leave the sort of causal stamp at issue? A straightforward way of understanding this process has the organism internalizing aspects of the structure of a coupled system of which it once was a part. The organism first couples with its environment, that entire extended system exhibits certain structural features, and the salient features of the dynamics of this coupled system are then copied or otherwise stored (implicit in neural connections, perhaps). Later, in off-line cognitive activity, this internalized stamp of prior coupling recreates the dynamics of what was originally an extended system.

This approach does not advance the case for the extended view. It requires that the organism copy and retain certain aspects of the patterns instantiated by the previously coupled dynamical system. In which case, the existence of the coupled system plays only a causal role in grounding cognitive capacities, while the internalized structure clearly plays the constitutive role in later off-line cognitive processing.

Notice that advocates of dynamical-systems-based modeling might resist my talk of internal copies; it might smack too strongly of representationalism. The organism's experience coupling with the environment may alter the organism's phase space, such theorists would allow, and as a result, the organism can engage in sophisticated cognitive processing off-line. Nevertheless, it might be claimed, there is no need to posit a representation standing proxy for the structures of the previously instantiated coupled system. Rather there is merely the historical fact that organism's phase space was altered by the prior coupling.

Fair enough, but the fundamental concern persists: the dynamical-systems-cum-extended theorist cites a historical fact, giving us no reason to think the previously encountered external items are part of the cognitive system at later times when the capacity in question is exercised. Builders constructed my house, an important historical fact about it that explains many of its features; but they are not part of my house, or part of a single house-builder system, nor do they possess the distinctive architectural properties normally associated with my house. For all I know, they are dead (cf. Adams and Aizawa [2001, 2007, 2009, forthcoming]).

The defender of the extended approach might deny the existence of any internal changes of the relevant sort, but this leads to a form of mysterianism. No explanation is offered as to *how* the organismic system, once decoupled, builds its cognitive activities from the structural features of the coupled system of which it was formerly a component; nor is there any explanation of why such a process would allot the historical interactions anything more than a causal–genetic role in explaining central cognitive processes.

7.3.2. Model-Type Two: Organismically Internal Dynamical Interactions

Now consider models that treat the activity only of the organism (or of its parts) as a dynamical system. As evidence of extended cognition, such models seem to be nonstarters. It is, nevertheless, worth saying a bit about them. This is partly to show that, although there may be successful dynamical-systems-based models in the field, many of them are not of the right sort to support the extended approach.

In some cases, the capacities being modeled by type-two approaches are clearly cognitive (the forms of behavior being explained are those that seem in need of a cognitivist explanation). For example, Townsend and Busemeyer (1995) describe a dynamical-systems-based decision theory. In respect of the *explanandum*, Townsend and Busemeyer's model is on the right track. Nevertheless, the model includes preferences, states that anticipate consequences and assign them values, and motor outputs, all of which are internal to the organism. At least so far as we have any reason to think Townsend and Busemeyer have modeled human decision-making, the external environment plays no direct role in the dynamical model, so this kind of model will not deliver the extended view. Of course, if it were established that there are extended cognitive systems, Townsend and Busemeyer's decision-making model could be applied to them: states encoding preferences might be carried by external vehicles. In the present context, however, this observation puts the cart before the horse. I am hunting dynamical-systems-based models that motivate the extended view, not ones merely consistent with it.

So, the extended view garners no support from models of type two. Problem is, it would appear that some of the most influential dynamical-systems-based models fall under this rubric. Consider Beer's description (1995) of his research on autonomous agents. Central to his presentation is the following pair of equations:

$$\dot{\mathbf{x}}_A = A(\mathbf{x}_A; \mathbf{S}(\mathbf{x}_E))$$
$$\dot{\mathbf{x}}_E = E(\mathbf{x}_E; \mathbf{M}(\mathbf{x}_A))$$

where A is the agent-system and E is the environment-system, $\mathbf{S}$ is a sensory function "from environmental state variables to agent parameters" and $\mathbf{M}$ is a motor function "from agent state variables to environmental parameters" (Beer 1995, 130; equations found on 131).

This seems to describe a heavy-duty coupling between organism and environment; in fact, though, in the models discussed by Beer, the environment is the agent's body! In particular, $\mathbf{x}_E$ is the state of various sensors.

7.3.3. Model-Type Three: Active External Control

The third kind of case involves an external control parameter without coupling. Consider first an example invoked by Michael Wheeler (2004, 2005), taken from work by Harvey, Husbands, and Cliff (1994). Harvey et al. use a genetic algorithm to evolve the control system of a robot that can distinguish between a lighted triangle and a lighted rectangle on the dark wall of an arena. The resulting, highly successful control system has two sensors that cause the robot to swivel back and forth, unless they take on the right combination of values: the combination that results from fixing on the oblique edge of a triangle. When this last condition is met, the robot rolls forward, arriving at the triangle.

Setting aside the question whether this model has any bearing on the human case, the model clearly does not provide a coupling-based argument for the extended view. As the robot rolls toward the lighted triangle, the triangle continuously affects the onboard motor control system. The robot does not, however, affect the external object's states: the movement of the robot does not change the light. Furthermore, perhaps contrary to initial appearance, Harvey et al.'s model does not, technically speaking, provide an example of an external control parameter. The behavior of the robot is not driven by any changes in the lighting of the triangle; the lighting remains constant throughout. Thus, beyond the fluctuations that might normally be associated with the emission of light, there is no change in an external control parameter.[4]

Granted, the robot's behavior is determined by delicate interplay between the state of the system and the values of the sensor units, and the value of the sensor units depends on the relation of the robot to the constantly lighted shapes. These observations, however, reinforce an embedded interpretation of this particular model: the robot's behavior depends in sensitive ways on input

---

4. To be fair, it is not clear that, when Wheeler invokes this model, he means to illustrate anything more than nontrivial causal spread.

from the systemically external environment. This is hardly revolutionary as a view of the fundamental relation between system and environment. Even in the most orthodox A.I. projects—Shakey, the robot, for example (Nilsson 1984)—the environment drives motor responses by stimulating sensors. The use of the tools of dynamical-systems theory to model the robot's internal processing distinguishes some of Harvey et al.'s robots from classical projects. One important, resulting difference may be in the amount or kind of internal representation used to complete the task (cf. Husbands, Harvey, and Cliff [1995, 103]). That difference alone does not, however, provide any support for the extended view. The environment makes its standard one-way causal contribution via the stimulation of the robot's sensors, which, in terms of the subject's relation to its environment is old hat.

One might reasonably worry that I have been uncharitable in my description of the work of Harvey et al. Discussions of dynamical-systems-based models frequently emphasize the agent's interaction with the environment (in connection with autonomous agents [Harvey, Husbands, and Cliff 1994; Husbands, Harvey, and Cliff 1995], developmental psychology [Thelen and Smith 1994], and perceptual psychology [Hurley 2001]). In all of these areas, dynamical-systems-based theories of perception and action hold that the agent's actions alter the information available to the agent (cf. Beer [2003, 218]). Fine, but in the sort of model under consideration, the actions do so not by changing the objects perceived but by altering the values of the input sensors. As emphasized above, when Harvey et al.'s light-seeking robot moves, it does not change the lighted triangle one jot. What changes as a result of the agent's movement is the stimulation at the periphery; regardless of the amount of exploration the light-seeking robot engages in, the triangle simply gives off light according to the laws of physics, without respect to the robot's movement. Compare Hurley's emphasis (2001, 23–30) on the correlations detected between, for example, motor signals and the sensory input that follows. In Hurley's terms, perceptual information frequently depends on reafferent input, exafferent input, and the effects of efferent copies. Reafferent input is normally thought of as perceptual input from the environment; exafferent input is the subset of reafferent input that distinctively reflects the movement of the subject's own body. The effects of efferent copies are a bit more complex, but here is the basic idea (for further discussion, see chapter 8). When motor cortex issues a command, it issues a copy of that command to other portions of the brain, which process it in various ways. The results of such processing can then be "compared" to or correlated with various bits of reafferent or exafferent input; and the latter two kinds of input can, as well, be compared and correlations detected. This entire process is, however, an entirely internal affair. It must be in order to maintain the distinction between the exafferent and the reafferent signals. Quantities in the extraorganismic world do not respect the difference between self-generated changes and nonself-generated changes. Even if, as Hurley would have it, the content and character of perception is determined by correlations between these three factors, the correlations detected (not consciously, mind you) hold between three kinds of internal signal, that is, three kinds of activity within the organism.

It appears, then, that many of the models that most inspire the extended view exemplify type two, rather than type three. Thus my plaint: as we get closer to model-types that would genuinely support the extended view if successfully applied to humans, it becomes very difficult to find working models of that type.

The search for type-three models should not, however, be called off too easily. In more recent work by Beer (2003), he evolves simulated autonomous agents that catch falling circles and avoids falling diamonds. His mathematical model (2003, 214) explicitly includes a changing external stimulus that can act as control parameter: the equations include a term for the rate of change in the location of the object to be caught or avoided.

Nevertheless, the role played by that variable is to determine only the state of the agent's sensors. As Beer makes clear, having fixed the state of the sensors at any given time, the behavior of the autonomous agent follows by the internal dynamics alone. "Discontinuities are introduced into the dynamics through the ray sensory neurons..." (Beer 2003, 223). Variations in the values of the seven input neurons drive changes in internal processing, that is, changes in the dynamics of the continuous time recurrent neural network (CTRNN) that controls the behavior of the autonomous agent. The autonomous agent's categorization behavior is explained by the interaction between changes in the values of the sensory neurons and the overall state of the agent-bounded system as those sensory values change (ibid., 228–30).

Of course, changes in the values of the input neurons are determined by the (simulated) location of the falling objects, but this fact introduces nothing unusual or unexpected into the agent–environment relation. This reflects precisely the traditional view of the agent–environment relation in perception. Beer intends that the extraorganismic environment play a much bigger role in cognitive theorizing, and his dynamical-systems-based models do explain beautifully how, for example, his agents navigate. The models do so, however, by adverting to an entirely internal dynamical system that takes inputs from the environment. In other words, to the extent that the external value acts as control parameter, it is only via the role of sensor values, which are themselves the immediate control parameters.[5] Thus, Beer appears to be offering a type-two model together with a causal story of how the values of the genuine control parameters—the internal sensor values—change.

Generally speaking, the operation of some mechanism must underwrite the organism's sensitivity to properties in the environment. The most effective

5. Similar remarks apply to Schöner and Thelen's dynamical-systems-based account (2006) of dishabituation in infants.

way to model the process of interaction involves variation in the activation of some sensory mechanisms; and this explains in what sense the behavior at issue rests on the exercise of the capacity of an organismically bounded cognitive system (regardless of whether this activation is cast in terms of representation).

If we are to accept the embedded gloss, we should want evidence of a local realizer of the capacities in question. Beer's analysis of his agents provides just this, a local candidate for the realizer of the agent's behavioral capacity. Beer's agent has a capacity to sense the environment and respond to it on the basis of those sensor readings; the values of the sensor readings, together with activation levels of other internal units, provide plausible realizers of the fine-grained states the appearance of which amounts to the exercise of the agent's capacity to interact with the relevant environmental structures.

Notice, too, that the behavior in question—the catching and avoiding that determined the evolutionary dynamic in Beer's agents—is entirely "organismic." As Beer puts it, "Clearly, whatever decomposition we choose should emphasize the factors underlying movement, since the agent's decision is expressed in its motion over time and *it is this behavior that we want to explain* (ibid., 228, emphasis added; see also 210). The behavior for which the evolving system is reproductively "punished" or "rewarded" does not include portions of the environment; it is a reaction to said portions. The environment remains constant, with falling circles and diamonds; some of Beer's simulated autonomous agents get beneath falling circles and dodge falling diamonds, but others fail. Thus, it is misleading for Beer to claim that "the evolutionary algorithm has been asked to structure the dynamics of the entire coupled system..." (ibid., 223);[6] rather, what is structured is the behavior of the agent-bounded system, given a fixed environment. The evolution of the agent does not alter the structure of the environment, and the evolved capacities of the agent do not maintain that environment.

Here is the upshot. The most impressive dynamical-systems-based models intended to explain genuinely cognitive processes do so by taking the approach of model-type two. These are purely internal models, however, and as such do not support the extended view.

Perhaps this is the place to comment on a certain style of dynamical-systems-based argument that I find perplexing. It is often noted (Beer 2003; Gibbs 2006) that the particular effect of a given peripheral stimulation depends on the current state of the organism. From this it is inferred that there is a single extended system. As stated the argument is not valid. Omitted is the principle bridging the gap from the contextual nature of effects to the extended view. I can see no plausible principle to insert here. The effects of the sun's

---

6. Beer acknowledges that only the agent evolves, not the environment. Nevertheless, he explicitly claims that "*it is a property of the dynamics of the entire coupled system that has been selected for*" (Beer 2003, 236). The grounds for this assertion are not clear.

rays on my skin depend on the state of the skin at the time the rays strike. This hardly creates a new, scientifically important entity, a sun-skin system. Furthermore, notice that the observation in question is entirely standard in orthodox cognitive science. Of course, the effect of a stimulus differs with over-all internal state of the cognitive system; someone who has learned Japanese is much more likely than a person who has not learned Japanese to respond appropriately to her companion's Japanese utterances. Chomsky, Fodor, and the rest of the orthodox community should not argue with this for a moment. So, why does the mere conditionalization of effects on present state entail any-thing more than a local cognitive system that responds in different ways to a single stimulus depending on, for example, its current goal state or what is in its short-term memory buffer?

Some proponents of the extended view (Gibbs 2006) are struck by the fact that no single neural structure realizes the same concept across all contexts. Nevertheless, it is quite a leap from the claim that, for example, there is no single unit activation of which represents the same property across all contexts to the claim that the cognitive system is extended. In Beer's model (2003), there is a set number of sensory units the activation of which then causes fur-ther internal processing; granted it is not the same combination of sensor val-ues that represents the same external item on all occasions, but why does this matter if, on every occasion of the system's representing, say, a diamond, *some combination or other of sensor values* does the representing? It can still be the case that, relative to a given agent, the compound set of sensor values, together with specific internal states of the relevant subsystems, always plays the same role. Moreover, given our prior reasons for thinking the organismic package is the cognitive system, such sensory units, were they to appear in humans as opposed to simulated autonomous agents, would provide the kind of interface we expect to appear between the organismic cognitive system and the external world. Granted, the semantics of such units is more complex than we would have liked, being fixed by a complicated function of both the degree of stimula-tion of activation of sensory units and the internal state of the organism at the time of stimulation (together with the facts about what is actually in the envi-ronment, facts that are relevant on nearly all views of representational content, extended and nonextended). By itself, though, the complicated nature of the semantics lends no support to the extended view.

All this being said, I wonder whether, even if we were to find a successful type-three model, it would advance the cause of the extended view. Slow music puts some people to sleep; listening to certain politicians speak causes such a cognitive phase shift in some people that they cannot think straight—perhaps they become furious or they are lulled into mindless complicity. In these cases, the phase profiles of the internal system change as the result of stimulation caused by an external source. Such cases, however, fit nicely into an ortho-dox organism-centered approach to individuating cognitive systems. (Perhaps these are simply further cases in which the activation of the organism's sensors causes a phase shift, in which case the successful modeling of these processes would return us to the realm of type-two models. This again highlights the difficulty of the extended theorist's task: to find a successful dynamical-systems-based model of a clearly cognitive process that is of the right sort to support the extended view.)

7.3.4. Model-Type Four: Organismic Collective Variables, Extended Realizers

The preceding discussion suggests a fourth kind of model, or perhaps more accurately a different way of explicating what I described as models of type two. In this kind of model, although the behavior to be explained is organismic behavior, the best model of the realization of the behavior or cognitive states appeals directly to external quantities. Models of type four, were they to appear, would involve lower-level processes that do not neatly factor into internal and external subsystems. In such cases, there may simply be no viable candidates for local realizers.

I doubt there are any extant models of type four that successfully explain important aspects of human cognition. Dynamical-systems theorists have modeled some aspects of motor behavior in ways that are tracked by single collective variables, but even here the relevant mathematical models include separate quantities for organismic contributions and contributions of the external environment. This allows a clean separation between the organismically internal and the external contributions. Given this separability, there is a viable candidate for the internal realizer of the organismic capacity to couple with the environment. Since we should want a local realizer for local cognitive or psychological states and capacities, the neatly separable internal state realizes the organismically local cognitive state or capacity; and such a view offers no support for the extended view.

Why, though, should we want a local realizer of the organismic capacity (or its token exercise)? First, recall worries about the mismatch of causal roles. Token realizers should satisfy the Causal-Structure Principle, discussed in chapter 4. To illustrate, assume that, on a particular occasion, a desire for apple juice causes the state of wondering where some apple juice might be. At a bare minimum, the token realizer of the desire had better cause—among whatever else it causes—the instantiation of token realizer of the wondering. This view follows from the standard philosophical accounts of realization and, more importantly, it plays a guiding role in the methodology of cognitive scientific research. An excellent way to decide between two competing psychological theories is to look at the lower level to see whether there are independently identifiable states and connections that play the causal roles of one model's boxes and arrows but not the other model's.

By hypothesis, the form of behavior to be explained in the cases at issue is an organismic capacity or the exercise of it. Consider a world-involving capacity for reaching for a cup of apple juice. At the personal level, the cognitive capacity or state at issue is organismically bounded. A model of type four suggests, however, that the cognitive state is realized by an extended portion of the world. This introduces causal mismatch. The reaching causally interacts with the thing for which the subject reaches. This is a feature of central importance in our characterization of reaching behavior. Furthermore, the intention or decision to reach is causally responsible for the arm movement. Extended realizers are not in a position to play this causal role. In fact, the thing that one might most naturally want to include in the dynamic-systems analysis of the reaching—that is, the object reached for—is certainly not in the right position to realize the cognitive state of reaching or the intention to reach. It is a necessary condition on the token realizer that it enter into causal relations that are structurally analogous to those into which the realized state or property enters. But, the object reached for does not have the effect of reaching for the object—and neither does any composite object of which it is a part; for then it would be causally interacting with itself.

In cases of interaction between cognitive states—desirings and wonderings, for instance—the kind of model in question introduces a different kind of causal mismatch. If my desiring causes my wondering, then the realizer of the former had better cause the realizer of the latter; that is, the extended realizer of the first must bear the right causal relation to the extended realizer of the second. I grant that things could work out this way: the entire extended realizer of the desire—external and internal parts working together—*could* bring about the right internal *and* external effects. At present, though, I know of no such model.

In contrast, Beer's model offers us a very nice account of the organismically realized capacity for catching circles and avoiding diamonds. It is a neural network story that explains, among other things, how the information fed by the seven sensor units to the rest of the system creates a dynamical pattern of action that normally leads to successful catching or dodging. This embedded interpretation is straightforward, stands a chance of respecting the Causal-Structure Principle, and does not introduce the mystery of realizers that are someplace other than the states they realize.

7.3.5. *Model-Type Five: Extended Collective Variable,*
Organismic Separability

A model of this type takes values of a collective variable of an extended system as *explanandum*. In this kind of case, we treat the behavior of a single extended dynamical system as the cognitive behavior to be explained. This behavior is characterized as a pattern in that entire extended system's phase space, which might then be explained in terms of the interaction between two or more sub-systems or between the larger system and the environment beyond it. Further-more, to support the extended view, this single larger system must include both a human organism and some material beyond the organism's boundary.

I have three reactions to the description of this kind of model. First, I am fairly sure there are no such models of cognitive behavior. The closest we get are models of walking, running, or sailboarding, not anything close to the abilities or capacities of central importance to cognitive science—such things as language-use, planning, decision-making, inference, memory, theory con-struction, and perception. Then again, motor control has *something* to do with cognition, so, this problem being flagged, I shall not risk being dogmatic by excluding models of walking or sailboarding.

This raises my second concern, however: even if we allow a model of, say, walking to count, extant models do not fit the description I gave of the model-type five. Walking is not the capacity of an extended system; it is the activity of an organismic system. Now, this reaction might be naïve. After all, Thelen and Smith have shown ways in which the ability to walk is context-dependent. Nevertheless, there is a perfectly straightforward sense in which the organism that walks. It begins walking when it is young; it walks on a variety of surfaces under a variety of circumstances. It requires no effort to describe walking as a capacity of the organism; true, the capacity can be exercised only in a limited range of conditions, but that is true of virtually *all capacities*. Similarly for a skill such as sailboarding. One who knows how to sailboard knows how to become one with the board, so to speak. Nevertheless, there is nothing about the phenomenon that resists easy and natural decomposition: Sally is the one who took lessons, who bought the sailboard, who rigged it up to her truck, who purposefully applied the skills she learned in her lessons, who borrowed her neighbor's board when hers went kaput, etc. As such, the behavior in question is her behavior, not the behavior of an extended system. These ways of conceiv-ing of behavior are, of course, negotiable but should be changed only in the face of highly successful empirical work resting on a reconception of the behavior as the behavior of a single, extended system. There appears, however, to be a dearth of such work.

Third, even were we to find a model of type five, the inference to the extended view would not be automatic. If an organismically local realizer can be neatly extracted from the dynamical-systems-based model, that alone might provide reason to attribute a cognitive capacity to the organism—that is, the organism's capacity to enter into *that* kind of relation (demonstrating toward the apparently unified cognitive behavior of the single dynamical system). This might seem ad hoc, but whether it is in a given case depends on considerations of theoretical coherence. Imagine an extreme case where the organism in ques-tion has been subject to highly successful psychological theorizing with respect to virtually all its other cognitive endeavors; furthermore, imagine that all of these cognitive endeavors correspond naturally to local realizers and, what is more, that the neatly separable realizer in the case of the dynamical-systems-based model at issue is systematically related to the realizers of other cognitive capacities that have been successfully subjected to purely local theorizing. In this case, the move that might have appeared ad hoc now appears well motivated. Even if we do not have a name for the organism's contribution to what appears to be the behavior of an indivisible extended system, we should coin one.

7.3.6. Model-Type Six: Extended Order Parameter, No Local Separability

In this kind of case, the *explanandum* is the cognitive behavior of an extended system; furthermore, in contrast to type-five models, there is no tidy decoupling of the organism and the environment. Imagine, for example, that it is reasonable to attribute behavior to an entire extended system, and when we look at the dynamical-systems-based model explaining such behavior, there is no natural way to decompose it into coupled subsystems; or, if there is a natural decomposition, it involves, say, the left side of the body plus part of the environment, on the one hand, and the right side of the body together with a different aspect of the environment, on the other hand. Successful dynamical-systems-based models of this type would clearly support the inference to the extended view.

At present, though, I know of nothing that even approximates such a model. To the contrary, most uses of dynamical-systems-based models to support the extended view appeal to models that are explicitly outside of this category: models that involve the coupling of the organismic subsystem to some aspect of the environment, in which the two subsystems are analytically separable. Thus, at present, models of type six do not motivate paradigm shift in cognitive science. They provide only a desideratum for those who would like to derive the extended view from dynamical-systems-based theorizing.[7]

7.4. Evolution, Context-Dependence, and Epistemic Dependence

To close this chapter, I address an argument that does not appeal to a specific kind of dynamical-systems-based model, but nevertheless appears in discussions of dynamical systems and the extended approach. Certain capacities of an

---

7. Andy Clark (personal communication) has asked whether my diagnosis of the debate about extended cognition is unfalsifiable, being so flexible as to accommodate any result. The discussion of model-type six shows that it is not. In this regard, note too that my previous appeals to successful research programs involve an appeal to contingent facts. Such research programs might not have turned out the way they did, and there is nothing in my approach that would have licensed me to interpret those programs as successful no matter what had happened.

organism are especially well tuned to the environment in which those capacities are exercised. Biological evolution provides a straightforward explanation of how this situation might arise: sometimes a creature evolves a capacity to do A in an environment where doing A increases fitness; if creatures of that kind continue to find themselves in a relevantly similar environment, then it is natural to see those creatures' capacity to A as somehow specially fitted to the environment. For instance, an animal's sensory system might be attuned to environmental conditions that change in cycles, and these changes may have exerted evolutionary pressure on the animal's ancestral populations. As a result, there may have been selection for sensory systems sensitive to the very changes in question. In an actual case of this sort, we might be inclined to say that the animal is built for or specially attuned to its environment.

Beer (2003) makes this kind of point concerning his simulated agents, claiming that because the agents were evolved by genetic algorithm in a particular environment—where their responses to falling objects determined their descendants' catching-related behavior—those external objects should be considered part of the cognitive system. Quoting Beer:

> First and foremost, this analysis has illustrated what it means to say that an agent's behavior is a property only of the coupled brain/body/ environment system, and cannot be attributed to any one subsystem. In a very real sense, the evolved CTRNN does not "know" the difference between circles and diamonds. It is only when embodied in its particular body and situated within the environment in which it evolved that this distinction arises over time through the interaction of these subsystems. (2003, 235–36)

There are a number of strands to Beer's argument for the extended view. One strand seems to concern the evolutionary argument outlined above. Taken in this way, however, the argument is unconvincing. Beyond cognitive science, the general form of argument is simply bizarre: the typical planet formed against the backdrop of a local gravitational field that caused the planet to form and to orbit in the way it eventually did; but this hardly shows that orbiting is not the behavior of the planet, or that the gravitational field is a proper part of the planet, or that there is an important natural kind, the planet-plus-gravitational field, of theoretical interest in astrophysics or astronomy. Even in the cognitive domain this inference seems misguided: the presence of the sun was a condition of the evolution of my visual capacity; but that fact provides no reason to think that the sun is a literal part of my visual system. This suggests a much more straightforward explanation of Beer's case: the genetic algorithm explains how the agent-bounded cognitive system acquires the capacity to discriminate between circles and diamonds within a certain range of conditions; Beer's model makes clear what the local realizers of this capacity are likely to be.

Note, too, Margaret Wilson's point (2002) that the evolutionary argument does not apply to many of humans' central cognitive capacities. These capacities are flexible and not tied to the particular context in which they evolved. Additionally, in many cases, it is likely that they were not even selected for their present-day online use (Wilson 2002, 626–27). Many human cognitive capacities evolved for one purpose and today, functioning as exaptations, are put to others. My visual system works in nonnatural light, an artifact created by humans very late in evolutionary history. Are we to infer that the sun is part of the realizer of a visual process that does not involve sunlight? If we were to infer that the backdrop against which a capacity evolves is part of that cognitive capacity, we would seem forced to this absurd conclusion. Wilson's general point seems beyond dispute, for throughout much of our day, we apply our cognitive resources to interact with technological and cultural creations that simply did not exist in the evolutionary environment. Moreover, and at least as worrisome as anything else, evolutionary facts are causal–historical considerations, the relevance of which to systems individuation has been rightly called into question.

Perhaps it is not so much the evolutionary consideration that impresses Beer, but the context-dependence of the agent's behavior, which the evolutionary point serves to emphasize. The agent does not know how to distinguish between diamonds and circles across the board; rather, the agent can do so only in a restricted range of contexts, in fact, the ones in which the capacity in question was chosen for.

This does no better as an argument for extended cognition. First, note that many skills and capacities are context-dependent, without this suggesting any addition to our ontology. I can shoot baskets only when I am on relatively flat ground. Thus, my basket-shooting capacity has context-dependent limits. This gives us no reason to posit a new natural kind—an organism-plus-flat-ground system. Similar remarks hold of nearly all capacities. The capacity to A is virtually always a capacity to A under certain conditions. I can see, but I cannot see in the dark. I can speak English, but not after taking large doses of Demerol. And so on. This is a garden-variety fact about dispositions, skills, capacities, and abilities. Sugar dissolves in water, but not when the water is frozen solid. This hardly makes the liquid state of water a part of sugar (Gillett 2007). Rather, sugar has certain capacities, triggered under certain circumstances and not under others. These capacities and their triggering are a function of the intrinsic properties of the substances and the laws of nature. We have been given no reason to treat humans' admittedly context-dependent capacity for categorization any differently.

Second, the view of human reasoning as context-dependent and interactive is, generally speaking, the orthodox view. Standard practice takes cognitive behavior to depend in important ways on (and to be constrained by) physical implementation and environmental context. Artificial intelligence (AI) researchers of the most orthodox stripe take pains that their hardware can do what they want it do and that their software is sensitive in the right ways to the changing environment. After the opponent makes a move, a chess-playing AI system had better be able to sense the move made, and it had better be able to update its ordering of strategies on the basis of the new board position. Has any influential AI researcher ever thought otherwise? Thus, the traditional view accepts context-dependence and assigns a substantive role to interaction in cognition; moreover, the general vision employed is easily extended to dynamical-systems-based models of the sort Beer presents. Without some reason to think that the traditional approach was confused all along—that orthodox cognitive science was, unbeknownst to its practitioners, committed to the extended view—the status quo remains in place, at least with regard to the agent–environment relation. Part I offered strong reasons for thinking the standard view has not been confused all along, and arguments throughout the current chapter show how natural it is to apply the extended view to extant dynamical-systems-based models.

Finally, Beer's argument might be an argument from epistemic dependence, of the sort touched on in chapter 2. If we wish to understand why a cognitive system functions the way it does, we should look to the environment in which it evolved for clues to that system's functioning. Fair enough, but it is unclear why this epistemic point carries any metaphysical weight. If we wish to understand why a coastline has the particular mixture of minerals it does, we might do well to investigate geological conditions at the fault where this coast was rent from the land to which it used to be connected; this may be the only practical way for us to understand some of the properties of the coastline in question. Nevertheless, it hardly makes the fault a proper part of the coastline.

Andy Clark sometimes offers a converse consideration: in cases where the environment is tailored to the organism, the organism's cognitive processes extend into the environment. One of Clark's most colorful examples involves the characteristics of certain programs, for example, search engines or software used on commercial web sites (2003, 30; cf. Clark [1997, 217]), that save information about the individual user, creating a profile that allows, for instance, the search engine to tailor future search results to the interests of the user. Similarly, but of greater importance in cognitive science, Clark (1998, 169) suggests that the form and structure of language may have evolved to fit our preexisting cognitive capacities.

It is difficult for me to see why such tailoring alone bears on systems individuation. A man might have a suit carefully tailored to his proportions, but that hardly makes the suit part of his physical body, even if he wears it fairly often. Imagine that we build a hospital emergency-room entrance with big lights and many signs, knowing that it will be used by desperate and injured people who are not thinking as clearly as they normally would be. The emergency room and the general placement of it in the hospital might be built to interact in a certain way with people (maybe the hospital is built in such a way that all entrances lead one past the emergency room). Thus, the hospital building is tailored to its social environment. That hardly gives the emergency room the properties normally associated with people or creates a new entity, the emergency-room-plus-society. We might say that the emergency room is attention-getting, but this is nothing more than a way of indicating how some separate systems—persons—are likely to react to that separate entity, the emergency ward.

8

The Experience of Extension and the Extension of Experience

In this chapter, I consider two kinds of argument for the extended view. One kind appeals to the contents of conscious experience or to reports concerning such experience. These arguments presuppose that we can learn about the location or operation of the cognitive system by introspection; thus, I refer to these as 'phenomenological arguments', using the term somewhat loosely. Arguments of the second sort appeal to a theory of experience itself. In particular, I focus on the sensorimotor contingency theory of visual experience (Noë 2004), arguing that the theory, in its plausible form, provides no support for the extended view.

8.1. Cognitive Science and the In-Key Constraint

Sometimes it is claimed that phenomenology explores the very ground of cognitive science, the very possibility of doing any scientific work at all, and, as a consequence, that phenomenology takes priority over science. After all, scientific enquiry presupposes our abilities to observe results and to reason about these observations; perhaps careful introspective examination of such processes is required in order even to understand what scientific thinking consists in. In response, however, the cognitive scientist might turn the tables, arguing that cognitive science explores the very ground of phenomenology: cognitive science explains how it is that anyone can examine her own experience or write a phenomenological treatise. Observations made in the lab may have phenomenological character, but such observations are also judgments of a sort; and their status as judgments (the patterns in the making of which are themselves judged to lead to successful results) may alone ground the scientific enterprise.

Regardless of how the priority dispute works out in the end, once we have decided to take our observations seriously and to draw standard scientific inferences from them, we find little reason to think that phenomenological reports—that is, introspective reports concerning how things seem to us in conscious experience—offer a direct window into the workings of our cognitive mechanisms. To the contrary, empirical results call into question the content of many first-person reports on cognitive processing, to an extent that undermines phenomenology-based arguments for the extended view.

Let me say a bit more about the opposing view. In his recent book, *Reconstructing the Cognitive World*, Michael Wheeler claims that we should strive to construct models that are phenomenologically in key (Wheeler 2005, 133, 199, 227), borrowing a phrase from John McDowell (ibid., 128). Take, for instance, a model that posits a system of rules and representations that guides our hitch-free use of tools, such as a hammer. A model of this sort falls under immediate suspicion, according to Wheeler. The expert, tool-using subject is not aware of the application of rules or the issuing of output commands. According to Wheeler, we should prefer a model that respects the phenomenology.

As Wheeler (2005, 226–27) would have it, the in-key constraint grounds an argument for the extended view. According to the most plausible version of the extended view, it is only in certain circumstances that a significant part of the physical process constituting cognition occurs beyond the boundary of the organism. Wheeler argues that in just these cases, we have no conscious awareness of the details of cognitive processing or our interaction with the world. Because the extended view of the implementation of cognitive processing meshes with the reports of conscious experience, the extended view is phenomenologically in key.

This argument presupposes that conscious experience is tied specifically to the organism. Otherwise, why would it be natural to think that if cognition happens beyond the boundary of the organism, it will be hidden from consciousness? It is somewhat odd to appeal to a nonextended view of consciousness in arguing for the extended view of cognition.

Set aside this concern, and consider the relation between Wheeler's argument and the scientific work. When one examines cognitive psychological practice, it is difficult to locate much support for this in-key criterion. Cognitive psychologists sometimes collect subject protocols; in research on expert problem-solving, for example, subjects are sometimes asked to track verbally the problem-solving steps they apply (Chi, Feltovich, and Glaser 1981). Moreover, it may even be possible to determine the general factors that improve or degrade subjects' accuracy in such reports (Ericsson and Simon 1980). Protocols are used as a starting point and as data to be accounted for, in an integrated way, along with other data. Sometimes this involves checking to see whether proto-col data correlate with other forms of data, which correlations can then be used to infer further details of cognitive processing. Nevertheless, cognitive psychol-ogy does not give trumping power to such reports or take them as revealing, in some unqualified way, the details of the cognitive processes occurring at the time of the report. As a general desideratum, then, the in-key requirement appears to be a philosopher's construction, not something that emerges from a naturalistic philosophy of cognitive science.

To make matters worse for the in-key constraint, a large body of empirical results directly calls into question the reliability of subjects' reports on their own cognitive processing. I briefly review a pair of examples. First, consider the work of Richard Nisbett and associates (surveyed, along with many similar results, in Nisbett and Wilson 1977), showing the extent to which subjects are unaware of their own motivations and reasoning processes. In one experiment, performed by Storms and Nisbett (1970), insomniacs are given sugar pills. Half are told that the pill produces what are, in fact, the standard bodily symptoms of sleeplessness—although not described to the subjects in those terms. The other half are told that the pill is a muscle relaxer of sorts: that it lowers heart-rate, reduces alertness, and the like. Members of the first group fall asleep significantly more quickly than usual. The best explanation of these results seems to be that the subjects in the first group attribute their insomnia-related symptoms to the pill, rather than to their typical causes (e.g., thoughts about personal problems). In contrast, members of the second group take longer to fall asleep than they normally do. These subjects, who believe themselves to have taken a relaxation pill, are presumably upset by the fact that the standard symptoms of insomnia appear and persist despite having taken a pill that coun-teracts such symptoms; plausibly, this results in higher levels of stress and thus more sleeplessness. In post-experimental questioning, though, the subjects fabricate reasons for the results and resist any suggestion that they engaged in the thought processes described above. When the entire experimental setup is revealed to the subjects, they deny having undergone the thought processes that seem best to explain the results.

A separate line of research concerns false memories. Elizabeth Loftus (Loftus and Bernstein 2005), Roddy Roediger, Kathleen McDermott, and others have spent much of the past thirty years showing how to manipulate memory reports—to create false recall, as it is sometimes labeled. Consider Roediger's list-learning experiments (Roediger and Gallo 2005). After having studied a list of words, many subjects report that a term merely related to those on list was itself on the list. In fact, under some conditions, subjects "remember" words that were not on the studied list at a slightly *higher* rate than those that actually were on the list. In more elaborate versions of the experiments, subjects' memories of the list-learning context are probed. Many subjects report a distinct memory of having heard the experimenter's voice pronouncing the nonlist word; others report what they were thinking at the time they allegedly heard the nonlist word. Subjects with introspective access to the cognitive processes by which those "memories" were formed and remembered should not make these drastic mistakes; they would be aware of how their own cognitive systems of encoding and recall function and of the kinds of mistake those systems tend to produce. Problems with recall are not, however, revealed phenomenologically, but rather by careful empirical research. The best explanation of subjects' mistakes almost certainly involves mechanisms of semantic association and storage, and we have no reason to think phenomenological reflection offers insight into the complex workings of these mechanisms.

Admittedly, a healthy debate currently exists over the role of introspection in cognitive science (Gallagher 2002; Jack and Roepstorff 2002a, 2002b; Schooler 2002a, 2002b). Defenders of introspection note a number of cases in which first-person reports about the workings of cognitive mechanisms have proven useful (for a list of cases, see Jack and Roepstorff [2002a, 336]). For instance, when investigating short-term memory, it has been useful to ask subjects whether they were aware of the use of a rehearsal strategy and what form it seemed to them to take. Nevertheless, research continues to produce cases in which subjects do not report accurately on the details of their cognitive processing (Cleeremans, Destrebecqz, and Boyer 1998; Schooler 2002a; Wegner 2002; Silverman and Mack 2006; Linser and Goschke 2007). Cases involving priming or implicit learning include an ironic twist: in these cases, cognitive psychologists can (and routinely do) cause the cognitive system to work in ways that severely reduce the likelihood of accurate introspective report. On balance, then, the state of the game remains as depicted above: first-person reports on the workings of one's own cognitive mechanisms should be treated as suspect till proven useful, case by case. More importantly, there is no doubt that we should reject the in-key requirement. Introspective reports may turn out to be useful in some contexts, but we should not expect that, in general, introspective reports have the same content as our best cognitive-scientific theories.[1]

In Wheeler's defense, he sometimes advocates a weaker version of the in-key criterion: on this view, for a cognitive-scientific model to be in good standing, it should make the associated phenomenology intelligible. Fair enough, but only insofar as one is out to explain the phenomenology in particular. If, instead, one's goal is to explain the processing of linguistic input, then one should want to make intelligible various processes and forms of behavior related to language processing; one might, for example, explain how these emerge from lower-level information-processing routines. The explanation of linguistic processing need pay very little attention to subjects reports concerning what it is like from a first-person

---

1. Wheeler acknowledges the primary concern developed in the preceding paragraphs of the main text: that phenomenology provides "a highly unreliable guide to the psychological mechanisms that underpin mind and intelligence" (2005, 123). Wheeler dismisses this worry, however, as the knee-jerk reaction of mainstream cognitive scientists. I hope to have shown that it is not a knee-jerk reaction but is based instead on a large body of reliable results. Wheeler does not address these results or explain exactly where the mainstream reaction goes wrong.

standpoint to process incoming speech; that would be to confuse two separate areas of research: one on language processing, the other on the phenomenology of language processing. Of course, the ultimate explanation of human cognition—cognitive psychology's final and true theory, if there ever is such a thing—should account for both. We should doubt, however, that the mechanisms producing the phenomenology are so connected to cognitive processing in general that an understanding of the mechanisms producing phenomenological reports will itself render language processing intelligible. Furthermore, given the extent of phenomenological error, we should in fact be quite surprised to find out that what makes language processing intelligible does so directly for the phenomenology of language processing as well, or vice versa. More likely than not, the mechanisms that segment and parse incoming speech differ in significant respects from those producing experiences (or reports of experiences) of hearing someone else talk.

Even in respect of the phenomenology itself, the demand for intelligibility does not vindicate the contents of phenomenology-based reports. To make something intelligible amounts no more than explaining that thing. Yet, it is generally false that if A explains B, then the content of B (when B is the sort of thing that has content) accurately describes A. Why should it be any different in the case of cognitive or conscious states? It is one thing to treat the characteristics of a verbal report as evidence of their cause—a standard approach to explaining the verbal reports. It is quite another, though, to take the contents of such reports to be accurate, even about the very processes that produce those reports. Making conscious experiences, or reports of them, intelligible does not require taking their content to be accurate.

8.2. The Phenomenology of Smooth Coping

8.2.1. The Argument from Smooth Coping

Consider now an argument for the extended view based specifically on the phenomenology of smooth coping, that is, the seamless way we interact with the world when engaging in, for instance, skilled hammering or typing.

ARGUMENT FROM SMOOTH COPING

Premise 1.   In smooth coping, we are not aware of a distinction between bodily self and the external resources being used.

Premise 2.   If we are not aware of such a distinction, then the correct cognitive theory of smooth coping probably appeals to no such distinction.

Conclusion. Therefore, chances are that the correct cognitive theory of smooth coping draws no important distinction between bodily and extra-bodily resources; in which case the extended view holds.

Moreover, smooth coping is a significant and widespread form of human cognition; thus, if the argument from smooth coping is sound, the extended view is likely to have significant scope. To the extent that online cognition is the *fundamental* form of human cognition and smooth coping is common form of online cognition, the extended view is likely to apply widely and to some of the most fundamental forms of human cognition (Wheeler 2005, 12–13, 222, 226).

Wheeler does not present his phenomenological argument in as bald a form as I have cast the Argument from Smooth Coping, but the latter captures the gist of his reasoning (most clearly at Wheeler 2005, 225–27). Wheeler claims that the extended view and a Heideggerian approach offer each other mutual support (ibid., 225), and the Argument from Smooth Coping reconstructs, in a straightforward way, one plank in this mutual relation: phenomenology's support for the extended view. The situation is a bit less clear with Clark. Sometimes Clark (2003, 28, 33–34, and chapter 2, passim) emphasizes smooth coping in the use of new technologies that augment or transform our cognitive capacities. It frequently seems as if Clark is merely illustrating what it would be like phenomenologically if our minds were extended by technology, while resting his arguments for the extended view on such separate considerations as the functionalist ones discussed above, in chapter 5. Sometimes, however, Clark seems to be saying that because we have the appropriate phenomenological experiences when using external resources—the very kinds of experience we have when we use our own brains during cognitive processing (ibid., 34)—the extended view is less implausible.

I doubt the Argument from Smooth Coping succeeds. In addition to my general concerns about the phenomenological approach, both premises of the present argument strike me as questionable. Take *Premise 1*'s description of the phenomenology itself. There is some sense in which, when we hammer, type, drive, play an instrument, play a sport, or engage in conversation, we seamlessly interact with the world. When typing smoothly, however, I feel the keys as items distinct from my body, and similarly in other cases of smooth coping. There is a certain thin-ness to this conscious experience, no doubt—a lack of awareness of many of the details of the interactions, as well as a sense of fluidity or lack of difficulty in producing successful motions. It is, however, one thing to transcend conscious planning and the deliberate issuing of motor commands; it is quite another literally to lose all awareness of external items as separate from one's body.

A promising account of motor control does not gibe with *Premise 2*. The account I have in mind is the control theory or emulator theory (Grush 1997, 2003, 2004). Here is the view in outline. When initiating reaching, motor cortex sends outgoing signals on their way to the apposite neuro-muscular junctures.

In addition, a copy of this signal, an efferent copy, is sent to an emulator unit in the brain, which, in effect, predicts the outcome of the subject's reaching on the basis of a simulation (or perhaps on the basis of stored results of past acts of reaching). The emulator thus provides feedback in a timely enough manner to allow real-time correction commands to be sent by motor cortex.

Motor control aside, there is evidence that other forms of cognition depend on the interaction among neural signals. Eagleman and Holcombe (2002) present evidence of this sort of process in cases of intentional action: when subjects act intentionally to bring about a tone, their correlation of visual (position of clock-hand) and auditory stimulus is affected by their having intentionally brought about the tone (cf. Linser and Goschke [2007]); on one reasonable hypothesis, their brains rely on the outgoing motor command to calibrate the correlation of stimuli from different sensory modalities.[2]

Now for a phenomenological approach. Take the example of reaching for a coffee cup. Borrett, Kelly, and Kwan (2000) describe the phenomenology this way:

> When I want to drink some coffee from my coffee mug in the morning I simply grab the mug in a single, smooth, undifferentiated movement. I do not constantly update my understanding of the place of my arm with respect to the place of my coffee mug on the basis of continuous sensory feedback about their relative positions in objective space. (217)

Borrett et al. then quote Merleau-Ponty approvingly, asserting that, at the initiation of the act, the action is already magically at its completion. I suspect, though, that there is nothing magical about the success of the action; reaching for a coffee cup is likely guided by an emulator circuit. Thus, Borrett, Kelly, and Kwan are partly correct. At least in the early stages of reaching, before proprioceptive information can be fed back to motor cortex, "continuous sensory feedback" does not guide the arm's reach; but Borrett et al. are right for the wrong reason. Introspection does not justify the conclusion; rather, it is a matter of the way in which the brain copes with certain temporal limitations: given the relevant transduction times, the proprioceptive loop cannot be closed quickly enough to provide corrective feedback to motor cortex, and so the brain relies on emulator circuits. *Contra* the conception of neuroscience suggested by Borrett et al. (as a science the primary goal of which is to explain conscious states—ibid., 214), the justification of the emulator-based explanation does not

---

2. I suspect this kind of process accounts for a bodily phenomenon that Clark (2006a, 373, 2007) adduces in support of the extended view: the use of gesture in problem-solving. Allowing subjects to gesture can significantly affect their ability to solve problems, and this suggests to Clark that the bodily gestures are themselves part of the cognitive system (for an overview of the empirical research, see Goldin-Meadow [2003]). It has yet to be shown, though, that the gesture itself causally affects problem-solving, as opposed to the neural command to gesture, an efferent copy of it, or a visual representation of gestures.

derive solely, or even primarily, from the way in which it accounts for the phenomenology. Rather, the justification derives from an emulator model's capacity to account for the behavioral data in a way that is physiologically plausible.
If a plausible mechanism of subconscious sensory feedback were discovered,
it would present a viable option as well, regardless of how the phenomenology
appears.

Thus, *Premise 2* is likely false, or at least far from established: our lack of
awareness of an important distinction between bodily and external resources
does not entail that a correct theory of motor cognition makes no such distinction. Emulator models, and the research they are based on, provide evidence to
the contrary. The emulator at least implicitly represents bodily parts; but insofar as it represents cups at all, it represents them quite differently: the emulator
sends signals correcting the movement of the arm, but it sends no such signals
correcting the movement of the cup—for obvious reasons.

8.2.2. The Heideggerian Framework

The preceding discussion might strike some readers as insensitive to the richness and complexity of the phenomenological approach. Wheeler, in particular,
lays out the phenomenological framework in some detail, employing specifically Heideggerian conceptual machinery. To be fair, then, we should ask
whether increased sophistication improves the phenomenological argument.

The fundamental Heideggerian picture presented by Wheeler is this.
Humans exist in a state of thrown projection: they find themselves always in
a meaningful environment, filled with meaning that the individual projects
onto that environment and its constituents. Which means that the individual
experiences in the environment are determined partly by a process of self-
interpretation: the human identifies himself with certain socially defined roles
and the norms of behavior and thought associated with those roles. Wheeler
gives the example of being a parent. Someone who identifies himself as a parent sees certain meanings in the environment, having to do, for example, with
safety or well-being of his child (Wheeler 2005, 122). Smooth coping consists
in the subject's acting smoothly in accordance with such norms, fluidly and
naturally acting to keep the child out of harm's way.

Here, though, I bring my exegesis of Wheeler's Heidegger to a halt. The view
suffers from an obvious and crippling foundational problem that the filling in
of further details does not alleviate. The Heideggerian view offers no explanation of how the human internalizes social norms or of how social norms come
into existence. (And similar remarks apply to the individual's capacity to react to
involvement-wholes and referential networks and the like—see Wheeler [2005,
146–48]). More importantly, one would expect the best explanations of the process
of creating and internalizing social norms to appeal to the standard constructs of
orthodox cognitive science: perception, memory, language-use, etc. It is not magic

that a parent in contemporary American society thinks he should have health insurance for his children. Rather, it is the result of a long process of persons perceiving others who are hurt, reasoning through possible ways to treat hurt people, hearing the people who treat wounds and illness saying that they would like money for their services, and so on. Likewise, for the process of learning what is available and expected in American society—for example, that one should ask at one's place of employment whether the company offers a health insurance plan. How does the average American parent become familiar with this standard procedure? Presumably, he has applied his suite of interconnected organismically bounded cognitive capacities, for example, those involved in reading about the standard procedures, hearing about them, remembering from childhood that Mom or Dad had health insurance through her or his employer, and so on.

Wheeler rests his philosophy of cognitive science on claims about social expectations and norms without acknowledging the extent to which this begs many of the most interesting questions in cognitive science.[3] We should find this unsatisfying. It takes for granted that the basic cognitive skills can go unexplained, then casts the remainder of cognitive science in a Heideggerian light; but the primary work of cognitive science is to explain those cognitive skills by which anyone can come to create culture, be affected by it, and apply the lessons learned from it. Culture, in some loose sense, may define what is meaningful— what hammers are for—but the subject must learn this and how to exploit this meaning to achieve her goals. Once an explanation of these latter processes is on the table, the inference from the phenomenology of smooth coping (fleshed out by talk of social norms) to the extended view loses its force. Cognitive-scientific explanations of learning and enculturation undercut Wheeler's appeal to phenomenology, partly by revealing the shape of an orthodox-cum-embedded account of the introspective facts. The thin-ness of the phenomenology offers us no reason to think cognitive processing takes place beyond the boundary of the organism, in the social realm of norms and meaning.

8.2.3. Wheeler's Appeal to Dynamical Systems Theory

In the final substantive chapter of his book, Wheeler recognizes the need for "an account of the subagential causal mechanisms that generate richly context-sensitive online intelligence" (2005, 274; cf. 277). On Wheeler's view, dynamical systems theory bridges the gap between the phenomenology of smooth coping and the subagential mechanisms that generate intelligent behavior. That is,

3. Toward the book's end, Wheeler seems to recognize that his appeals to Heideggerian throw-*ness* presuppose an account of enculturation (2005, 277), but he presents this as a positive aspect of his account, rather than acknowledging the extent to which it leaves fundamental questions unanswered. Elsewhere Wheeler mentions the issue of socialization (Wheeler 2005, 150) and cultural initiation (p. 158) without recognizing the need for a cognitive-scientific account of these processes. Here, as well as in the discussion of smooth coping, Wheeler does not seem to come to grips with standard models of learning and the development of expertise (Stillings et al. 1995, 129–35).

dynamical systems-based models explain the causal sources of online intelligent behavior, typically in a way that involves nontrivial causal spread. In particular, dynamical-systems models can show how online intelligence can be exhibited by systems with nontrivial causal spread of an extreme type, where mostly external forces are causally responsible for the behavior at issue (which also explains why we have no conscious access to the workings of these processes, at least so long as we take consciousness to be an organismically limited affair).

What should we make of Wheeler's appeal to dynamical-systems models with nontrivial causal spread? First, we should be worried about the empirical claim. Wheeler appeals to a small number of not-very-compelling examples, of the infant-walking variety. Perhaps dynamical-systems-based models with extreme nontrivial causal spread would explain the Heideggerian phenomenology of cognition, if there were such models. As it is, though, Wheeler's view lacks empirical meat.

Second, even if Wheeler succeeds in appealing to dynamical-systems theory to explain the phenomenology of smooth coping, this does not support the extended view. Any theory of the causal antecedents of behavior will be consistent with a Heideggerian view of the phenomenology of smooth coping, so long as that theory places the causal antecedents of the behavior outside the reach of the mechanisms that directly produce conscious awareness. The forces causally responsible for behavior might be inside the organism (brain states not involved in the production of introspective reports) or outside the organism (the sun, e.g., or a sheet of notebook paper). The forces causally responsible for skilled behavior might be within the boundary of the cognitive system, or they might not; it depends on where the cognitive system is located. The demand (or even mere preference) that the cognitive science of skilled interaction with the world be consistent with Heideggerian phenomenology entails nothing of interest about the location of the cognitive system. In the end, then, Wheeler's support for the extended view rests on claims about nontrivial causal spread; this is a casual-dependence argument, which, as a general form of argument, is unsound.

8.3. The Sense of One's Own Location

Turn now to a different kind of phenomenological argument:

SENSE-OF-LOCATION ARGUMENT

Premise 1. In some cases, human subjects have the sense that their body (or self)[4] extends beyond their organismic boundary.

---

4. There is, of course, a difference between self and body. In the present context, though, it is relatively unimportant. In the cases at issue, subjects experience a sense of extended self inasmuch as, or for the sole reason that, they have a sense of extended bodily action.

Premise 2.   At least in some of these cases, the subject's sense of her bodily location is a reliable guide to the location of her cognitive processing.

Therefore, the extended view is true.

It is not clear that any influential philosopher or cognitive scientist endorses the argument in this stripped down form. The phenomenological sense of an extended body serves as a recurring theme in Clark (2003, 23–24, 45, 58, 61), playing what strikes me as an evidentiary role. Clark appeals to other considerations in support of the extended view: the persistence and reliability of the underlying correlations that give rise to the sense of an extended body or self (ibid., 105) as well as sense of control (ibid., 131, 135). Nevertheless, sometimes the talk of a phenomenological sense of extended presence seems to play an argumentative role in its own right. In summarizing the results of the chapter in which the plasticity of our sense of self takes center stage, Clark says, "The intimacy of brain and body is evidenced in the very plasticity of the body-image itself" (ibid., 190), which plasticity is partly supported by an appeal to the subject's shifting sense of where her body is located (and here Clark emphasizes cases in which subjects experience the body as beyond their organismic boundaries—specific examples are discussed below). For Clark, the intimacy of body and world is of a piece with the intimacy of brain and body—the intimacy of the latter being used to argue for (at least by providing a model of) the intimacy of the former. Furthermore, in Clark (2003, 3), the extended view is announced right off as the main thesis; in which case it would be odd to go on at length about phenomenological facts if they are not meant to provide any evidentiary support for the extended view (or the hypothesis of extended mind).

Enough about motivation. What about the content of the argument? Which cases is *Premise 1* meant to cover? A representative example comes from the work of Vilayanur Ramachandran (Clark 2003, 59–60, citing Ramachandran and Blakeslee [1998]). In one experiment, two subjects sit in chairs, one behind the other and both facing the same direction, as if in single file. They sit so that the subject in the rear can extend her arm fully and touch the nose of the person in front. The subject in the rear is blindfolded and one of her hands is taken up by the experimenter. The experimenter causes the rear subject's finger to tap against the nose of the subject in front in an irregular rhythm; in synchrony, the experimenter herself taps the same irregular pattern against the rear subject's nose. About 50 percent of subjects in the rear report the sense that they themselves are tapping their own nose; in fact, the rear subjects report experiencing their nose as extending two to three feet in length.

What should we make of these results? First, it is not clear that they tell us anything about the location of cognition; the location of my nose has no direct connection to the location of my cognitive processes or cognitive system. Second, the subjects reporting the sense of an extended nose are simply wrong. Any subject who claims that she is tapping her own two-foot-long nose is sorely mistaken about the location and shape of her nose. Third, we have some idea of what underlies the illusion. In general, the brain uses various mechanisms for correlating different sources of stimuli, including mechanisms dedicated to the correlation of stimuli from different sensory modalities. One such mechanism involves bimodally sensitive neurons in the intraparietal sulcus, or at least it does in Japanese macaque monkeys (Iriki, Tanaka, and Iwamura 1996; Iriki, Tanaka, Obayashi, and Iwamura 2001; cf. Graziano, Yap, and Gross [1994]). These neurons fire in response both to tactile stimulation of the hand and to the visual impression of the location of the hand. Quite plausibly, the nose-tapping experiment exploits neural mechanisms of a similar sort, which normally converge accurately on a single model of the body's current situation. Given a lack of agreement between different sources of information, the brain's drive to construct a single consistent model allows one source of information to dominate, even if the resulting model of the situation diverges from reality. This kind of process, not the literal extension of the body, self, or the cognitive system, explains the experience of an extended nose (cf. Clark [2003, 105]).

Iriki and associates provide a different gloss of their results, however, one that seems to buttress the sense-of-location argument. In one experiment (Iriki et al. 2001), macaque monkeys were trained to use a video monitor to guide the retrieval of food (either by hand or by using a small rake); they learned to retrieve food getting visual feedback only from a monitor. The monkeys then were exposed only to the video images of their hand. Functionally, they treated the video image as if it were their real hand, in that, for example, if a snake were shown approaching the image of the hand on the video screen, the monkeys would withdraw their real hand (occluded by a screen). Perhaps more impressively were the responses of bimodal neurons in monkey intraparietal sulcus. After the monkeys have been trained using the video screen to guide manual retrieval of food, the neurons in question respond to a visual probe on the screen as they normally would to objects approaching their hands. Iriki et al. describe the moral in terms of seeing-as: "Now the visual receptive field is located on the monitor, as if the monkey sees the image of its hand shown on the monitor as a part of or an extension of his own body" (2001, 166–67).[5]

Do these results support *Premise 1* of the sense-of-location argument? This depends partly on how comfortable one is attributing conscious experiences or a subjective sense of self to macaques and how much one makes of the physiology humans share with macaques (as of 2004, single-cell recordings of this sort had not been done on humans—see Holmes, Calvert, and Spence [2004]). Problem is, even if the results in question support the sense-of-location argument's *Premise 1*, they simultaneously undermine the sense-of-location

---

5. Obayashi, Tanaka, and Iriki (2000) describe their results in more explicitly phenomenological terms, in terms of the monkey's subjective image of its own body.

argument's *Premise 2*, by identifying the neural states that represent the location of the hand or arm. As Iriki et al. put it:

> Thus, the presently observed properties of the visual RFs [receptive fields] would represent neural correlate for this sort of internal representations, indicating that macaque monkeys...attained a neural machinery which can become capable, when extensively forced, of representing an intentionally controllable visual representation of their own body. (2001, 171)

This offers us a natural, nonextended interpretation of the situation. What happens at the cognitive level? The monkey thinks about its body in a certain way. Where is that thinking taking place? Wherever its realizer is. Where is its realizer? Precisely where Iriki et al. have shown it to be. Their neural evidence for a change in body image also locates the realizer of the relevant cognitive state. The relevant realizer is that of the monkey's cognitive state of taking her own body to extend beyond the boundary of the organism; and that realizer is located in the brain, at least partly in the firing of the bimodal neurons.[6] Thus, the conclusions of part I—in particular, that we should expect an organismically internal realizer of cognitive states—undermine any support the work of Iriki et al. might have otherwise provided for the extended view.

8.4. Control-Based Arguments

Can the basic thought underlying the sense-of-location argument be fleshed out in a more convincing way? The cases discussed in the preceding section seem to involve a misrepresentation of the body's location by an organismically internal cognitive-cum-neural process. Perhaps, though, the subject accurately represents something else of greater relevance to the location of cognitive states: it represents the kind of control the system has over various resources. Consider, then, a further phenomenological argument:

SENSE-OF-CONTROL ARGUMENT

Premise 1.   In the cases of some kinds of action, humans have a sense of unmediated control over external objects.

Premise 2.   If a subject has the sense of unmediated control of some resource *R*, then *R* is part of that subject's cognitive system.

Therefore, the extended view is true.[7]

---

6. Others have offered similar diagnoses of results both experimental and clinical. An example of the former kind involves a rubber hand, which, under the right conditions of stimulation, subjects will take to be their own (Ehrsson, Holmes, and Passingham 2005). An example of the latter case involves clinical patients who deny ownership of limbs that lack normal function (Ramachandran 1995, 33). Also see Markman and Brendl (2005).

7. It is much clearer that Clark has this form of argument in mind (2003, 91, 131–32).

Think now about the way in which one senses the location of one's body in the course of *doing* something. Iriki and associates show (Iriki, Tanaka, and Iwamura 1996) that if one gives macaque monkeys practice retrieving items with a rake, certain changes occur in the receptive fields of the bimodal neurons described above: these neurons' visual receptive fields become keyed not only to the hand, but to the rake as well, at least when monkey is actively using the rake to retrieve food. In some sense, then, the monkeys' brains are treating the rake as an extension of their own bodily selves.

In these cases, we might describe the macaques as having a sense of unmediated control of the rake, at least insofar as their neural systems treat the rake as part of their own physical bodies.[8] Compare this to other examples discussed by Clark. Someone controlling a robotic arm from a distance (Clark 2003, 96–99) may begin to feel as if she controls the robotic arm in an unmediated way; and in fact, one might think she experiences the arm as part of her own body because she experiences unmediated control of it. Furthermore, insofar as the blind person using a cane (Clark 2003, 62) develops a sense of an extended body, it results from her sense of controlling, in an unmediated way, an external object in the course of carrying out a cognitive task—that of gathering information about the environment.

I have three objections to the argument. First, the general concern about phenomenological reliability must be faced. The subject holding a rake might report an intention directly to reach (as opposed to reaching with her rake); nevertheless, the realizer of this intention—that is, the outgoing neural signal that causes the arm to move, rake in hand—may well represent separately, the arm, the rake and the causal dynamics of their interaction. It is simply not up to phenomenology to decide this issue.

Second, I wonder about the characterization of the phenomenology itself. I suspect that the phenomenology of cane-use or of the remote use of a robotic arm is indeterminate in an important way. As in the cases of smooth coping discussed above, the subject almost certainly experiences some sense of the presence of the cane or the glove; it is not the phenomenology of simply feeling the world, but rather the phenomenology of easily feeling the world with, or through, a cane. I suspect that the latter more accurately describes the phenomenology at issue. More cautiously, if the phenomenology can be described just as well either way, then we need some sort of tiebreaker to decide where the cognitive system is located, given the phenomenology. The argument developed

---

8. Only in a limited sense, though. Recent studies on humans (Holmes et al., 2004) seem to show that personal space is not simply extended; rather, the body image seems to be selectively projected to the tips of the tools used, excluding their shafts. Thus, we should interpret Iriki et al.'s results more cautiously. Insofar as they show anything about the human case, they show that humans represent the point of causal contact or control, which is often the hand.

in part I—as well as the other objections raised in the present section—acts as a tiebreaker here, favoring the nonextended view.

Finally, unless the proponent of the extended view has in hand an extension-friendly theory of phenomenological experience, she must account for the privilege of organismically located phenomenological experience. If phenomenological experience serves as the arbiter of the location of cognitive activity, and phenomenological experience is organismically local, then it appears that the organism plays a deeply privileged role in cognition. Such privilege seems to confer special status to the organism, which suggests an embedded view. This is part of a pattern. A variety of theoretically important asymmetries have emerged between the organismically internal and external materials relevant to cognitive processing. This point about phenomenological experience adds another point of asymmetry to the list.

In contrast, if the sense-of-control argument is beholden to an extended view of conscious experience, it rightly invites suspicion. Perhaps it is plausible on independent grounds that bits of matter are proto-conscious (Chalmers 1996a). Regardless, the sort of internalist intuition of robust conscious experiences (the kind of intuition that drives zombie arguments and the like) has no compelling application when it comes to pencils, rakes, and the like. Thus, the proponent of the extended view lacks compelling grounds for attributing a sense of control (and of phenomenological experience in general) to an extended system.

8.5. Control *Simpliciter*

At this point, the advocate for the extended view might opt for a purely control-based approach, phenomenology be damned. In this connection, Clark (2003, 130) echoes Dennett's claim, "I am the sum total of the parts I control directly" (from Dennett [1984, 82]). The idea might be fleshed out in this way. If one were to analyze the composite system including the body and the portion of the world with which it interacts, one would find natural boundaries—perhaps a steep drop-off in the kind of activity present (cf. Hutchins [1995, 157]). These might be identified as points of causal leverage, where changes in the position of some physically recognizable component are disproportionately responsible for a cognitive phenomenon. Such points of causal control can then be identified as the boundaries of the cognitive system.

To my mind, the argument from control provides a more compelling case for the extended view than many of the more popular arguments. Nevertheless, it has its own problems. Notice that it has much more limited application than advocates of the extended view would like. The argument might deliver an extended cognitive system in the case of sketching or solving a mathematical problem using pen and paper; but these extended systems include less than is typically claimed: only the body and writing implement, not the sketch pad or the piece of paper (these are merely acted upon). In the case of a cell phone (Clark 2003, 8–9) or the game Rush Hour (Wilson 2004, 193–95), this argument does not yield an extended cognitive system at all; the point of direct causal influence lies precisely at the boundary of the organism.

Moreover, in many cases, the sphere of causal control may not have a tidy boundary. The artist has more control over her hand than she does the pencil. The point of contact between the artist's hand and her pencil involves quite a bit of variation: changing grip, changing angle, changing degree of pressure—all of these involve changes in the way the artist's hand interacts with the pencil. On the other end of the process, she can use the pencil to push the sketch pad around to some further end—to knock that pesky bug off the edge of the table, however awkwardly. Each point of interface has some of the characteristics of a locus of control. Both the interface between the subject and the tool and the interface between the tool and the further part of the physical world being acted upon—which might itself be used as a tool—are of theoretical interest. How do we decide which point of interaction marks the boundary of the cognitive system?

Here we should defer to the considerations of part I, partly as a matter of principle but also because the systems-based view offers a natural explanation of the processes of interest. The cognitive system can use a tool to solve a further problem; the cognitive system has learned how to hold a tool steady so that the locus of causal influence is at the end of the tool.

This nonextended approach is reinforced by one further observation. It is not clear why bodily action should be taken as the appropriate arbiter of the location of cognition. To the contrary, it seems that the neural representations of action and the neural guidance of action on the basis of these representations constitutes all the *cognitive* explanation necessary. I grant that many advocates of the extended view hold relatively unorthodox views about mental representation (Rowlands 2006). Nevertheless, in generic cases of problem-solving, it is not clear what compelling reasons one could offer, in the face of such a neural explanation, to support the view that the movement of the body is cognition. If the movement of the body is not cognition, then neither is the action of a rod rigidly wedded to the body. Moreover, my talk of neural explanation is not idle speculation. The process by which motor signals effect action by stimulating the end plate is well understood (Purves, Augustine, Fitzpatrick, Katz, LaMantia, and McNamara 1997, 121–27). Here is located a well-defined interface that controls, in a systematic way, movements of the muscles holding, for example, a cane.

8.6. Extended Cognition and Extended Experience

For the most part, the preceding sections consider attempts to derive the extended view from the contents of first-person experience. In this section,

I consider a somewhat different tack: an attempt to derive the extended view from an independently motivated theory of conscious experience, of perceptual experience, in particular.

Consider the sensorimotor contingency view of sensory experience (Noë 2004). According to this view, having a conscious perceptual experience of a particular kind—say, the seeing of a tomato—consists in the mastering of certain sensorimotor contingencies; it is a matter of knowing what to expect if one were to move in certain ways, given that one is having certain sensations. Take the phenomenon of perceptual presence. In the typical case when one looks at a tomato, one sees only the facing side, yet there is some sense in which one sees the whole tomato. Advocates of the sensorimotor contingency view hold that the seeing of the whole tomato amounts to knowing the contingent connections between certain motor movements—leaning forward, grasping the tomato, taking a step sideways—and the sensations that would result from those movements. One sees the whole tomato, even though one has a sensation only of the facing side, because one knows that certain kinds of movement would lead to sensations of the backside of the tomato.

It is not my charge here to evaluate the sensorimotor view (Block 2005; Aizawa 2007).[9] I shall focus instead on the supposed connection between the sensorimotor view and the extended view. Noë argues that the former, together with certain empirical facts, supports the extended view, or something much like it (Noë 2004, chapter 7). Assuming, then, that perceptions are constituted by sensorimotor activity or knowledge of sensorimotor contingencies, does the extended view follow?

How, then, does Noë get from the sensorimotor view to extended cognition? The basic idea seems to be that the external world is part of the "physical substrate" (2004, 220) of perceptual experience, where this conception of the substrate is of whatever portion of the physical universe serves as a necessary condition for the perceptual experience. Given that causal interaction between the organism and the external environment is a necessary condition for certain kinds of perceptual experience, these experiences extend into the environment, in the way cognition does on Clark and Chalmers's view (Noë 2004, 210–11, 221).

Noë packs many ideas into his argument, however. In a single paragraph (220–21), he characterizes the relevant external factors as necessary for the experiential state, he characterizes the experiential state as depending on external factors, and he emphasizes the nontrivial causal responsibility of the

---

9. Here is one critical point, though. It is sometimes suspected that the sensorimotor contingency view is a recycled behaviorist account of sensory experience. Noë (2004, 32) argues that it is not, partly on the grounds that experience involves knowledge of sensorimotor contingencies. The explanation of that knowledge, however, often sounds behaviorist: it is simply a matter of having a skill or expecting certain results, where these amount to acting a certain way upon moving a certain way. If the sensorimotor contingency view is behaviorist in an objectionable way, it matters little whether it supports the extended view.

external facts. Nevertheless, each distinct line of reasoning rests on an assumption I have criticized in earlier chapters. It is not in general true that all of the necessary conditions of the occurrence of a state are part of that state; and whether Noë has metaphysical necessity in mind or merely nomological necessity matters not, for the reasons given in chapter 2. Moreover, it is not true that any time state A's existence depends on state B, state B is part of state A, or the characteristics distinctive of As are possessed by Bs, or the system of which A is a state is partly constituted by B. Lastly, it is not true that any time B is nontrivially causally responsible for A, then state B is part of state A, or that the kinds of characteristic distinctive of As are possessed by B, or that the system of which A is a state is partly constituted by B. Numerous intuitive counterexamples have been given, and more to the point, the systems delivered by these principles appear to be of no particular use to cognitive science.[10]

Does the case of perceptual experience exhibit mitigating features that render sound a domain-limited dependency premise? Noë emphasizes the distinctive nature of the content of perceptual experience. He argues, convincingly enough, that some perceptual content is virtual. We take ourselves to have a perceptual experience with a certain content, but we do not explicitly represent that content; rather, we have ready access to that content, and given our implicit knowledge of sensorimotor contingencies, we anticipate ways of gaining access to that content. If the content of perceptual experiences is always virtual—always a matter of having access to the content without explicitly representing that content—this warrants the extended view of perceptual experience.

This line of reasoning invites the following response. Admittedly, there is a distinction between virtual representation and genuine representation, and conscious perceptual states involve a relatively small amount of genuine representation. Nevertheless, vision might work in the following way. In response to foveal stimulation, visual processing stimulates a small number of explicit representations, the activation of which constitutes the conscious visual experience. On any particular occasion of seeing, the limited genuine content of a visual experience matches the content of these representations. At the same time, the conscious sense of, for example, seeing the far side of a tomato is explained in terms of various other cognitive states to which the explicit representation of the facing side of the tomato is connected. Assume that visual processing involves multiple layers of representation and that the visual process producing an explicit visual representation of one side of the tomato also causes the activation of a context-free 'tomato' element downstream (perhaps in the 3-D model of the environment—Marr 1982). This element is itself connected

10. Keep in mind a further point made in chapter 2. Noë's discussion might succeed as a criticism of certain arguments for internalism (arguments supposing it is possible to have perceptual experience in a world with no external matter), without establishing that perceptual experience extends into the environment. It can be a necessary condition for A that B (and therefore impossible to have A without B), without B's having A-like properties (or being part of a single, scientifically interesting A–B system, etc.).

to a set of representations of sensorimotor contingencies (or some other kind of internally represented knowledge that influences the subject's expectations). Thus, the presence of tomatohood is represented by a visually activated explicit representation of whole tomatoes, but a representation that is nevertheless not part of the immediate visual percept. This would explain the relevant aspects of conscious visual experience without requiring that such experiences are rich with explicit representation and, moreover, without appealing to any states beyond the boundary of the organism.

Noë (2004, 216–17) objects to this kind of approach because it presupposes a clear distinction between genuinely, explicitly represented content and virtual content. According to Noë, content is virtual all the way down, in the sense that no matter what the subject would take herself to representing at a given time, that very content could be further refined or elaborated. Noë says, "[Y]ou cannot factor experience into an occurrent and a merely potential part. Pick any candidate for the occurrent factor...It is present only in potential" (ibid., 217). The qualities that you might think are represented explicitly, that is, occurrently, "are available in experience as possibilities, as potentialities, but not as completed givens" (ibid.). Therefore, Noë concludes, there is no set of local, occurrent conscious states with genuine content distinct from the processes responsible for perceptual sense of further possibilities. On Noë's view, all perceptual content is virtual and, moreover, virtual content depends on a physical substrate that goes beyond the boundary of the organism. Thus, there is something special about dependence in the cognitive case. One of the essential features of a perceptual experience, its content, is constituted by a set of contingencies that are manifest only in the interaction between the organism and material beyond its boundary. When theorizing about perception, we cannot grasp onto one part of experiential content—the genuine content— then explain the further sense of potentiality by appealing to internal mechanisms that would, say, govern the transition from one explicit conscious state to another.

Noë's presentation of the argument is fairly impressionistic. At some points, the premises are missing; at others, they seem unclear. How do we get from the idea that the content of any representational state can be refined to the conclusion that there is no determinate content? The reasoning seems to rest on a pair of dubious assumptions: (a) that if the subject can refine the content of a perception, then that perception did not initially have determinate content (it has content only "in potential") and (b) that the process of refinement cannot itself be explained in terms of the organism's existing cognitive states or mechanisms. I shall argue that (a) is questionable and (b) almost certainly false. In the course of arguing that (b) is false, I show that Noë begs the question against the kind of embedded view I am inclined to press. What is more, the only obvious way Noë offers to avoid begging the question returns us full circle to the unsound dependence arguments.

In connection with (a), consider this possibility. A subject experiences a series of conscious states, which individually have the following contents: *That thing is red. That thing is red and slightly wrinkled. That thing is red and slightly wrinkled and has a small, rectangular divot in its surface.* Now imagine that the states come in this series as a result of exploration of the sort Noë emphasizes: the subject leans forward, peers at the object from a new angle, and so on. Nothing about the narrowing of truth-conditions from one state to the next suggests that the first in a given pair represented the world only potentially or only possibly. The first in the series represented precisely that the surface in question is red; it is a veridical perceptual experience if and only if the surface is red. The fact that the subject can act so as to cause herself to enter another perceptual state with more demanding truth-conditions (or conditions of veridical perception) is simply irrelevant to the truth-conditions of the first state.

Noë worries, however, that even in the case of the red surface of a tomato, the viewer does not take it in all at once: "But if you are careful you will admit that you don't actually experience every part even of its visible surface all at once. Your eyes scan the surface, and you direct your attention to this or that" (Noë 2004, 217). Perhaps, but this shows very little. It shows only that, in my example, *S*'s initial state represents as red a smaller surface than one might have thought; but *S* might still represent *that smaller part* determinately as red. If Noë's example has any persuasive force, it is because the subject tries to, or takes herself to, represent a bigger item than she can hold in visual consciousness at once. Try a smaller item, say, an individual letter on a page. One need not flit one's eyes about to see the character 'a' in its entirety; look at it, straight at it, and attend to the whole thing—it is easy.

Now consider (b), the claim that the process of refinement cannot itself be explained in terms of the organism's existing cognitive states or mechanisms. Noë should accept the distinction between, on the one hand, the entire collection of conscious perceptual states and, on the other hand, the implicit mastery of sensorimotor contingencies. Here (b) runs on the rocks. The orthodox approach tells a rich story about the causal interaction between the organism and the environment, a story according to which mastery of sensorimotor contingencies involves alterations in the causal relations among a great number of internal states. Think of this in terms of the experience by which these contingencies are learned. Learning these contingencies involves causally interacting with various aspects of the world, and whatever is learned from these interactions, the cognitive system takes with it: having learned that certain contingencies hold is a matter of alteration in the physical structure of the organism only. In contrast, the subject leaves behind the environment with which she interacted. On pain of our having to commit to a gerrymandered spatiotemporal worm of no use to cognitive psychology, the objects interacting with the organism are here and gone, necessary to learning but not part of the realization of the sensorimotor knowledge that results.

One cannot respond effectively to this concern simply by emphasizing the complexity of the internal relations, that they, for example, involve complex functions from various sensory stimulations and various aspects of the current state of other parts of the brain or body to a resulting subpersonal expectation (or analogous cognitive structure). Pointing out this complexity (Hurley 2001) is surely informative in many respects, but impertinent here. My point is simply that the most plausible way to implement visual experience as described by the sensorimotor contingency view is cast in terms of organismically instantiated dispositions shaped by learning; having sensorimotor knowledge is to have organismically instantiated capacities to interact with the world in certain ways.

Noë might resist this view, but his grounds for doing so would seem to consist only in unrefined considerations of dependence: since causal interaction with the extra-bodily environment is nomologically necessary for the organism's mastering of sensorimotor contingencies, the external stuff becomes part of the implicit knowledge of sensorimotor contingencies.

Perhaps Noë would instead emphasize the short timescales involved in sensory exploration. Doing so would shift us away from knowledge of sensorimotor contingencies—which presumably is a relatively stable affair—to an emphasis on the exploration itself. Why, though, should the act of exploring itself, including the thing explored, constitute the relevant kind of physical substrate? Here the argument concerning realization discussed in chapter 4 applies. If seeing were the actual exploration, including the thing explored, the Causal-Structure Principle would be violated. We should not bother trying to finesse this problem when we have, near to hand, an acceptable, even superior, alternative that does not require metaphysical and methodological contortions. The psychological state of knowing sensorimotor contingencies is realized by physical structures of the organism that were shaped during learning and that facilitate and guide exploration of the environment.

This brings us to the end of part II, the survey of arguments in support of the extended view. I have not found much here to encourage the proponent of the extended view. Many of the fundamental forms of argument offered in support of the extended view rely on premises that would be immediately rejected if applied in other domains; and proponents of the extended view offer us little reason to think that cognitive science comprises a special domain for which a circumscribed form of those premises holds. Even in the cases most amenable to an extended interpretation, the discussion seems to end in stalemate, with a choice between an orthodox view (possibly of the embedded variety), an unsatisfactory version of the extended view, or a version of the extended view that is empirically adequate but is a trivial variant of the orthodox view. In keeping with the results of part I, we should endorse the first option, the orthodox-cum-embedded view.

Many questions remain concerning the relation between the nonextended view, generally speaking, and the narrower orthodoxy often taken as target by advocates for the situated program. In part III, I take up such questions, examining the claims to innovation and heterodoxy made by advocates of the embedded and embodied views. Even if cognition is an organismically local affair, it may take a much different form than has often been assumed in standard rules-and-representations-based cognitive science.

Finally, recall a line of reasoning suggested at the outset, reasoning that brings our primary discussion to bear on questions about the human mind. Imagine we identify an important division between the human mind and the resources it uses, a division embedded in our everyday concept of a mind. Philosophers then ask whether cognitive science delivers anything that mirrors this division. Can we fill in the following blanks: the mind stands to the resources it uses as cognitive-scientific construct A stands to some B? Locating values for A and B at least suggests that cognitive science has located the mind: the value of A. If my arguments have stayed on track, A is the integrated set of cognitive capacities and mechanisms; moreover, this system appears, for most humans most of the time, inside the boundary of the organism. Thus, the moral of parts I and II extends beyond the philosophical foundations of cognitive science to philosophy of mind: insofar as cognitive science delivers a human mind, it is organismically bounded.

PART III

The Embedded and Embodied Mind

9

Embedded Cognition and Computation

Parts I and II criticize the extended view and various arguments for it. Some of the criticisms rest on a claim about the embedded view: it accounts well enough for phenomena that impress proponents of the extended approach. This claim needs little argument. The extended view is normally developed in two stages: first comes the description of an interactive process, then the claim that the interaction in question extends cognition. By detailing the organism's interaction with the environment, the proponent of the extended view, in effect, presents an embedded model of process in question. Disagreement concerns the status of the environment's contribution to that interaction; we can ask whether it literally constitutes part of a distinctively cognitive process, and I have argued that it does not.

Many questions remain, however. Assuming the embedded approach is on the right track, we should wonder what it brings in its train. This issue is especially pressing given the striking theoretical claims made on behalf of the embedded view (e.g., in Wheeler [2005] and in Gibbs [2006]). These authors claim, for example, that the embedded view (or the undifferentiated situated view) is at odds with computationalism, that it does without mental representations, or that it deploys representations of an entirely new sort: action-oriented, egocentric, and context-dependent.

In this chapter, I set out the embedded view and address the role of computation in embedded models. In chapter 10, I address questions about the embedded approach to mental representations. Throughout, the discussion focuses on the issue of heterodoxy: given the clear value of embedded models, to what extent and in what ways do such models depart from the orthodox rules-and-representations-based approach in cognitive science? Are the differences merely a matter of degree, of interest primarily to working cognitive scientists who must decide precisely how to model cognitive processes? Or, are these differences of grander philosophical importance, differences in our theoretical understanding of human cognition, computation, or mental representation, differences that thereby alter our philosophical understanding of the human mind and self? In chapter 11, the final substantive chapter, I address parallel questions about the embodiedview.

9.1. The Embedded Approach

The embedded approach aims to model human cognition using less elaborate computational structure and fewer internal representations than orthodox practice tends to presuppose (Clark 1995, 1997, chapter 8; McClamrock 1995, chapter 6; Ballard et al. 1997; Gigerenzer 2000). On the orthodox view, when the human subject is faced with a problem, her cognitive system performs a complex analysis of the situation before she acts. In the case of vision-based cognition, such complex analysis involves the subconscious construction of a detailed, internal representation of the immediate environment. In the case of a more abstract cognitive process, for instance, the choice of a college to attend, the subject might begin by explicitly representing[1] the maximum acceptable tuition, the costs and benefits of each of a range of options, and the likelihood of success of each option.

In contrast, on an embedded view, the subject exploits context-specific correlations to simplify the problem-solving process. Using the case of visual perception to illustrate, consider Andy Clark's example (1995, 97) of finding the photo-development counter at a drugstore. Given the market dominance of Kodak, the area above or around the photo-development counter is normally splashed with yellow. This suggests a simple strategy to the consumer in search of the photo counter: enter the drugstore, and swivel one's head looking for a large patch of yellow; walk toward the yellow patch. Or, consider the way in which a reader might find an entry in a list of works cited. In the main text, the reader sees "(Meyer, Thomson-Forshay, Gabowitz, Taylor, and Repucci 2004)," which refers to a work in which the reader is particularly interested. Rather than committing five surnames and a date to short-term memory, the reader simply remembers "Meyer plus a bunch"; given contingent facts about the academic milieu, this information almost certainly corresponds to only one entry.

---

1. A representation's being explicit does not entail that it is a constituent of (or otherwise specially related to) a conscious state. Explicit representation requires a physically identifiable structure—a word or a data structure, for example—that itself carries the content in question. Contrast this with what is implicit, that is, derivable from the content of physically individuated structures without actually being carried by any such structure.

At work in these examples are three strategic principles by which embedded models minimize the subject's use of internal resources. First, the subject need not explicitly represent any very elaborate theory of the domain of interest. In the case of photo counters, she need represent only the local, contingent correlation between patches of yellow and the location of photo counters. Second, the subject represents what might be called a 'coarse-grained' property: the subject looks for a large patch of yellow, not one of any very definite shape or size. Third, the subject collects only the information she needs. Mind you, the requisite representational resources far exceed nil. The subject must, for example, represent the project or plan she is engaged in: a person should not wander through life looking for yellow patches. Once the goal has been determined, though—for example, to get one's photos developed—and the subject has found and entered the store, the amount of information needed, at that moment, is fairly small. The subject need not represent the general layout of the building, the location of the restrooms, the number of cashiers on duty, or which cashiers' lines are open. The subject might need to represent some of these facts at some time during her visit; but when she enters the store and begins looking for the photo counter, she can ignore these other matters. Note, too, that a more general idea binds these three principles to the embedded theorist's minimalist approach: as much as possible, let the environment do the cognitive work (Clark 1989, 64; Brooks 1999).

Perhaps surprisingly, all of these principles apply equally to the case of decision-making, where many of the points about embedded vision seem to have little application. Consider first the overarching strategy of letting the world do the cognitive work. In many actual environments, there is a contingent correlation between *being a college that is treated as respectable* and *being a satisfactory option* (where a satisfactory option is, say, a school that provides the subject with a decent education and a marketable degree). Thus, although this oversimplifies most actual cases, a subject can set her mind on the first reasonably respectable school she comes across, then ask about its cost. Applying this heuristic requires *some* internal calculation on the subject's part and thus some internal representation; but it is much less demanding than an optimizing comparison of a substantial range of options. Now, if there were only a weak correlation between these properties, or none at all, the subject who acts in keeping with the suggested heuristic might expend her cognitive resources inefficiently, performing a series of quick and dirty analyses of the many possibilities that present themselves, determining serially that every one is either too expensive or (by dint of some red flag that arises along the way) not likely to provide a solid education. Humans, however, tend to structure their environments, institutions, and social interactions in such a way as to strengthen the kind of correlation at issue.

Think now about the three strategic principles listed in connection with the example of visual cognition. A subject can follow the college-selection heuristic and represent very little in the way of a theory of universities: she might know (or believe) very little about how universities are organized and run, and about what determines a university's quality or the esteem in which it is generally held. Also, given that the subject makes no detailed comparison of options, she can represent coarse-grained properties—such as *being a fairly respectable school*—instead of attempting a fine-grained determination of, for example, relative degrees of prestige of a substantial range of alternatives. Imagine that two or more options fall in roughly the same ballpark in terms of costs and benefits; if the subject's charge is to figure out which is more prestigious overall, she cannot coarse-grain; coarse-graining leads to a tie. Decision-making under such conditions required fine-grained comparison. If, however, the subject considers the first fairly respectable opportunity that presents itself, she is off to the races, at least if the school's tuition does not exceed the maximum acceptable cost. Lastly, notice that the amount of information one needs to gather to determine that a single college is respectable falls far short of the amount the subject would need to gather to determine which of a number of respectable schools is more prestigious than all others in the group.

For the remainder of this chapter I focus primarily on the relation between the embedded program and computation (returning, in chapter 10, to questions about embedded representations). As suggested by some of the preceding discussion, embedded models of cognitive tasks appear to require computational structure. Even if the embedded mind relies on heuristics and local correlations to achieve its goals, it must apply the appropriate heuristics at the appropriate times. Embedded models must explain how humans pursue various short-, middle-, and long-term goals in a structured way; some mechanism must, for example, control the timely abandonment of one goal and the substitution of another, in a way that is not merely random or triggered by an environmental cue.

As obvious as these observations might seem, proponents of the embedded approach take varying views of the role of computation in the embedded program. Some explicitly embrace a computational approach (e.g., Ballard et al. [1997], Gigerenzer [2000, 64–65], Gray and Fu [2004], Gray et al. [2006]); and of those sympathetic to the embedded approach, these authors appear to have had the greatest success in modeling genuinely cognitive phenomena. In contrast, some supporters of the embedded approach express ambivalence or downright hostility toward computational cognitive science (Thelen and Smith 1994, 331–38; Brooks 1999; Wheeler 2005). This hostility flows partly, I think, from mistaken views about the kinds of representation essential to situated and to computational models, a claim I substantiate in chapter 10 (and, to some extent, chapter 11). Additionally, anticomputationalist views sometimes rest on concerns about rules (Dreyfus 1992/1972, 271) and timing (Thelen and Smith 1994, 333–34; Wheeler 2005, 106; cf. Clark [1995, 99])—the latter particularly in connection with the dynamical-systems-based embedded approach. A comprehensive comparison of computational and dynamical-systems-based models requires more space than is available here. In the sections to follow, I have more modest aims. I argue (a) that embedded models' elimination of (some) explicitly encoded rules does not support an anticomputationalist reading of the embedded program and (b) that temporal considerations do not favor a non-computationalist dynamical-systems-based embedded approach over a computationalist one.

9.2. Computation, Implementation, and Explicitly Encoded Rules

Computational processes (Minsky 1967; Boolos, Burgess, and Jeffrey 2002) compute *functions*, pairings of the members of one set—the domain—with elements of another set—the codomain. As such, functions are abstract entities, as are *algorithms*, which constitute particular ways of computing functions. An algorithm is a set of dependence relations among states-types; this can be thought of as a partial ordering—say, in the form of a flow chart with conditional branching—of the application of a series of basic operations. Subsets of these state-types correspond to the arguments and values of the function being computed.

Take, for example, multiplication. It is a function, in that it maps pairs of numbers onto a number. The partial products method constitutes one algorithmic procedure for computing the multiplication function. Certain aspects of the problem are conditional: if one of the two place-holders to be multiplied in a given step is zero, write zero and move to the next step. Furthermore, although some steps are independent of others, the final step of adding products together depends on having already multiplied the relevant pairs of place-holding numbers.

What is it, though, for a physical system to compute a function? The implementation of a specific algorithm requires that a series of the physical system's causally connected states map onto the algorithm's abstract state-types, such that the causal relations of the concrete states map onto the stepwise dependence relations holding among the state-types in the algorithm (Chalmers 1994). Thus, the algorithm can be seen as a recipe for the concrete, causal mapping of the function's arguments to the corresponding values. A certain flexibility also seems required for genuine computing. The concrete system must be so constituted as to pass reliably through the series of causally connected states corresponding to steps in the algorithmic ordering of state-types, for a reasonably wide range of input and output values, as well as counterfactual cases (Chalmers 1996b), if the concrete system is to count as computing the function in question.

The preceding description of computation does not mention explicitly encoded rules (or instructions or programs). Nevertheless, there is a strong association between computing and explicitly encoded rules, which grounds our first objection to embedded computationalism. Embedded models show that many cognitive processes that we might have thought are governed by explicitly encoded rules need not be. If this result is generalized to the claim that our best embedded models contain no explicitly encoded rules at all, this might ground a thoroughly noncomputationalist reading of the embedded program—at least given the additional premise that computation must be governed by explicitly encoded rules (Harnad 1990, 336; Horgan and Tienson 1996, 24). So far as I can tell, though, anything but a modest embedded opposition to explicitly encoded rules lacks support: it may be that cognition is not guided by explicitly encoded rules in some cases where we might have expected it to be, but there is little evidence that human cognition proceeds entirely in the absence of explicitly encoded rules. Moreover, and of more interest to me in what follows, the objector misses an important theoretical point: that computation need not be governed by explicitly encoded rules.

First, a bit about rules themselves, particularly the kinds likely to appear in computational models of human cognitive processes. Some such rules are low level, in that they pertain to fairly specific values: a production-rule (Rosenbloom, Laird, Newell, and McCarl 1991) might explicitly represent the taking of action "a" under specific conditions "c," and nothing more (although production rules might be more abstract—Anderson 2007, 36). Also, rules can be represented algebraically, as expressions of relations among symbols of general types (Marcus, Vijayan, Rao, and Vishton 1999; Marcus 1999). Rules might also dictate how a system learns—by, for example, explicitly specifying the conditions under which the computing system should add or change rules of the first two types (by, for instance, chunking together, into a single production rule, what was originally a chain of independently executed rules).

It cannot be, however, that every computational step requires the application of an explicitly encoded rule (Fodor 1987, 21–26). Otherwise, computation would be bound to an infinite regress, and no algorithms could be implemented in concrete systems: every step in the implementation of an algorithm would require the application of a rule, and the process of applying that rule would have to be guided by a further explicitly encoded rule, and so on (cf. Carroll [1895]). Thus, some essential steps in the execution of an algorithm are not controlled by explicitly encoded rules. Some must be hard-programmed, the result of physical processes that, in the absence of explicitly encoded rules, nevertheless cause the system to move through a series of states in a problem-solving procedure.

Why is the association between rules and computing so tight in the minds of so many, when the straightforward regress argument shows that not all computing is rule-governed in the relevant sense? In what follows, I offer a diagnosis, which amounts, as much as anything, to a series of psychological hypotheses.

First, a computing machine controlled by explicitly encoded rules allows for a valuable kind of flexibility in computers. If a single piece of hardware is to compute a wide variety of functions, there must be some way to cause the machine to compute one function rather than another. Explicitly encoded instructions provide the requisite means (Piccinini 2008).

A second point rests on a more theoretically oriented, yet still practical, consideration. For any algorithm, there exists a set of instructions (say, the description of a Turing machine) that uniquely specifies that algorithm. As a result, one can prove things about all possible algorithms by proving things about all members of a well-ordered set of all possible instructions. This, too, creates the impression that instructions play an essential role in the implementation of an algorithm.

Third, a number of important debates might be resolved by the identification of explicitly encoded rules in the human mind or brain. For example, the presence of explicitly encoded rules entails the presence of an internal code, a language of thought, if you will (Fodor 1975). In a similar vein, the presence of such rules would show that certain connectionists are wrong when they claim to be able to do without representations of the abstract categories designated by symbols that appear in explicitly encoded rules (Marcus et al. 1999; McClelland and Plaut 1999; Marcus 1999). Moreover, the viability of the computational view of thought could be established by the demonstration of explicitly encoded rules. Nevertheless, these debates make perfect sense when we take explicitly encoded rules to be sufficient conditions for computation (or some important portion of a set of jointly sufficient conditions), rather than necessary conditions; finding the rules decides the issue in one way, although failing to find explicitly encoded rules in a given case does not decide the issue.[2]

Finally, the context of learning has created strong, shared associations. Theoretical introductions to computing often emphasize the foundational role of Turing machines, the behavior of which accords with explicit rules, which are naturally taken to be encoded in the tape head and thereby to be causally efficacious. Practical introductions to computing also emphasize explicit instructions. In my beginner's guide to programming in C, the topic *variable declarations* appears very early; and one purpose of defining variables is to encode rule-like commands explicitly. It is no surprise that, in describing computational models of cognition, explicitly encoded rules are sometimes considered essential.

How, then, should we conceive of computation in the absence of explicit instructions? Even if it is not a necessary condition of computation that each

2. Setting aside questions about explicitly encoded rules, explicit mental representations may, for other reasons, be necessary for computation-based cognition. Such units might, for instance, be needed to represent input.

step be governed by an explicitly encoded rule, could a human implement an algorithm without the contribution of any explicitly encoded rules? Imagine that we come across what appears to be a physical implementation of a Turing machine. We watch the head run over the tape, writing, erasing, and so forth, and in doing so, passing through a series of discrete states that could be paired with steps in a problem-solving process (say, multiplying). Nevertheless, our most thorough investigation of the head does not reveal the states we expect to find. Why not consider this a computational solution of the problem?

Of course, the question remains how a real-world physical system could compute without rules. To the extent that humans compute without rules, it may be by dint of epigenetic programming—innate structure caused to develop in one way rather than another by interaction with the environment. Humans can do without rules as well as they can because the structure of the environment causes the developmentally flexible brain to implement some algorithms in the absence of explicitly encoded rules; and this process may be ongoing, even reversible in some respects. Compare this to early, hard-programmable computers (Piccinini 2008), which certainly were computing: when the operator wants the machine to compute a new function, the operator physically alters the hardware. It is possible that human cognitive systems are hard-programmable computers the "hardware" of which is tuned up, and regularly reprogrammed, by interaction with the world.

In the end, the question whether there could be an entirely rules-free computational system is, I think, beside the point. There are no embedded models of any significant chunk of human cognition that do entirely without explicitly encoded rules. So, for many purposes, we can bracket the question of whether such a system genuinely computes. Nevertheless, in cases in which some rules are "eliminated," we should think properly about the result; we should not conclude that computation has thereby been eliminated from that portion of the cognitive process.

To reinforce this conclusion, consider the kinds of rules embedded models are likely to eliminate. Explicitly encoded rules can appear at different levels. Even an embedded model that appears to do away with explicitly encoded rules at something like the conscious or personal level does not necessarily do away with rules at a lower level (cf. Dreyfus [2005]). Take a cognitive model of memory that exploits spreading activation. The basic operation *pass activation in accordance with association strength* proceeds as a fundamental operation from the standpoint of a high-level cognitive description: as a result, the passing of activation may not appear to be governed by any rule at the level of the cognitive model; yet the implementation of the model may well involve the explicit encoding of rules at the lower level, as a means to carry out what counts as a basic operation at the higher level. The virtual machine that is human memory may not be rule-governed, but the computational process on which the activity of that virtual machine supervenes may still be rule-governed. Arguably, the use of such lower-level rules helps to ground the intuition that computation essentially involves the execution of explicitly encoded instructions; when higher-level rules are explicitly encoded, this ultimately serves the purpose of encoding lower-level ones. Similarly, the appearance of a rule in the textbook presentation of a model does not automatically implicate an explicit representation of the rule by the system the behavior of which is being described. Rather, it can indicate the presence of lower-level mechanisms—perhaps themselves involving explicitly encoded rules—that enforce behavior in accordance with the higher-level rule included as part of the behavior of the system. This distinction between explicitly encoded higher-level and explicitly encoded lower-level rules should be kept clearly in mind when evaluating any claim that an embedded model eliminates altogether the use of rules.

9.3. Computationalism in Principle and Computationalism in Practice

As a theory of human cognition, computationalism asserts that human cognition proceeds computationally, where this amounts to the implementation of Turing-computable algorithms. Defined this way, computationalism offers a very large umbrella, large enough to cover a surprising amount of situated research. Much of what seems to be a departure from standard computational approaches—in the connectionist and dynamical systems camps—can in fact be computationally modeled; most connectionist and dynamical-systems simulations are run on computers, after all. Yet, although the connectionist's functions are computable, via algorithms that specify rules for updating the activation of nodes, and although a neural-network simulation run on a computer thereby proves the existence of an algorithm that might, in principle, be implemented by human brains, the connectionist's modeling *practice* can depart significantly from the computational models developed by historically influential computationalists. The connectionist algorithms do not look at all like those used to model problem-solving in GPS, SOAR, or ACT (although see Anderson [2007, 37–38]). Computationalism in practice consists in a concrete family of research programs, each typically patterned after some small number of paradigmatic models or applications and employing variants on the architectures used in these paradigmatic cases.

Thus, we should distinguish computationalism in principle from computationalism in practice (Clark 2001, chapters 1 and 2). It is clear enough how the two computationalist views might come apart. Computationalism in principle tolerates computational models of a sort that no leading or influential researcher has pursued. Conversely, computationalism in practice makes commitments dispensable from the standpoint of computationalism in principle. In order to evaluate an anticomputationalist claim, then, one must identify its target. Successful embedded research might be recognizably computationalist, even though it involves such different styles of computation as to constitute a genuine departure from prevailing computational approaches; by rejecting standard computationalist practice, the embedded approach might reasonably bill itself as anticomputationalist, in practice, but the limited nature of this claim must be kept in mind.

Is this limitation substantive, though? Barsalou, Simmons, Barbey, and Wilson (2003, 87) claim that computationalism in principle is unfalsifiable, so flexible as to model any cognitive process. Although computationalism in principle offers a broader umbrella than sometimes thought, it is not unfalsifiable. If a human could compute the halting function (Minsky 1967, chapter 8)—in the bare sense of mapping inputs to correct outputs—then that human's cognitive process would not be entirely computational and computationalism in principle would be proven false; there is no effective procedure for computing the halting function. More likely to be relevant are implementation-related factors, which heavily constrain computationalism as a framework for explaining human cognition: successful models of human cognition invoke only states and basic operations that plausibly appear in human beings. For example, the standard execution time for a basic operation had better not be smaller than can be carried out by the human neural mechanism implementing that operation. This is no minor constraint. Neither, though, is it simply handed down by computationalism in practice, viewed as a set of historically important research programs or models. Thus, the rejection of computationalism in practice leaves unaddressed the broader, substantive (and falsifiable) thesis that human cognition proceeds computationally.

9.4. Timing, Computationalism, and Dynamical Systems Theory

It is often claimed that, given the embedded nature of human cognition, dynamical systems theory should replace computationalism as cognitive science's overarching theoretical framework. The argument runs as follows (Wheeler 2005, 106; cf. Clark 1995, 99): Embedded cognition depends heavily on the timing of subjects' interactions with their environments: as the body moves through the world during cognitive processing, the human's internal cognitive process must develop in synchrony with the series of events in the environment with which the subject causally interacts. The dynamical-systems approach employs differential equations, which are intrinsically suited to the modeling of fine-grained temporal dependencies. In contrast, computational tools are not suited to the modeling of fine-grained temporal dependencies. Thus, dynamical systems theory, and not computational theory, offers the appropriate framework for modeling embedded human cognition.

This argument does not depend on claims about the explicit representation of rules. Neither does it require that the processes modeled be noncomputational. The superiority in question need concern only the potential for scientific illumination. Even if computational models accurately describe human cognitive processes, such models may not shed much light on the underlying principles of cognition; thinking in computational terms may obscure important generalizations about cognition. In contrast, a dynamical-systems-based alternative might capture patterns or principles that lead to more fruitful theoretical developments and practical applications—and particularly via their intrinsic ability to model complex relations of timing (Wheeler 2005, 108).

It is not clear to me, however, that the dynamical-systems approach offers an intrinsic advantage in modeling timing. The contrary view seems to rest on two mistakes. The first involves a mistaken interpretation of differential equations. The second underestimates the role of considerations of timing in computational modeling. I take these in order.

Consider the basic definition of differential calculus: $f(x + h) - f(x)/h$. What is its intrinsic connection to time? There is none. It simply allows us to talk meaningfully about limits: the value of $f(x)$ as h approaches zero. We can conceive of h as a temporal interval if we like, but it is not an essentially temporal quantity. This is true of differential equations in general; the use of Δt and talk of instantaneous rate of change may remind us of the intended temporal interpretation of a certain derivative, but that temporal interpretation is not part of the mathematical structure itself.

Think of my point in this way. Either mathematical symbols denote abstract objects or they are mere notation to be manipulated according to certain practices. As mere bits of notation or objects of concrete practice, the symbols bear no intrinsic connection to fine-grained temporal structure. Of course it takes time to write symbols, and there might be a standard amount of time it takes to solve a certain kind of equation, but these are not the temporal characteristics at issue. If mathematical notation picks out abstract objects, however, these are structured objects. This structure can be mapped onto fine-grained temporal structure, but it need not be. It can equally productively be mapped into, say, price relationships in economics (a standard textbook illustration) that reflect *ordering* information, *sans* temporal metric. Wheeler claims that orthodox computational cognitive science reduces "time to mere sequence" (Wheeler 2005, 105); considered at the same level of generality, however, the formal tools of dynamical systems theory effect the same reduction, providing information only about sequence and thus no more temporal information than abstract algorithms provide.

Turn now to the actual practices of modeling. Computational explanations of cognitive phenomena normally begin by positing an architecture (Anderson 2007, chapter 1; this is sometimes called the 'functional architecture'—Pylyshyn 1984, 30–31): the set of basic operations and representational primitives that constitute the cognitive system's resources. In many cases, the time that it takes to apply a given basic operation is a fact about the architecture, a fundamental posit necessary to modeling within a particular computationalist framework. For instance, in modeling memory, the speed with which activation spreads can determine outcomes, particularly when multiple operations compete with each other for cognitive resources; in a winner-take-all race to recall, one parameter setting might produce one winner (i.e., one accessed memory), and a different setting, a different winner. Estimating the values of such parameters is seen as a central task in, for example, the ACT-R and SOAR research programs (Anderson et al. 2004, 1042; Anderson 2007, 110; Cooper 2007, 524).[3] Thus, the claim that a series of basic operations is performed, with given architectural parameters set, entails a fine-grained temporal profile, which can then be tested against human data.

The preceding points defuse the time-based argument for the principled superiority of dynamical approaches over computationalism. As general analytical tools, differential equations are no more intrinsically temporal than are algorithms. That parts of such equations map onto the temporal order is a basic posit of the dynamical-systems-based explanatory project; it is part of dynamical-systems-based modeling in practice. Similarly, it is a basic posit of prominent computationalist explanations of human cognition that each basic operation takes a fixed amount of time or that various processes have relative implementation values that can be mapped into the temporal order. Thus, neither approach uses tools that are essentially temporal, but as a central part of their practice, both schools connect their modeling formalism, in a deep way, to temporal relations.

9.5. Conclusion

The embedded program is not at odds with computationalism, at least insofar as the embedded approach (a) attempts to minimize the use of explicitly encoded rules in cognitive modeling and (b) might encourage an interest in fine-grained temporal profiles of human cognitive processing. With respect to case (a), we should keep two points in mind: first, that minimizing the use of rules does not necessary eliminate all rules—some explicitly encoded rules are likely to be needed for the control of embedded interaction, long-term planning, and the like—and second, that a lack of rules does not entail the absence

---

3. Daniel Weiskopf's (otherwise excellent) discussion (2004) of these issues does the present line of reasoning a disservice by describing such values as auxiliary hypotheses (p. 98) or strictly supplemental (p. 99). If we engage with the dynamical-systems-based view on its own terms—as an attempt to model specific real-world cognitive processes—the role of parameter setting in cognitive models is no less a part of the cognitive model, and no more peripheral to it, than the dynamical-systems theorist's mapping of her mathematical formalism into temporal structure.

of computation. As regards (b), the importance of timing does not alone favor a dynamical-systems-based version of the embedded approach over a computationalist version. Both approaches provide the tools to model fine-grained temporal processes, but neither approach is essentially temporal in the way sometimes claimed for dynamical-systems-based theorizing.

In closing, I offer a diagnostic point. Many early cognitive scientists were impressed by the generality of computational theory: a universal Turing machine can, in principle, carry out any effective procedure. This engendered claims about intelligence *simpliciter*, for example, that physical symbols systems were necessary and sufficient for general intelligence (Newell and Simon 1997/1976). Critics of computationalism have tended to take these very abstract remarks as their target, rather than focusing on the equally early and important attempts to model actual human cognition (Anderson and Bower 1973); here, although computational theory was assumed to provide sufficient resources to model human cognition, the modeling process was highly constrained so as to produce performance of the sort exhibited by humans. The comparison to dynamical-systems-based cognitive science should *not* be made along the former dimension; so far as I know, no one in the dynamical-systems camp has offered a theory of general intelligence—that is, a theory of the particular kind of dynamical system that meets the necessary and sufficient conditions for general intelligence. More importantly, inspiration for dynamical-systems-based anticomputationalism comes from actual modeling, in which case the only fair comparison is to the second strain of computationalist research, that aimed at the modeling of real-world human data. Comparisons of the two theoretical frameworks are all well and good, so long as it is abstract theory versus abstract theory, and actual modeling versus actual modeling. And on the fair playing surface, computationalism seems to fare quite well; fans of the embedded view should not hesitate to bear the computationalist standard.

10

Embedded Cognition and Mental Representation

This chapter addresses the claim that embedded models exploit a form of representation not available to computational theorists (Wheeler 2005, 72, 196). Embedded representations are supposed to be partial, action-oriented, context-dependent, and egocentric (Churchland et al. 1994; Clark 1995, 1997, 49, 160), representations that can fluidly guide our messy, real-time interaction with the world. In contrast, computational models are said to deal only in context-neutral, inflexible, prespecified, detailed representations of the world (Edelman 1987, 38, 43–44; Varela, Thompson, and Rosch 1991, 100, 133–36), capable of handling only toy domains containing static properties.[1] Given the central role of representation in cognitive science, embedded modeling thus constitutes a radical departure from the orthodoxy.

In the sections to follow, I cast a critical eye on this alleged contrast between the two approaches' respective sets of representational resources. My conclusion is conciliatory: to the extent that the embedded approach offers something plausible and new, its approach to representation supplements orthodox computationalism, without departing from it in a philosophically significant way. In the first section, I examine positive characterizations of embedded representations arguing that such representations do not differ in principle from those employed in

---

1. Related concerns about representation arise in connection with the embodied program. According to proponents of the embodied view, orthodox representations are objectionably arbitrary, amodal, and abstract. These issues are discussed in chapter 11.

orthodox cognitive modeling. In the second section, I argue that plausible embedded models must include context-independent representations of the standard computationalist sort. In the final two sections, I emphasize the way in which the embedded approach complements the existing theory of mental content, then apply the results of this discussion to the debate over the innateness of mental representations.

10.1. What Is Special about Embedded Representations?

10.1.1. Detailed or Partial?

Since the cognitivist revolution, mental representations have played a central role in the modeling of human thought and problem-solving, memory and language-use, and inference and theory construction. Although some situated theorists have taken an antirepresentationalist approach (Varela, Thomson, and Rosch 1991, 9, 172–73; Thelen and Smith 1994, 338; Keijzer 1998), many others have advocated instead for a new, situated approach to representation.

The movement toward a situated account of visual processing is often used to illustrate the distinctive characteristics of embedded representations (Churchland et al. 1994). For at least two decades, computational accounts of vision presupposed that the visual system produces a rich and detailed model of some substantial portion of the subject's immediate environment. Computational vision scientists attempted to explain how the differential stimulation of a subject's retinal cells could yield a detailed internal model of the object or scene perceived. Typically, such a model includes categorical information about those objects as well as information about their features, for example, their shapes and colors.

About twenty years ago, experimental results began to challenge this picture (O'Regan 1992; Simons and Levin 1997). The human's range of visual focus, peripheral acuity, and awareness of detail are far poorer than one would expect of subjects who have constructed rich and detailed models of their immediate environments. Alternative theories came to the fore—situated, animate, and enactive theories of vision—according to which the human sees by sampling only those small bits of the external environment pertinent to her immediate interests and the task at hand. Vision scientists were forced to change their theoretical strategy, simplifying the internal processing assumed to be at work and deferring more broadly to the environment as the store of information the visual system might gain access to if needed. In visual processing, humans create partial representations, which can then be altered or supplemented as necessary by further interaction with the environment.

These suggestions constitute genuine innovations in the theory of vision, but we should doubt that they underwrite a new form or style of representation. Consider first the partial character of internal representations. Note first that not even the most expansive computational model of vision contains a fully detailed model of everything. So, the contrast at issue cannot be the contrast between a complete model of the universe hypothesized by the computationalist and something short of that offered by the embedded approach. Even within the more limited domain of, say, the immediate environment, computational models frequently contain incomplete information. David Marr and associates developed the most influential and widely known computational model of vision, and they do not attribute to the seeing subject a representation of everything in the immediate environment. Some things are too small; some things are behind the viewer; some things are in front of the viewer but occluded. When one looks at a limited portion of the environment, of course one does not see everything! In fact, Marr's theory explains how information from the immediate environment is lost in visual processing: Gaussian filters sample at different grains (Marr 1982, 56–61, 68–71); if a bit of information at one grain does not correspond to what is yielded by the application of the filter with a different sampling grain, that information is lost—even if it is veridical.

This point holds in other domains, for example, the study of reading and memory (Gathercole and Baddeley 1993, chapter 8; Baddeley 1999, 66–68). Orthodox theorists would like to explain why some subjects construct a more detailed internal representation of a story they have read than other subjects do. Perforce, then, the orthodox approach is consistent with both more and less detailed internal representations of the relevant information in the task domain. Similarly for the varying degrees to which subjects can commit material to memory; some subjects commit more to memory—that is, create a more detailed model of the information presented—and some commit less, and computationalists attempt to explain this using standard computational tools (Lovett et al. 2000).

We might begin to wonder whether the entire discussion of partial representations is beside the point. After all, why should the nature of a given representation depend on the amount of representing going on? It would seem that how much of the world is represented at a particular point in cognitive processing is, other things being equal, a fact about how many representations there are, and that is not a deep fact about the nature of the individual representations involved.

If one is inclined, as many computationalists are, toward an atomistic account of mental representations, the irrelevance of the accompanying quantity of representations is especially clear. On the atomistic view, a computational system has a stock of basic symbols the representational values of which are independent of (in the sense of not being literally constituted by) the values of other mental representations. Combinatorial rules allow the construction of compound formulae from this stock of atoms, and in the most straightforward of such systems, an atomic symbol contributes the same representational value to the value of any compound in which that atom appears, no matter how long the compound string, according to categorially defined combinatory rules (of the sort used, e.g., in Montague grammar—Dowty, Wall, and Peters 1981).

Consider an empirical result that has inspired some embedded theorists to claim that visual representations are partial. When reading, the typical subject attends to only about twenty characters, a fact revealed by the following kind of experiment (Churchland et al. 1994). By using a device that tracks eye movements, experimenters can change the text on a page while the subject is reading it. If experimenters turn the text entirely into junk text, save for a three-character window that moves along with the subject's eyes, the subject notices that something is wrong. If, however, experimenters extend this moving window beyond about eighteen characters, with a minimum of about fifteen ahead and three behind, subjects fail to notice that the entire remainder of the page is made up of nonsense. These results may well show that the computationalist's modeling task is easier than previously thought, for she need include only twenty representations at a time stored in a visual buffer or working memory, rather than having to include the entire page's worth of characters. Relative to any single letter found within the twenty characters attended to, however, the embedded theorist has given us no reason to think *it* is represented differently from the way in which it would have been represented were it accompanied by five hundred other representations of letters.

10.1.2. Context-Dependent and Action-Oriented Representations

Let us try, then, to locate the embedded approach's new form of representation somewhere else, in some form of context-dependence. We can quickly set aside one kind of context-dependence: the dependence of a variable's value on context. Computational models comprise quite a lot of variable-binding, and thus, the dependence of a variable's representational value on context is nothing new to the computationalist.

Some authors tie context-dependence to the action-oriented nature of some representations (Wheeler 2005; Gibbs 2006). The cognitive system employs representations of actions likely to be useful given the subject's particular needs and interests; the cognitive system thus constructs a partial representation, of only what is relevant to the subject's context-specific purposes. Given the differences in needs and purposes from one occasion to the next, two representations of the same thing might have significantly different effects on action. This suggests that different representations are used depending on context and thus that the subject represents what might normally be characterized as the same thing in different ways depending on context.

The natural interpretation of such claims does not, however, move us beyond the realm of mundanely classical representations. Consider that much of the talk about action-oriented representations stems from J. J. Gibson's perceptual psychology (1979). Gibson claimed that in perceiving the world, we gain direct access to affordances, that is, to what the environment allows us to do with it or in it. The subject immediately perceives the chair as, pardon the grammatical violence, sit-upon-able and a hefty rock as smash-with-able. Spelling out the psychological processes at work here has been a challenge to Gibsonian perceptual psychologists (Fodor and Pylyshyn 1981). Although not terribly Gibsonian, the most plausible tack hypothesizes the use of complex representations. Representing the sit-upon-able-ness of the chair involves a complex representation assembled from representations of the properties *being a chair, sitting,* and *human.* This does not introduce any new sort of represen-tation. Each of the properties involved is one that a computationalist would want a primitive or complex representation to take as content: the orthodox computationalist of course wants to claim that a person looking for a place to sit instantiates symbol strings with such contents as *that's a chair, chairs can be sat upon by humans,* and *I am a human.*

Proponents of the embedded approach typically have further concerns, however. Action-oriented representations express something specially rel-evant to the behavior of the agent, something that computationalist repre-sentations do not capture. The fact that chairs can be sat upon by humans expresses nothing about the system's *actions*; computational models—at least in practice—do not take this connection to actions into consideration. Put in this way, the embedded critic of the orthodoxy aims at a straw position. The famous robot Shakey—supposedly a paradigm of all that is wrong with computationally oriented A.I. (Dreyfus 1992/1972; Shapiro 2004; Wheeler 2005)—used to roll around the laboratory at the Stanford Research Institute. Shakey contained representations pertaining directly to its actions, TILT and ROLL, for example (Nilsson 1984, 29–30). In general, computational model-ing has included outputs pertaining to the cognitive task being modeled, and typically the cognitive task involves, as output, a command to the body to do something—produce speech, press a button, move a chess piece, etc. To the extent that these commands take the form of explicit representations, as they often are, they specifically represent the agent's actions, and thus are action-oriented.

Notice that such commands are generated in response to the demands of the situation—that is, to what the model produces as a response given the problem at hand. Therefore, it does no good for the advocate of the embed-ded approach to claim that action-oriented representations differ from com-putationalist ones because the needs of the subject or the details of the context determine which representations are tokened or how they are used (Wheeler 2005, 64, 140). Which representations are tokened at which times in com-putational processing clearly depends on factors of the context: the input, the system's state at the time of the input, and which algorithms the system imple-ments—the last of these being determined to a great extent by the system's history, either developmental or evolutionary.

It may be useful here to distinguish between two kinds of context-dependence. A symbol might be context-dependent in the sense that it represents a property, individual, or kind only as it appears in a given context: the subject might have an unstructured symbol the condition for the correct application of which is *property-p-in-context-c*. This kind of symbol is not really context-dependent; it applies in a context-*in*dependent way to a narrow property. We happen to designate this property in natural language via the conjunction of terms each of which expresses a more broadly instantiated property, and this produces the illusion of context-dependence. Contrast this with the case where a subject has more than one symbol with the same representational value, one of which is activated in some circumstances and the other of which is activated in different circumstances. For example, a cognitive system might contain a symbol with representational content *square* that is activated only when seeing a square and have a distinct symbol with the same content that is activated only when touching a square.[2]

Neither possibility seems at all heterodox. The former case involves the representation of fine-grained features, but this is standard fare in, for example, computational—or at least computation-friendly—theories of vision (Marr 1982; Biederman 1990; Palmer 1999) and linguistic knowledge (Halle 1990): the property of being a voiced, bilabial stop is a highly specific physical property. The fact that, according to some models of speech production and recognition, we represent fine-grained features does not indicate that these models depart from the orthodoxy; rather, such models appear prominently in standard presentations of orthodox cognitive science (Osherson and Lasnik 1990; Stillings et al. 1995). These remarks apply to atomic representations as well as to compound ones. *Being a stop* is a more broadly instantiated property than is *being a voiced bilabial stop*, but the former is nevertheless a fairly narrowly instantiated property, compared to, say, *being an electron*.

On a more abstract note, the use of such representations does not, in itself, suggest a new representation-relation of any sort. Presumably, for representations to have fine-grained context-specific content, that content must be available in the world. There is an objective property, or environmentally valid complex, or something real in the environment, to which the context-specific representation is specially sensitive. A variety of theories have been proposed to account for the external content of computational symbols. Some emphasize a kind of tracking, others a privileged historical relation, either developmental or evolutionary (for instance, see Dretske [1981, 1988], Millikan [1984], Fodor [1987, 1990], Rupert [1999], Ryder [2004]); but I am not aware of any argument showing that, across the board, such theories run specially on the rocks when the properties to be represented are fine grained or appear in only a narrow range of contexts.

---

2. In such a case, I am inclined to think that both symbols activate a further context-neutral symbol with content *square*, but that is beside the point here.

The second of the two kinds of context-sensitivity distinguished above holds that single subjects have multiple representations of the same property, kind, or individual. This is standard fare in modular computational architectures (Fodor 1983; Pinker 1997). The visual system has a proprietary representation of a dog (in terms of generalized cones, perhaps—Marr 1982), while the tactile system has a different one and central processing has another. It may be useful for many programming or modeling purposes to assume that each referent has only one name or designating predicate, but this is not at all essential to a computational view of mind.

Gibbs (2006, 48–49) takes this second kind of context-sensitivity to be a significant departure from the orthodox view, suggesting that an orthodox view cannot explain the use of different bits of cortex at different times (by different subjects) to play the same representational role. To the contrary, this possibility falls directly out of orthodox functionalist accounts of realization (Fodor 1974). The trick is to get one's quantifiers in the right place. It is not that, on the orthodox view, there is a single physical realizer R, such that for any subject who represents P at any time, that subject instantiates R. Rather, on the orthodox view, for any subject and any time at which she represents P, there exists some physical realizer or other that the subject instantiates and that represents P. The former view—the one that Gibbs seems to be criticizing—is a type–type identity theory of the sort that philosophers occasionally toy with but has not had much influence on orthodox computational cognitive science.

Moving on, consider a further result supposed to illustrate a kind of context-dependence the orthodox approach cannot handle: subjects describe a given category or kind differently depending on the context of the query (Gibbs 2006, 84). This is an interesting enough result, but it should not be taken to support any unorthodox form of context-dependent representation. On the standard view (Fodor 1975), the system of mental representations contains a stock of atomic—that is, unstructured—representations of different categories that can be combined into well-formed strings in accordance with formation rules. The atomic units are what we might call 'concepts' and the strings, or at least certain collections of them, what we might call 'conceptions' (Woodfield 1991; Cummins 1996, 88). For instance, COW might be an atomic concept and COWS ARE BROWN a string of symbols that constitutes part of the subject's conception of cows (a conception that, for the typical subject, contains many other strings as well, although not necessarily the same strings for every subject). Conceptions are sometimes described as knowledge structures concerning, or simply sets of beliefs about, a given kind, property, or individual. Regardless of how we label the distinction, it plays an important role at a number of points in this chapter and the next. With regard to the question at hand, it grounds a straightforwardly orthodox explanation of the effect in question. Different contexts activate different aspects of the subject's conception of cows; so in some contexts, during a discussion of mammalian hides, for instance, the subject is inclined to think of brownness first, and in other contexts, just after a discussion of cheese, say, the subject is inclined to think first of cows' milk-yielding properties. The causally contributing atomic representation of cows, the subject's COW, remains precisely the same unit across contexts, however.

The tendency to think otherwise results, I suspect, from a tendency to conflate concepts and conceptions. This is exacerbated by a tendency in the psychological literature (Smith and Medin 1981) to use 'concept' to refer to certain compound structures and to refer to their components as 'features', without much comment on the role of the features as atomic units or, more importantly, on the question whether a concept is identical to a structured set of atomic feature-representations or is a distinct atom causally associated with a set of atomic feature-representations. Either way, however, it is no surprise that context affects processing, so as to cause variations in output, without atomic concepts themselves being context-dependent.

10.1.3. Relational and Egocentric Representations

Consider another of the supposedly distinctive properties of embedded representations. The embedded theorist sometimes characterizes computationalist representations as too objective, too detached from the subject. Actual mental representations are egocentric, it is claimed (Brooks 1999): the properties represented are relational properties, one *relatum* of which is the subject or cognitive system itself. In contrast, computationalist models include only what are called 'allocentric' representations, subject-neutral descriptions of the world. On this interpretation of the computationalist view, the symbol string expressing "There's a chair" binds the symbol for chairhood to some region in space, specified within a perfectly general coordinate system (e.g., "Chair at coordinates $x13$, $y275$, $z2$").

This criticism of computationalist representations also takes a straw target, which we can appreciate by returning our attention to Marr's computational theory of vision. Marr's model does place objects in the categories we normally designate using subject-neutral nouns, such as 'chair'. Nevertheless, according to Marr, one integral part of visual processing is the construction of an explicitly viewer-centered representation: the two-and-one-half dimensional sketch. This is, in Marr's words "a viewer-centered representation" carrying information about such relational properties as "the distance from the viewer of a point on a surface" (Marr 1982, 277). At this stage in computational processing, the environment is represented perspectively, and Marr makes no move to disavow his explicit talk of representations and computations. It is not essential, then—not even central—to computationalist representations that they represent locations only allocentrically.

Do embedded models' relational representations presuppose a concept of the self not available to computationalists, perhaps, as it is sometimes called, an essential indexical (Perry 1979)? I take it that they do not. A computational model can have any number of representations that refer to the cognitive system itself or to the body in which the system is realized, and it will, of course, be quite important to have some of these rigged up to action. A perceptual representation 't' that happens to take as its content the subject herself may not have much effect on action; but many perceptual representations that happen to be of the self will appear in compound symbol structures the effects of which are partly to activate one or more action-controlling representations of the self. These are robustly self-reflexive representations, in that the symbol appears as part of further compound formulae that represent bodily commands and cause action. In contrast, the cognitive system does not treat some representations of itself in a way that we expect the subject to when she is thinking about herself. Such a representation might be visual, caused by a system of mirrors and activated in circumstances in which, as we would normally say, the subject does not realize she is seeing herself. This is no big surprise, however. Different representations with the same externalist (i.e., referential) content can play different functional roles in the cognitive system. Nothing in the computationalist view precludes the existence of a mental representation of the self that is integrated with self-preserving programs and the control of action (e.g., avoidance behavior).

10.2. Atomic Affordance Representations

Advocates for the embedded approach frequently claim that cognition is *for* action, and this is meant to be a deep principle motivating the embedded view. On certain obvious interpretations, though, the claim is a truism, contested by no one. Of course, cognition serves action; if cognition had historically had no effect on human action, it almost certainly would not have evolved in the complex form it now takes. It is a matter of everyday experience that cognitive processes often eventuate in action. Most importantly, action provides the point of departure for cognitive science; it is because people use language, act out complex plans, etc. that we posit cognitive processes as the causes of these phenomena. Once we have in place a theoretical framework for explaining the behavior caused by cognitive processing, we can see how even the most arcane theoretical positions *could* cause action—if nothing else, the action of describing one's positions (e.g., my writing this sentence).

Thus, for the action-oriented tenet to be interesting, the proponent of the embedded view must have something more robust in mind, and the idea seems to be that action somehow constitutes cognition (Noë 2004). Chapter 11 investigates some ways of spelling this out in particularly embodied terms, for example, in terms of a sensorimotor basis for representations. At present, though, let us focus on a claim more closely related to the discussion of embedded representations. If there is a radically noncomputationalist view in this vicinity, having to do with representation, it would seem to be the view that such properties as *sit-upon-able-ness* are represented by atomic, not compound, representational units and that these exhaust, or at least dominate, the basic stock of mental representations. According to this view, the subject does not separately represent herself, the chair, action-types, and relations between these, and then act upon beliefs about those properties. No, that would be perfectly amenable to the orthodox approach. Instead, the *sit-upon-able-ness* of the chair acts as an immediate and simple stimulus to the cognitive system, causing it to behave in ways that depend in the first instance on the unmediated detection of *sit-upon-able-ness*.

This view does not hold much promise. If the embedded approach is to provide a plausible account of human cognition, embedded models must include representations of a decidedly context-independent sort: repeatable representations the externalist semantic values of which remains constant across activations and that do not represent affordances. It might be that we represent possibilities of action during cognitive processing, visual or otherwise. Any model of cognition must, however, account for the way those possibilities are bound to objects and to each other so as to facilitate a wide range of cognitive processes. I do not see how these requirements can be met by the view on offer, according to which atomic affordance representations provide the fundamental and primary materials of cognition. The only plausible strategies for modeling cognition within an affordance-oriented framework seem to forfeit the advantages of the embedded view (Clark 1995, 100).

Consider a subject who comes upon a coconut tree. He cannot climb the tree, and he is not sure how he would crack open a coconut were he to get one down. He sees a lone, medium-sized rock in the vicinity. He also notices that the coconut tree is up against a steep cliff. So, he picks up the rock, walks to the side of the tree, and throws it toward a coconut from the cliff side of the tree (as much as he can without losing his balance). Why? Presumably, he reasons as follows: "This rock would be good for knocking down a coconut *and* for cracking it open. If the rock falls over the cliff, I will not be able to retrieve it, and will not be able to use it to crack open the coconut. If I get around behind the tree and throw in the direction away from the cliff's edge, I am less likely to lose the rock in the process of knocking the coconut down." And so on. This way of describing the subject's reasoning presupposes a representation of the thing, the rock, as the single thing that can be used to knock loose the coconut, that can be used to crack open the coconut, that flies with a certain sort of trajectory such that it might be lost over the cliff, etc. Similarly for the coconut: There is a single thing that must be knocked down, cracked open, then drunk from and eaten.

In fact, if our man is typical, he is prepared to do all manner of things with the rock, in the short, medium, and long term, things that may seem completely irrelevant to him when he first confronts it (Wilson 2002, 632). How might the radical embedded view explain the subject's behavior? She might appeal to some kind of internal enactment of past sensorimotor experiences (Glenberg 1997). Doing so, however, likely forfeits either the distinctive claim of the embedded view or the supposed advantages it offers to cognitive modelers, particularly to do with the minimization of the use of computation and representation. Imagine the subject internally enacts a sensorimotor pattern of himself throwing-to-knock-loose from an angle facing the cliff. This internal enactment causes the sensorimotor enactment of sitting pathetically, unable to open the coconut. Perhaps, but why should the first enactment cause the second? Circumstances can vary in all sorts of ways not previously experienced, and a subject must be able to pick out the relevant aspects of the situation and plan accordingly. If we, as modelers, smuggle in representations of the rock's features and the standard properties of cliffs, then the subject can access all sorts of knowledge—perhaps including sensorimotor routines—having to do with rocks, cliffs, gravity, and so on. These can help to set the parameters of the first simulation so that it has an outcome relevant to the second simulation; if the subject assumes the presence of a rock, possessing its standard complement of properties, and a cliff with its, he can enact, in sequence, heaving the knock-loosable-ness and losing the crack-withable-ness. This, however, presupposes a context-free representation of rocks and cliffs and their properties and a theory (loosely speaking) of rocks and cliffs. Sensorimotor enactments guided by such conceptions, theories, or background knowledge may be useful, but they hardly project the picture of a radical embedded break with the orthodoxy.

I am concerned partly about the shortcomings of a purely association-based account. A subject might encounter knock-loose-able-ness and smash-with-able-ness together frequently, but the typical subject often encounters them separately, as well. A long stick might have the first affordance property but not the second. What, then, causes an appropriate binding of these two properties, given that such action-neutral categorical representations as STICK and ROCK are off limits? The subject might identify nonaction-oriented-properties having to do with, for example, shape, texture, size, and color, in order to recognize the object as being of a kind likely to share any two affordance properties located at the same spatial coordinates. This view, however, makes free use of representations of nonaffordance-based properties. Object features themselves might be bound associatively, but absent a theoretical (in the loose sense) understanding of the principles of objects—that is, of the kinds of categories they fall into—this seems unlikely to succeed; observable features come in all sorts of mixed-up and overlapping patterns, not strict and regular associations. One might think the subject effects the association by locating property instances in a spatial map: two properties might be bound together because they are represented as being located at the same objective spatial coordinates. This proposal raises difficulties of its own, though, for most embedded theorists reject allocentric spatial coordinates (Brooks 1999). Furthermore, unless speci-fied in fine-grained detail (inimical to the embedded program), even *egocentric* spatial coordinates will not do; for sometimes two distinct objects appear in the same space in a coarse-grained framework of coordinates; in which case, the affordance properties co-located in that region probably do not move together. One property might go over the cliff without the other. Finally, in this regard, we should not ignore questions about processing. A single "object" can be presented in numerous perspectives. Thus, if egocentric coordinates are to be used, the embedded theorist must explain how these are transformed so as to keep track of co-instantiated atomically represented affordance properties, while preserving all of the supposed advantages of doing away with rich and complicated computational apparatus.

Part of my concern pertains to a potential regress. When attempting to explain the property of crack-open-with-able-ness, the consistent advocate for action-oriented representation cannot freely use context-independent repre-sentations of features of the situation (the object to be cracked open, the fea-tures of the object that guide the process of cracking it open, the visual features perceived upon cracking it open) (cf. Glenberg [1997]). I have not seen any serious attempts to translate such talk into purely affordance-based language. Moreover, such translation seems no less daunting, and no more plausible, that behaviorist reductions of mental state-talk and phenomenalist reductions of object-talk. I can understand what knock-loosable-with-ness amounts to on the assumption that I have a representation of something's being attached and something's knocking into something else. I have no hope of understanding what being knock-loosable is, however, if it is to be understood relative to some-thing's being nondetachable and the like, and being nondetachable is cashed out in terms of more action-oriented representations, those to be explained by taking for granted an understanding of further affordance representations; this results in either regress or circularity. I suspect that examples of pure affor-dance properties seem to make sense only because, when we consider them, we take for granted our own representations of background objects and fea-tures in nonaffordance-based terms, which themselves ground the description of the actions afforded.[3]

10.3. Embedded Models and External Content

The preceding sections argue that the external content of embedded represen-tations does not differ much from what one expects to find in orthodox models: embedded models emphasize representations of actions, the self, and relations

---

3. If anything specially situated is meant to anchor these descriptions, it is embodied experience, touched on above in connection with internal sensorimotor enactment. Chapter 11 argues against the view that distinc-tively embodied content anchors our conceptual repertoire.

between the self and environment, all of which find a natural home in orthodox models. Moreover, preservation of the supposed advantages of the embedded approach—with regard to cognitive processing—seems to require the free
use of representations of nonaffordance-constituted individuals, features, or
categories.

The embedded theorist might, however, claim innovation with regard to the
theory of externalist content-fixation (or content-determination), as opposed to
any innovation with regard to the contents so determined. Perhaps the embedded approach's emphasis on interaction with the environment grounds a novel
account of the process that fixes the externalist content of mental representations. I think the embedded approach can add something important to the discussion of externalist content-fixation; but rather than grounding a new theory
of content, it sheds light on the ways in which a standard content-fixing relation
might obtain. This matter merits discussion on account of its intrinsic interest;
such discussion also sets the stage for the argument of section 10.4.

A few preliminary remarks may be in order; for, although the semantic
externalist might welcome help from the embedded approach, the embedded
theorist might wonder about her stake in the bargain. Some situated theorists
reject talk of representation (Varela, Thompson, and Rosch 1991; Thelen and
Smith 1994) or distance themselves from the so-called objectivist metaphysics according to which subjects represent objective properties, individuals, and
kinds in the environment (Lakoff 1987; Glenberg 1997; Lakoff and Johnson
1999). Such theorists would seem to have no use for externalist semantics.

In my view, embedded theorists embrace antirepresentationalist views too
readily. It is one thing to emphasize the cognitive-scientific study of internal
processing, quite another to advocate for solipsism. Lakoff and Johnson claim,
"What makes concepts concepts is their inferential capacity, their ability to
be bound together in ways that yield inferences" (1999, 20), while rejecting a
metaphysics of independently existing objects, properties, and individuals that
mental representations can be about (i.e., take as externalist content); on their
view, "there is no such metaphysics–epistemology split" (ibid., 114). If, however, there is no metaphysics–epistemology split, it is not clear how, from, say,
Lakoff's standpoint, Johnson can be anything more than a construction from
Lakoff's own epistemological materials—sense-data, experiences, or the like.
Why is this not simply solipsism with a lot of cognitive scientific talk thrown
in as whitewash?

This is a special case of a general meta-problem. If a situated view is to
have a scientific basis, the view's theoretical pronouncements had better not
undercut the relevance of scientific research. Experiments reported in journal
articles are written up as if subjects enter the room, sit at computer screens,
take instructions from experimenters, etc. The situated theorist should thus
be quite interested in a theory of mental content that explains how researchers can think about subjects, computer screens, journal articles, editors, other

researchers, and all the rest. Lakoff and Johnson (1999, 109, 113) respond by embracing a pragmatist view, according to which what is real and what statements are true are nothing more than a matter of what we find useful. They talk freely of neurons and the like but argue that this amounts only to a kind of successful practice.

This seems to me to be a dodge, at least until some substantial portion of the reduction to usefulness is carried out. My beliefs in books and colleagues and family members are not merely useful constructions, so far as I can tell; after all, sometimes the things I believe in frustrate my aspirations as much as they facilitate them. When these beliefs do not seem useful, they persist partly because their content best explains various findings—including *why* the state of affairs represented by a given belief might frustrate my attempts to achieve my goals.

The more general point is this. Unless we cast our goals independently as truth-oriented, then pragmatic theories of truth have no plausible metric for ordering the usefulness of beliefs. Humans have an incredible variety of goals and methods of interacting with the world, and thus the only privileged or unifying goals—the only ones with epistemic punch—are truth-seeking ones, for example, the desire for solid scientific explanations. Resting one's pragmatic account of truth on these values, however, results in circularity: the true beliefs are the useful ones, where useful means the ones exhibiting properties conducive to finding the truth.

Think of this in a way that addresses the pragmatic view in its own terms: the most useful belief about objects and properties is that they exist objectively; ongoing investigation, critical reflection, correction of our beliefs in light of new experience—as well as interaction with others in our personal and professional lives—is all best motivated, and best executed, when we believe we are investigating the actual properties of things. This seems to be the best way to make sense of Lakoff and Johnson's appeals to basic-level categories, evolution, and the human bodies' interaction with the environment (1999, 26–27, 114). None of this carries much weight, though, if I treat evolution as merely a useful hypothesis, as opposed to an objective fact about human history: if there were no people—whose objective existence does not depend on what *I* find useful— then why should evolutionary theory be relevant? Similar remarks apply to objective properties, individuals, and kinds in the environment: if there were no objective properties of the environment, say, to shorten the lives of some of people in the evolutionary context and reduce their rate of reproduction— properties the existence of which does not depend on what I find useful—why should I put any stock at all in evolutionary theory? Why should I not find it merely a fanciful story? If all of science is metaphor, why not read Lakoff and Johnson's pragmatist theory (as well as evolutionary theory) as metaphor? Why should I not simply reject pragmatism, then, as a misleading, not very useful metaphor? This illustrates what appears to be the self-defeating nature of pragmatism: the most useful view is that the pragmatist theory of truth and reality is false!

Distinctively embedded claims might also come into play here. For example, on the embedded view, we structure our environments to facilitate problem-solving; we create scaffolding on which human cognition depends. Okay, but how do humans do this if they do not somehow home in on genuine properties of the environment (including properties exhibited by other humans), properties that can be reidentified and manipulated so as effectively to scaffold our cognition? Perhaps these properties are not the properties of interest in fundamental physics, but at the very least they are "special-purpose" physical properties—grounded ultimately in fundamental physics—and constitute part of the objectively existing external world. We do not bring them into existence ex nihilo or from an undifferentiated blob that is the external world: the blob must already be differentiated along lines that we can track before we start doing the tracking; otherwise, tracking would be a failure and the scaffolding, useless junk.

These are deep waters, though, and there is no chance of doing justice to substantive debates about truth and knowledge here. Suffice it to say that for the purposes of situated cognitive science, a theory of externalist content should be of interest, even if one ends up giving a nonstandard account of the external relata of the content-bearing relation. (If Bishop Berkeley is correct, his idea of a table is *about* something unexpected, an idea in the mind of God; but Berkeley still must explain the aboutness relation.) Even embedded theorists who have little interest in grand metaphysical debate should be moved by the extent to which cognitive science itself focuses on the individual's relation to the environment, which, as noted above, is especially strong on the embedded view. The cognitive phenomena with which we begin—the very explananda of the enterprise—are largely relational, humans' capacities to interact with the environment in various ways. Our brief is to explain how humans get into a regular relation to environmental individuals, properties, and kinds, with regard to which they exhibit the regular patterns of behavior that constitute cognitive phenomena. This should motivate interest in at least a bare-bones externalist semantics for mental representations.[4]

Turn now to the primary topic of this section, the wedding of externalist semantics and the embedded view. Assume the human cognitive system is two-layered; this is surely an oversimplification, but it allows us to focus on the relevant issues without, I think, distorting the conclusions reached. One layer consists of perceptual systems. Call the representations employed at this level 'peripheral representations'. These include such representations as the

---

4. Fodor and Lepore (1999) provide a host of further reasons to take intentional properties seriously in cognitive science.

proprietary visual representation of a tree, as well as visual representations of fine-grained features of the tree. The second layer is what some theorists call 'central processing' (Fodor 1983). Call the representations appearing at this level 'central representations'. Theoretical, abstract, and nonsensory concepts, such as PROTON and JUSTICE fall into this category, as do amodal concepts that share their externalist content with distinctively sensory concepts, for example, my general concept GREEN, separate from the concept directly involved in my distinctively visual experience of the color green.

It might seem that the embedded program has no special bearing on the discussion of central representations, except perhaps to tell us that central representations play a less prominent role in cognitive processing than it is often thought. I incline toward a contrasting view. Peripheral representations mediate the causal relations that fix the content of many central representations; peripheral representations help to bring central representations into the causal relations that determine what the latter represent. Moreover, in ways to be explained below, embedded modeling sheds light on this process. This view does not require that central representations inherit their content directly from some selection of peripheral representations or from external symbols; neither does it require that peripheral representations or external symbols define central representations. Thus, the current proposal is not empiricist in the traditional sense: many unstructured central representations have content distinct from—that is, not constituted by—the content of representations that mediate the activation of those atomic central representations.

A recurring theme in the embedded literature has been the extent to which humans simplify their cognitive tasks by structuring their external environment in ways that facilitate the performance of those tasks (McClamrock 1995; Dennett 1996; Clark 1997). Some such simplification can be effected through the use of language as well as by the assignment of a privileged role to certain observations. Straightforward examples involve the construction of written descriptions or visual diagrams meant to convey a new concept to others, that is, to get others' central representations causally connected in the right way to certain properties or kinds in the environment. In some cases, the individual formulates her own observation-based heuristic, for example, of the form "when I see such-and-such, there is a C present," where C is a newly coined, atomic central representation. In all of these cases, one or more peripheral representations come to mediate the activation of a newly coined, atomic, central representation, or a central representation to which the peripheral representation had not previously been connected (Rupert 1996, 1998, 2001; Margolis 1998; Laurence and Margolis 2002; Weiskopf 2008b). Adverting to the human habit of actively structuring her environment so that, under certain circumstances, she has certain sensory experiences, and not others, constitutes a powerful psychological explanation of how a human comes into the content-fixing relation to, say, electrons. (In fact, in the case of some kinds, this process seems the only plausible way for a human to acquire a representation with that kind as its content—see Fodor [1987, 118–22, 1994, 98, 1998, 156–58].)

10.4. Innate Representations and the Inflexibility Objection

In this section, I discuss what I call the 'inflexibility objection' to computational modeling, the claim that computational representations are unacceptably static, allowing successful interaction only in artificially restricted environments (as illustrated, e.g., by Winograd [1971]). On this view of computationalist commitments, a particular stock of representations must be prespecified by the modeler to fit the salient properties or kinds in the subject's environment and, accordingly, the environment must be strictly controlled by an outside observer so that it provides only acceptable inputs. For such models to explain actual cognition, we must imagine that the world in which the human agent acts is prepackaged or prelabeled, so that its elements or kinds correspond properly to the components of the computationalist's prepackaged stock of representations.

Gerald Edelman expresses nicely some of the concerns motivating the inflexibility objection:

> One of the fundamental tasks of the nervous system is to carry on adaptive perceptual categorization in an "unlabeled" world—one in which the macroscopic order and arrangement of objects and events (and even their definition or discrimination) cannot be prefigured for an organism, despite the fact that such objects and events obey the laws of physics. (1987, 7)

Computational models presuppose a stock of symbols. Presumably, this stock of symbols contains all of the representations needed to model the cognitive activity of the agent in question; otherwise, the computational model would be inadequate as an explanatory construct. The presupposition of this stock, however, seems to build into the computational model weighty assumptions about what must be represented; the computational models come with a set of "labels" appropriate to the environment in which the cognitive system is to operate, rather than letting the environment determine what, given the interests or needs of the organism, will be represented.

The situated theorist thus identifies a kind of flexibility that our cognitive models should capture. We might wonder, however, why situated critics take orthodox computationalism to be at odds with such flexibility. A certain reading of Fodor's views about innateness likely inspires this reaction (Varela, Thompson, Rosch 1991, 135–38). Fodor (1975, 1981b) argues that roughly all of our lexical concepts (those encoded by single natural language terms) are innate. His reasoning runs as follows: A concept is innate if and only if it is not learned (modulo worries about deviant causal chains, which are not relevant here). At present, the process of hypothesis formation and testing provides the only available model of learning. In order to acquire (i.e., learn) a new concept by hypothesis formation and testing, the subject must be able to frame a definition of the concept to be acquired. Most, perhaps all, lexical concepts cannot be defined. Therefore, they are not learned; thus, they are innate. Critics, I suspect, add a certain view of innateness: that if something is innate, it is present at birth, and the picture emerges of a cognitive system with a set of representations, already fixed at birth, that "magically" fit the subject's environment.

This reasoning misses one of Fodor's essential points. It might be that, as 'innate' is often used, it means 'present at birth' or 'has its appearance fully determined by what is present at birth'. Nevertheless, Fodor means something very different by 'innate'. As he puts it, "The view presently being proposed doesn't require that the innate conceptual system must literally be present 'at birth', only that it not be learned" (1975, 96).

This suggests a strategy for defusing at least part of the inflexibility objection: explain how symbolic units appear over the course of development in a way that allows interaction with the environment partly to determine the resulting stock of representations, over which computations then operate. Notice that this project is not committed to any particular view about the proper application of 'innate'. Fodor's liberal criterion of innateness (i.e., having been acquired by some process other than hypothesis testing) might yield one judgment: that very many such concepts are innate. A more restrictive criterion (e.g., not being acquired by a process any significant component of which is psychological in nature—Cowie 1999; Samuels 2002) yields a much smaller set of innate units. For present purposes, though, it matters not how we use the term 'innate'. In order to rebut the inflexibility objection, we need only account for the epigenetic appearance of units in the domain of the computational operations used to model cognition at a given time. Such a view might allow for literally millions of *possible* atomic concepts—each of which a human could acquire under some circumstances or other—that are innate by Fodor's standard, even though, for a given realistic environment, a human will acquire only a small proportion of these millions.

How might such a strategy be fleshed out? Begin with the assumption that to acquire a concept with a given content C, the subject must have some physical unit or other[5] that bears the content-fixing relation to C. In my view, laid out more fully elsewhere (Rupert 1998, 1999, 2001), this process of concept

5. For evidence of repeatable units that correspond to natural language terms and are susceptible to neurological characterization, see Pulvermüller (1999); for suggestions as to how mental representations corresponding to linguistic elements develop epigenetically and as to how the nature of developmental interactions affects the character of the nonsemantically individuated mental representations of words, see Pulvermüller (1999) as well as Müller (1996). The stability required here is intrasubjective stability; different subjects need not possess the *same* nonsemantically individuated concepts. An alternative to the straightforwardly neural approach identifies the vehicles of content with activation vectors or regions in a state space (Rupert 1998; Tiffany 1999).

acquisition has two aspects that, at least in some cases, run hand in hand. A physical process firms up and makes functional the neural assemblies that serve as realizers of mental representations, the 'units' referred to above. This process is interactive, its outcome determined largely by the subject's causal interactions with objects in the environment and by the effects of those interactions (e.g., the extent to which the interaction satisfied the subject's needs). The second aspect of the process is content-fixation. I contend that in the most developmentally basic cases, the very same pattern of causal interaction that helps to stabilize and give a cognitive function to the emerging physical units also fixes the externalist content of the unit so stabilized. The very process of causal interaction with the world necessary from the neural standpoint to produce an assembly that can play a cognitive role also is a process of interacting with the property or kind that becomes the content of that very unit, and it is by this very interaction that content is fixed.

On this view, atomic concepts are acquired—perhaps by intentional mediation, perhaps not—without hypothesis formation or testing, and thus are innate by Fodor's standard. Nevertheless, which stock of atomic concepts is so acquired depends heavily on which kinds and properties happen to be in the subject's environment, as well as on the range of physical properties to which the brain is sensitive. These are genuine constraints. Assuming, however, that the physical matter of the brain is consistent with the subject's acquisition of quite different sets of atomic concepts under different environmental conditions, there is no sense in which the world is prelabeled or prefitted to a preexisting stock of representational units. Instead there are quadrillions (at least?) of possible neural assemblies and the environment could be populated by an inestimable number of possible properties or kinds to which some of those neural assemblies might get into the content-fixing causal relation.

What can be said for such a view? Consider the neurological aspect of this developmental process. Brains grow and change in numerous and varied ways. Despite what looks like a messy, nonlinear process of growth and change, stable neural structure emerges, which subserves the subject's representational capacities. In an attempt to understand this process of emergence, neuroscientists ask such questions as (1) How does the overall functional structure of the brain appear without there being a tiny map of the brain's ultimate layout contained in the genetic material? and (2) How does experience contribute to the development of the functional properties of various neural structures? A commonly given answer to the first question leads immediately to prosecution of the second. It is widely thought that overall structure emerges via the delicate interplay of multiple factors: there is, it is said, an epigenetic dance, causal interaction with the environment appearing as one of the key participants. To a significant extent, the subject's experience shapes her neural substrate, determining the way in which the physical material of her brain eventually realizes its function as the center of cognitive processing. The interesting debate here is not over whether experience affects neural development—the experimental evidence seems to have settled that issue—but over the precise role of experience in shaping the structure of the brain (Churchland and Sejnowski 1992, 132, 307; Purves et al. 1997, chapter 22).

On one side in this debate stands Edelman's selectionist (1987) approach (also see Changeaux [1997]). According to selectionist views, genetically programmed growth provides a wealth of raw material that experience, among other factors, then winnows to create functional neural structure. Early development consists partly of the spreading of billions of dendritic and axonal arbors. Rich in synapses (approximately 100 trillion in the average human brain), these overlapping branches provide a mind-boggling number of possible ways in which groups of neurons might excite or inhibit each other. Of these various patterns of connections, experience reinforces and strengthens those that have proven most useful to the organism, or which have simply been used more than competing ones. The activity of strengthened patterns of connectivity overshadows the less useful or less used patterns of connections, resulting in ineffective activity in the overwhelmed connections; dendritic or axonal retraction or withering; or even cell death.

Constructivism offers an alternative (Quartz and Sejnowski 1997). Constructivists agree with selectionists that experience contributes to regressive events. They assign a further role, however, to experience: it guides the generation of axonal and dendritic arbors and can selectively increase the number of synapses in a given area of the brain or a given neural circuit; experience does so at least as early as the perinatal stage and as late as adulthood. Constructivists claim that such environmental instruction causes the growth of the very neural resources that are needed to represent aspects of problems the subject will solve using those resources: the specific character of experience catalyzes the growth of the neural resources needed to process more effectively the input that triggered the development of those resources. While some selectionists accept that there are multiple waves of growth and pruning within the life span of one organism, this is the fundamental point of disagreement between the two camps: whether experience can, as constructivists claim, cause axonal and dendritic growth or an increase in the number of synapses in a way that is sensitive to the content or structure of the input itself (ibid., 581).

The preceding discussion of perspectives on neural development gives some indication of the prevalence of epigenetic views among contemporary neuroscientists. Although various views differ in significant respects, there is widespread agreement that interaction with the environment in one way or another causes the appearance of mental representations conceived of non-semantically. Many causal theories of mental content (Millikan 1984; Dretske 1988; Fodor 1990; Rupert 1998, 1999; Ryder 2004—all of which are available to the computationalist) cohere well with this epigenetic view of the appearance of the vehicles of mental content, even if the concepts acquired are innate by Fodor's liberal standard.

The critical reader might worry, though, that I have strayed too far from the computationalist orthodoxy. The basic framework of a computational system— its stock of primitive representations together with its primitive operations—is sometimes characterized as the system's "fixed" functional architecture, which offers critics of computationalism all the more reason to think that the representational stock presupposed by computationalist cognitive models cannot be sensitive to the contingent experiences of the subject whose cognitive processes are to be modeled.

It is important to bear in mind, though, the sense in which this architecture is, and is not, fixed. Consider the view of a prominent computationalist, Zenon Pylyshyn, who holds functional architecture fixed for explanatory purposes:

> The architecture must form a cognitive "fixed point" so that
> differences in cognitive phenomena can be explained by appeal
> to arrangements (sequences of expressions and basic operations)
> among the fixed set of operations and to the basic resources
> provided by the architecture ... If the functional architecture were to
> change in ways requiring a cognitive rule-governed explanation, the
> architecture could no longer serve as the basis for explaining how
> changes in rules and representations produce changes in behavior.
> (1984, 114; also see 131)

Appeals to functional architecture are supposed to account for cognitive phenomena: when successful, such appeals explain semantically characterized actions and processes in terms of series of applications of nonsemantically characterized, simple operations, which operations are not themselves affected by processes described in semantic or representational terms. This provides an important sense in which the functional architecture is fixed: functional architecture is not subject to changes that must be characterized in cognitive terms; instead, functional architecture's being mere physical mechanism, following laws of nature stated in nonsemantic terms, explains how cognitively characterized behavior can arise from, or be instantiated in, an underlying physical system (ibid., 132–34).

Notice that the preceding picture of functional architecture and its role as an explanatory fixed point does not require that each aspect of the functional architecture be unchanging, only that such changes be explained ultimately in noncognitive terms. Pylyshyn himself describes the way in which the architecture instantiated in a single human system can change:

> Thus biological factors interact with symbol level generalizations
> by causing modifications in the basic computational resources,
> which I call the *functional architecture.* Such modulations may be

due to biochemical influences, maturation, the triggering effect of environmental releasers, dendritic arborization, atrophy of neural function from disuse, and so on. (1984, 259)

According to Pylyshyn, then, changes at the physical level alter the resources available to be described at the cognitive level; primitive operations and representations can emerge in the system largely as a result of changes at the physical level. New architectural features can emerge from maturation, experience-dependent synaptic growth, etc. Computationalism allows the appearance of new representational primitives as the result of noncognitive causes.

It is a mistake, then, to think that the standard approach to computational explanation of human cognition saddles humans with a preformed, pregiven set of representations for use in a prelabeled world. To the extent that changes in the representational stock arise from biology-based interactions with the environment, new representations can emerge in a way that is sensitive to some combination of the organism's needs, its prior biological structure (some of which is innately determined), and causal interaction with the environment, just the sort of codetermination that critics of the computational view seem to want (Varela, Thompson, and Rosch 1991).

In formulating a computational model of a current subject's ability to process sentences (or play chess, or remember digits, or whatever), the typical computationalist does not intend to offer a developmental model. Rather, the computationalist offers a hypothesis: the current subject now possesses such-and-such representational primitives processed in such and such a way so as to produce the behavior in question. This kind of modeling is consistent with a wide range of developmental stories and hypotheses concerning what different primitives the system would have had if it had developed under different conditions (even slightly different ones). No computationalist thinks that the human parachutes into a prelabeled, prefitted world: to think otherwise would be to confuse the purpose of prominent computational explanations—to account for a skill or capacity present in the subject at a given time—and the wide range of developmental and metaphysical theories consistent with goals of synchronic computationalist modeling.

The inflexibility objection—and with it the claims that computationalist representations are static and pre-fitted to a pre-labeled world—has been laid to rest. It may be worth mentioning, however, a certain narrowness of vision that lies behind the complaint. On the computationalist view, as I see it, humans come to represent a variety of objective properties from what may be an enormous range of possibilities. This does not entail that the human comes to represent the one true complete description of the world (cf. Lakoff and Johnson [1999, 96]): if there is one true description, it involves all of the possible properties available to be represented; it is, in a sense, the conjunction of all of the true descriptions of the world. Is there any reason to think an individual human or community will arrive at the sum total of all accurate descriptions? No. Is there any reason to think computationalism is, or has ever been, claimed otherwise? No, neither in principle nor in practice. The world possesses an enormous number of objective properties including properties of brains and bodies. The latter properties interact with properties in the environment, and as a result, humans come to think about various of those environmental properties and relations between them. This allows many objective properties and truths about them to go unrepresented; and it allows for different individuals and different groups of people to describe the world accurately but differently.

10.5. Conclusion

The present chapter focuses on embedded cognition and externalist representation. The conclusions are conciliatory. Advocates for the embedded view focus on such things as the action-oriented, context-sensitive (not pre-fitted), egocentric aspect of mental representation. Doing so does not, however, constitute much more than a difference in emphasis. It introduces neither a new stock of representational primitives—different in principle from those used in orthodox cognitive science—nor a new kind of representation-relation. The embedded claims about representation are consistent with a developmental story favored by at least some computationalists and the mainstream metaphysical picture of objective properties causally interacting to produce cognitive phenomena.

The central message of part III differs in important ways from that of parts I and II. In earlier chapters, I criticized the extended view, partly because it rests on an untenable theory of cognition but also because it appears not to have substantive implications for basic cognitive scientific practice. Chapters 9 and 10 question the more radical aspects of the embedded view but, in contrast, recognize various ways in which it supplements our theoretical understanding of cognition and contributes to cognitive scientific methodology. Chapter 11 treats the embodied approach in a similar fashion.

11

The Embodied View

According to the embodied view, human cognition relies heavily on imagistic representations, sensory and motor processing, and other features of human bodily experience. This chapter does not examine in detail, or take exception to, these basic themes; rather, it scrutinizes the more radical theoretical claims made on behalf of the embodied program, many of which set the embodied view at odds with the orthodox computationalist approach. In this way, I hope to dispel some conceptual confusion and clear the ground for a fruitful integration of the embodied view and the computational orthodoxy.

Proponents of embodied cognition claim that the standard rules-and-representations-based approach places too much emphasis on symbolic computation, a process that can be characterized in abstract mathematical terms disconnected from the physical body (Lakoff 1987, chapter 19; Varela, Thompson, and Rosch 1991; Glenberg 1997; Lakoff and Johnson 1999; Barsalou et al. 2003; Gibbs 2006; Spivey, Richardson, and Zednik forthcoming). In place of the orthodoxy, cognitive science should, they argue, attend to embodied experience, bodily based metaphorical thinking, sensorimotor routines, and the variety of ways in which we use our nonneural bodies in the performance of cognitive tasks. These claims need a lot of fleshing out. Thus, much of the current chapter consists in the articulation and evaluation of a series of possible—though not always mutually exclusive—interpretations of the claim that

Parts of this chapter are adapted from my extended review (Rupert 2006b) of Raymond Gibbs's *Embodiment and Cognitive Science*.

cognition is embodied (cf. Wilson [2002], Shapiro [2004, chapter 7, 2007]). My point here is to try to make sense of the embodied approach's central thesis and its relation to orthodox cognitive science. Throughout, I argue that a plausible theoretical understanding of the embodied program is significantly less radical and anti-orthodox than partisans of the embodied view claim.

11.1. Preliminaries: Where the Disagreement Is Not

Proponents of the embodied view frequently present their perspective in critical terms (Lakoff 1987, Part II; Varela, Thompson, and Rosch 1991, chapter 7; Glenberg 1997, 1–3; Shapiro 2004, chapter 6), that is, in terms of what the embodied view rejects. Often such critical discussion is misleading, however: it contrasts the embodied view either with a straw version of the orthodox view or with characteristics of the orthodox view that, in the end, embodied models are themselves likely to exhibit. This section reviews four such aspects of embodied theorists' critical stance.

11.1.1. Materialism

Advocates for the embodied view describe the orthodox position as disembodied (Lakoff 1987, 340). The choice of terminology suggests that standard cognitive science is premised on mind–body dualism and that it embraces supernatural minds, souls, or spirits. This way of thinking about the issue does not distinguish orthodox cognitive science from the embodied approach, for orthodox cognitive scientists accept the contemporary materialist view associated with modern science. The great innovations of contemporary cognitive science—computational theory as well as the construction of physical computers—impressed the scientific community largely because these innovations showed how human thought is mechanistically possible in a physical medium (see, e.g., John Anderson's recounting [2007, 1–2] of Alan Newell's final lecture). All parties to the discussion agree that human cognition is a physical process taking place in the human body.

   This introductory point is no small matter. For even though some embodied theorists seem to acknowledge the shared commitment to materialism (e.g., Lakoff and Johnson [1999, 20]), proponents of the embodied view often fail to appreciate what materialism amounts to in the hands of orthodox authors. Proponents of the orthodox view have expended substantial effort trying to explain how psychological properties, states, and laws fit into the physical order, partly by addressing such issues as realization and reduction (e.g., Fodor [1974]). These issues are central to the materialist metaphysics of mind; and according to common treatments of them, much of the embodied research seems either predicted by, or at least consistent with, the orthodox view. Such issues have been examined in particular detail in connection with functionalism.

11.1.2. *Functionalism*

Proponents of the embodied view sometimes target a certain kind of ortho-dox research program; on this approach, the researcher reflects, from the arm-chair, on some cognitive process, conceives of a possible model of it, gives the model life as a computer program, then runs a simulation—all without paying any attention to the particularities of the human body in which the process is supposed to take place. This strikes the advocate for embodied cognition as ill advised, and perhaps it is; but the embodied theorist's consternation tends, mistakenly, to spread to all manner of functionalism and computationalism, for reasons that are unclear. It is one thing to condemn analytical functional-ism (see chapter 5); it is another to eschew all forms of functionalism—includ-ing psychofunctionalism—and computationalism.

Driven largely by considerations of multiple realizability (Putnam 1967; Fodor 1974), many philosophers reject the outright identification of psycho-logical properties and physical (e.g., neural) ones. Functionalism provides an attractive alternative; according to the functionalist view, causal–functional roles constitute the very nature of psychological properties (insofar as they have natures). Even though every actual thing that plays a functional role is physi-cal, descriptions of the causal–functional roles themselves make no mention of the material that instantiates them. Herein lies the rub for the embodied theorist: if, according to functionalism, any old physical material can realize a given cognitive state or property, then functionalist theorizing is inherently disembodied, that is, inherently out of touch with the material structure of the body (Gallagher 2005, 134).

The embodied theorist's complaint extends beyond philosophical func-tionalism to computationalist cognitive science (see, for instance, Lakoff's dis-cussion [1987, 340] of algorithms). This association between functionalism and computationalism is no accident. Perhaps the first version of functionalism widely known to philosophers—machine functionalism (Block 1980a, 173)—was directly inspired by computational theory, and computational properties are typically given a functionalist interpretation: to be a memory register in a computing system is just to play a certain causal role in the overall workings of that system, regardless of what physical material constitutes the system. The embodied theorist takes aim at this entire approach.

So far as I can tell, the criticism rests mostly on a misunderstanding of the metaphysics of functionalism and computationalism (cf. Dennett [2005, 17–21]). Although functionalism has been associated with a number of research strategies (Churchland 2005), functionalism is, first and foremost, a theory of the relation between mental, psychological, or cognitive properties, on the one hand, and physical properties (properties of the brain, for instance), on the other hand. On the functionalist view, causal-role properties are not identical to physical properties; they are individuated by (i.e., bear relations of identity and difference in virtue of) their causal roles, characterized, for example, in the manner of the Ramsey sentences discussed in chapter 4. Functionalism makes no commitment whatsoever to the manner by which researchers formulate their characterizations of functional properties in psychological theories. A functionalist model of a cognitive process can be more or less inspired by the details of the physical body and remain a functionalist view. The rejection of type–type identification of physical and mental properties and the characterization of the latter in terms of their causal role decides the issue.

Consider how this point bears on the embodied program itself. If embodied theorists accept *any* multiple realizability at all of psychological, mental, or cognitive properties, they are functionalists, no matter how closely their models' functional properties track, or are inspired by, the fine-grained properties of human brains or bodies. Assuming the embodied theorist rejects type–type identity theory (and rejects eliminativism—Churchland 1981), she embraces the same functionalist metaphysical relation between mind and body as orthodox functionalism (and computationalism) does.[1] It matters not whether attention to the fine-grained workings of the human body caused the researcher to describe cognitive properties in a certain way; if these cognitive properties are not literally reduced to physical structures (and not eliminated), then, from the standpoint of the metaphysics of mind, the same old functionalist picture prevails.

Think of the point in terms of Ramsey sentences. Imagine one formulates a highly complex Ramsey sentence, the complexity of which—as well as the choice of input and output predicates for which—was motivated by contemplation of physical properties of the human body. The metaphysical status of the properties picked out by this Ramsey sentence is the same as in a Ramsey sentence constructed by a priori reflection on everyday concepts of mental states. Attention to human bodily processes may tell us which functions or which algorithms to care about (Clark 1997, 154), but they are abstract functions and algorithms all the same. If functionalism is, in itself, objectionably disembodied, so is the embodied view.

Thus, the embodied theorist's disagreement with the orthodoxy is not over functionalism or computationalism in principle. The embodied theorist seems, instead, to recommend a change in practice: cognitive science should search for more fine-grained functionalist or computationalist models, rather than more coarse-grained ones that have often dominated practicing cognitive science (Clark 2001; Shapiro 2004, 174–75). Notice, however, that even in terms

1. It is difficult to find embodied theorists who are either mind-brain (or mind-body) identity theorists or eliminativists. For instance, Gibbs (2006) reviews an enormous range of research from the embodied perspective, but none of the influential researchers—Lakoff, Glenberg, Barsalou—appear to fall into either category, and for good reason: they deal in cognitive constructs that stand little chance of being identified with types of brain (or other bodily) states. Such things as image schemas, for example, are abstract constructs (Gibbs 2006, 139), and as such, are clearly multiply realizable.

of computationalist practice, the recommended departure is not so great; prevailing computationalist models vary in the extent to which they are inspired by the fine details of the human body, particularly the brain; some orthodox models (Marr 1982; Anderson et al. 2004; Anderson 2007) keep a fairly clear eye on the relation between functionally characterized cognitive properties and the fine-grained physical properties that realize cognitive properties.

Consider one final point of clarification, which partly explains the embodied theorist's apparent mistake. Functionalists generally maintain that any physical material, if it is arranged in the proper way, can realize a given functional property (or set of properties). Nevertheless, this does not entail that functionalism places no constraint on the physical materials that realize a given functional property. Rather, there is one absolutely essential constraint: that the physical properties of the realizing material are interrelated in the appropriate way. Thus, any functionalist cognitive science of human minds—including orthodox cognitive science—tells us something very directly about the human body (contrary to what is suggested by Shapiro's discussion [2004, 167] of the Separability Thesis): the body must consist of materials with properties that satisfy the Ramsified realization formula (or machine-table description) in question. The more complex one's Ramsey formula, the more one's functionalist view entails about the body realizing the functional properties so characterized. At the same time, no functionalist cognitive science—embodied or otherwise—entails all of the precise characteristics of the materials of the human body.

11.1.3. Arbitrary Symbols and Embodiment

A further critical attack on the orthodox view does more to differentiate the embodied approach from the orthodoxy, but the importance of the criticism can easily be overstated. Proponents of the embodied view sometimes reject the orthodox approach because of the *arbitrary* nature of computationalist symbols (Glenberg 1997, 2). We should ask, however, in what sense computational symbols are arbitrary, and furthermore whether a plausible embodied view can do without units that are arbitrary in this very sense.

Here is one characterization of arbitrariness: A symbol in a model is arbitrary if there is no obvious relation between the mark or sound we use to designate that symbol and the things represented by instantiations of that symbol (or realizers of it, or objects onto which that symbol is mapped during modeling, etc.). Say that I use the inscription 'A1' to pick out an unstructured unit in a model of human reasoning about the domain of mammals. Let us say that this unit, when realized in the human brain, is about horses. The inscription ('A1') used to pick out the element in the model bears no obvious resemblance to horses. Notice moreover, that the inscription bears no obvious resemblance to (a) the abstract object in the model or (b) the physical states that realize A1. On this view, computational symbols are arbitrary, but in a way that all symbols used in all models are—or at least can be. Whatever style of cognitive modeling one prefers, one might choose to designate a model's abstract entities in an arbitrary way. Even on the embodied view, all mental representations and cognitive processes are repeatable (i.e., abstract) types, which must be picked out somehow. Nothing hangs on the choice of sounds or inscriptions for designating them (cf. Anderson [2007, 37]).

This might seem like a trivial point, but consider how it plays out in a familiar context, that of John Searle's example (1980) of the Chinese room (cf. Harnad [1990]). To put the example in a nutshell, Searle asks us to consider a person who knows no Chinese but can follow instructions for correlating strings of Chinese characters with other such strings; in doing so, the person produces reasonable answers, expressed in Chinese characters, to questions about a story written in Chinese. It seems obvious to Searle that the person in the Chinese room does not understand Chinese—even when the situation is so altered that the person has internalized all of the rules for manipulating Chinese symbol strings.

Why, though, should Searle have such confidence that if the man were to internalize the highly complex computations—which in a complete computational model would include relations to computationally characterized perceptual and motor states—the man would not understand the stories in question? Here is a possibility. When Searle himself looks at a Chinese character designating an element in a computational model of story comprehension, that symbol does not "look like" the subjective experience Searle associates with his own understanding. On this hypothesis (and it is merely a hypothesis), Searle is confronted by an image or a description of the processes that, according to the computationalist, constitute cognition or understanding. Searle supposes that if the visual image or description were accurate, he would recognize them as such (talk about Cartesian assumptions!), or at least that if some inscription were not a representation of the accurate model, he would know that it is not. When he looks at inscriptions designating computational units or hears auditory descriptions of them, the resulting internal states are not the ones he associates with understanding. So, he deems computational models neither constitutive of nor sufficient for cognition. Reading the word 'understanding' causes different internal states from those caused by reading the typical inscriptions used to designate a computational model of reading comprehension. This alone provides us with no reason to think that computational models of reading comprehension are incorrect.

Similarly, objections to the arbitrariness of symbols might rest on a concern about phenomenological feel or conscious experience, and this might also be at work in Searle's discussion. When I see a horse, I have an experience that I might describe as that of an image of a horse. I should not, however, conflate this visual experience with the processes constitutive of, say, reasoning about horses (or with experiences of representations that designate the processes constitutive of seeing or reasoning about horses). The experience of the visual presentation of the correct theory of cognitive processing may not strike the subject as resembling in any way the subject's experience when confronted with, say, a word that initiates such cognitive processing. That is, hearing the word 'horse' may cause an experience in me that strikes me as quite different from the experience I have when someone describes to me a computational model of my cognitive processes concerned with horses; nevertheless, that perceived mismatch alone tells me nothing about the accuracy of the cognitive model in question, and thus constitutes no objection to a computational theory of my horse-related cognitive processing.

Note that embodied views might be presented in a way that generates a new version of the Searle's Chinese room argument. Consider, for example, a variation on Searle's example, the sensorimotor room, which could be used to "disprove" the embodied hypothesis that all cognitive processing takes the form of sensorimotor reenactment. If Searle were in a room processing cards on which were written mathematical or discursive descriptions of sensorimotor processing, I suspect that they would not seem to him to amount to comprehension. This reasoning would rest on a mistake, though. One should not expect the inscriptions or sounds (or the experiences of the inscriptions or sounds) that designate the true model of cognitive processes to seem, from a first-person perspective, like the thought processes or experiences so modeled. (Searle might respond by saying that there is some way or other to present the embodied theory that alleviates this mismatch. Perhaps, but one might wonder why there is not also a way to do so in the computational case, by, e.g., using pictures to designate computational models, in place of the dry symbols of programming languages.)

Consider now a different sense in which computational symbols might be arbitrary: any bit of cortex (or the body) can realize any symbol. This is no complaint against a standard computationalism or functionalism; the preceding subsection explains why computational symbols are not arbitrary in this way. A physical state can realize a functional (or computational) property only if that physical state is part of a network of physical states the parts of which have appropriately interrelated causal structure (of the sort discussed in chapter 4 in connection with realization). Relative to a given functional or computational property, some parts of cortex (or the body) are almost certainly not candidate realizers.

Notice that this point applies to the externalist content of a mental representation, even if we assume a causal, not strictly functionalist, account of externalist mental content. Assume that part of what it is to be a mental representation is to bear the right causal relation to the external property, kind, or individual so represented. Surely some parts of cortex are not in the right position—say, not rigged up to the perceptual apparatus in the right way—to enter into the content-determining causal relation to the external individual, kind, or property in question.

Ultimately, the concern about arbitrariness has, I think, a substantial read-ing. It expresses a dissatisfaction with the format of typical computationalist mental representations. Most computational models employ symbols that are not inherently imagistic (Block 1981), and the accusation of arbitrariness can be interpreted in this light. Embodied theorists are saying to orthodox compu-tationalists, "More images!"

Although the use of imagistic structures in cognitive modeling may be well advised, embodied theorists are not in a position to claim cognitive-scientific revolution, for four reasons. First, the use of images, or terms that designate images, to describe one's cognitive models does not show that one's model is essentially imagistic. One must make it clear that the elements of the model function in a distinctively imagistic way, that is, that they have distinctively imagistic effects. Critics of the image-based approach (e.g., Pylyshyn [1981]) have long argued that effects suggesting the use of images in cognitive pro-cessing can be produced by computational systems with no essentially pictorial elements—in other words, no elements the distinctively imagistic properties of which play a role in cognitive processing. Something with imagistic properties might nevertheless have the role of an atomic symbol in cognitive processing. It sounds odd, but the realizers of unstructured representations in an orthodox computational model might themselves be pictures! Unless the distinctively imagistic properties of the representations (say, a constrained isomorphism they bear to the objects depicted) play a role in cognitive processing, the model remains entirely orthodox.

Second, note that the lion's share of work on embodied cognition does not address distinctively imagistic effects on cognitive processing. It may be that, in the human cognitive system, associations between linguistic terms and spatial relations influence sentence-processing (Glenberg 1997) or that stimulus items in human short-term memory are given an articulatory cod-ing (Wilson 2001); but these results do not in themselves demonstrate pic-torial effects, for example, effects resulting from the analogue properties of images.

Third, although a portion of the image-based research may support dis-tinctively imagistic processing, this is a far cry from the construction of a cognitive architecture that relies on imagistic representations alone. A hybrid model might contain computational control of processes that extract informa-tion from images (cf. Clark [2001, 133]). This represents an intriguing depar-ture from straightforward computationalism. Notice, however, that it does not seem to contradict functionalism at all, for the distinctive processing effects of images will, I take it, be functionally characterized, not literally identified with particular kinds of physical structure.

Lastly, the embodied theorist pursuing this form of the arbitrariness objec-tion stands in need of an image-friendly theory of external content. Assume that images and the distinctively imagistic processing of them constitute a cognitive model, and that this itself is what marks the component symbols as nonarbitrary. The semantics for such symbols had better appeal to their distinctively imagistic properties, then. Otherwise, even if the imagistic properties do explanatory work in cognitive processing, the images, qua symbols, will be just as arbitrary as computational symbols are claimed to be, at least with respect to their externalist contents.

11.1.4. *Abstract Symbols*

Proponents of the embodied view sometimes criticize the orthodox view for dealing in abstract symbols (Gibbs 2006, 142, 143, 151, 158, 165, 174, 205, 207). As in the case of arbitrariness, it is a bit difficult to get hold of the embodied theorist's precise complaint. On one version of the criticism, it concerns imagistic representation, discussed already in 11.1.3, so I set this aside. A further conception of abstractness holds that a concept is abstract if and only if it correctly applies to more than one thing; in which case, all parties to the debate are up to their ears in abstract concepts. Any given image schema, metaphorical mapping, or sensorimotor representation applies, at least in principle, to more than one thing. To try to differentiate between the embodied and the orthodox approaches, we might conceive of abstractness as comparative, one concept being more abstract than another if and only if the first, in fact, applies to more things than the second. This measure of abstractness yields precise comparisons, but it does not seem to be of any import in cognitive science. Often it is simply a contingent matter, subject to change at any time, which of two concepts has more instances than the other: there used to be more Dodo birds than democracies; the numbers are now reversed.

A more important measure along these lines focuses on principled reasons for differences in the ranges of things to which two concepts apply. Perhaps the embodied theorists are lobbying for more finely grained representations over coarse-grained ones. For at least some pairs of mental representations (e.g., ANIMAL, MAMMAL), it is matter of nomological necessity that the more fine-grained of the two never applies to more things than the other.

Fair enough. Yet, although many orthodox models deal in fairly coarse-grained representations, it is not an obligatory or essential part of the computationalist (or functionalist) program; the choice of representations depends to a great extent on the task being modeled. Consider again Marr's computational theory of vision, taken by the philosophical community to be an exemplar of computational modeling (see Egan [1994, 1999], and the many works referred to therein). Here the features represented are quite fine-grained, for example, degrees of disparity or differences in shading gradients. Cast in terms of a fine-grained approach to cognitively relevant properties, the present disagreement covers no ground beyond that covered in 11.1.2 in connection with functionalism.

11.2. The Constraint Thesis

Perhaps the distinctive nature of a plausible embodied view shines through more clearly when we turn to positive theses. Some authors (Ballard et al. 1997; Shapiro 2004, 2007; Gallagher 2005; Gibbs 2006) take the embodied view to express a bodily constraint or a determinative contribution of the body. On this view, human bodily structures, in their fine detail, highly limit the form cognition can take in humans and determine which cognitive properties the human instantiates (either causally or constitutively—say, by supervenience—but often this is not made clear).

In terms of the metaphysics of mind, the Constraint Thesis contains nothing new or surprising. Of course the arrangement of the materials of the body limit, in fact, it determines, which functional properties the body realizes. The functional and computational structure of the human mind supervene on its physical structure, that is, is completely determined by it. That view is standard, non-reductive materialist metaphysics, explored in either gripping or tedious detail (depending on one's proclivities) in analytic metaphysics and philosophy of mind (Fodor 1974; Kim 1993).

It is not even clear that the Constraint Thesis breaks ground as computationalist methodology. Historically, computationalists have taken for granted that the gross properties of the human body constrain human cognition. No one bothers formulating a computational model of visually guided action that presupposes direct visual inspection of objects behind large obstacles. Human perception is constrained by the gross bodily feature of being roughly four to seven feet tall. Computationalists preemptively eliminate models that presume otherwise, thereby accepting at least a crude form of the embodiment constraint.

Moreover, empirical evidence for the Constraint Thesis seems oversold. It is not the fine-grained physical properties of the nonneural body that matter in cases of many prominent embodied research results; rather it is the fairly high-level (and neurally realized) representation of such properties (Markman and Brendl 2005, and see chapter 8). We must distinguish between the content of such thoughts or experiences—for example, the content *the food-gathering rake is part of my arm*—and the units causally responsible for, or constitutive of, those thoughts or experiences; we have good reasons to think that the representing units are themselves in the brain, not in the location where the self or control is represented as being.

11.3. The Content Thesis

In this section, I explore what I call the 'Content Thesis' (cf. Shapiro [2004, section 7.2]), which holds that the content of all our mental representations depends, in some important way, on bodily experience. As put, the thesis is too vague. In what follows, I explore specific formulations.

11.3.1. External Content

Consider the following possibility: The human conceptual system consists of a basic stock of bodily concepts, together perhaps with such logical concepts as AND and OR; all other concepts are constructed entirely from this stock. What are bodily concepts? These come in two kinds. They might represent properties of the physical world beyond the body, say, certain kinds of forces or motions that are detected immediately by bodily movement or contact with the world. Alternatively, bodily concepts might represent properties of the physical body itself, a view suggested by the frequent talk of embodied experience; on this latter view, a basic concept might represent one's own body moving in some characteristic pattern. In either case (or a mixture of the two), these bodily concepts limit the contents of all other concepts, modulo the contribution of logical concepts.

What, however, is being constructed from the content of this basic stock of concepts? On standard accounts of external content, a representation's externalist content is the actual individual or collections of individuals represented—what is sometimes called its 'extension'. Alternatively the content might be the abstract property shared by all elements of the representation's extension. On the present proposal, then, all of the external individuals, kinds, and properties that humans mentally represent—that is, *the things or properties themselves*—are logical constructions of the individuals, kinds, and properties represented by the basic stock of bodily concepts.[2] This view is incredible. What would the world have to be like for palm trees, universities, justice, etc. to be literally constructed from the extensions of my concepts of force or bodily experience? A palm tree is not a cluster of force and motion (at least not of the particular kinds picked out by the average thinker's concepts of force and motion), and certainly is not a cluster of bodily experiences. Similarly for justice, quarks, universities, and grandmothers.

A more moderate reading of the Content Thesis pitches the semantic reduction a bit differently: it has more to do with definitions, something more like sets of necessary and sufficient conditions, of the sort often associated with Fregean senses.[3] This does not seem very promising. The view that embodied concepts can literally define the remaining concepts is only slightly more

2. Some embodied theorists (Lakoff 1987, chapter 15; Glenberg 1997, 2–3) reject the notion of external reference. I do not review their arguments here; to a great extent they depend on Hilary Putnam's model-theoretic criticism of externalist semantics (Putnam 1981, chapter 2). These results are far from conclusive (Lewis 1984; Levin 1997); moreover, it is not at all clear how to square this rejection of externalist content with the reasons given in chapter 10 for being interested in it.

3. Compare Jesse Prinz's view (2002); he advocates a kind of sensory reductionism together with a relatively standard view about the external kinds and properties represented; thus, although he attempts to show how the concept of justice can be built up out of sensory experiences, he does not attempt to show that the property *being just* is a Boolean function of other properties referred to by basic sensory experiences.

plausible than the extension-based view above. It is one thing to say that our bodily concepts, perhaps of balance, affect the way we reason about justice; it is another to promise to fill in the following schema: an action, institution, or arrangement is just if and only if such-and-such bodily concepts in fact apply to it.

Notice the connection between both of these versions of the Content Thesis and a grand tradition of semantic reductionism—the tradition that includes concept empiricism, logical positivism, phenomenalism, and logical behaviorism. On all of these views, there exists some set of primitive units, and all other thoughts (of the relevant sort) are claimed to be nothing more than arrangements of the primitive units. It is a grand tradition, but a failed one. In light of such failure and the prima facie implausibility of the embodied reductions themselves, the burden of proof is clearly on those who propose embodied externalist semantic reductionism. The sort of results commonly produced in the embodied literature—that, for instance, the position of a subject's body during an experiment affects the speed of sentence-processing—lend very little support, if any, to this project of semantic reduction.

11.3.2. Content-Determination by Causal Mediation

Perhaps, though, the content-based view has more to do with the fixation of concepts' externalist contents. Consider, then, a weaker form of the Content Thesis: Every human mental representation is either a bodily concept or acquired its content via causal mediation by at least some bodily concepts. On this view, humans acquire (or perhaps innately come by) some set of bodily concepts; and although that set can grow over time, some must have been acquired before any nonbodily concepts can be acquired. Let us take a developmental perspective. From a very early age, physical interaction with the environment plausibly involves bodily concepts. By the time nonbodily concepts are acquired, the child's moment-to-moment cognition is shot through with the activation of bodily concepts, in which case they are bound to play some causal role in mediating content-fixation for new mental representations.

This weak Content-Determination Thesis, though plausible, does not alter our fundamental conception of the mind or of the context-fixing process for mental representations; neither does it depart much from orthodox cognitive science, at least as it has been interpreted by such philosophers as Jerry Fodor. Computationalists think (or should think) that mental representations acquire external semantic content somehow. It is plausible enough that for many atomic concepts (those not defined as, or constituted by, Boolean combinations of others), the content-fixing relation is mediated by other mental representations (Fodor 1987, 118–22, 1994, 98, 1998, 156–58). It is not clear, though, why this should affect nondevelopmental computational modeling, that is, the attempt to model the processes that produce a given behavior at a given time. Moreover, as described, the Content-Determination Thesis's historical story of content acquisition itself seems amenable to orthodox computational modeling.

A stronger reading yields a more controversial version of the Content-Determination Thesis: Every human mental representation is either a bodily concept or acquired its content via causal mediation *only* by bodily concepts. On this view, a subject can acquire a nonbodily concept of justice or palm trees, but some bodily concepts must mediate the content-fixing causal relation and none other than bodily concepts can do so. This seems far too strong, precluding various plausible routes to content-fixation. Consider, for example, the process of reference-borrowing. I might form a concept and intend specifically that it refer to what someone else's word refers to: an expert uses 'lepton', which I know is supposed to refer to a family of subatomic particles. This requires that the concepts EXPERT, PARTICLE, and REFER all themselves be, or be wholly composed of, bodily concepts. I see no reason to take that proposal seriously. Certainly some bodily concepts are involved; perhaps any time I listen to a speaker, I mentally represent various things about the way my body is positioned, the way the speaker makes me feel, and whatnot. Here is an interesting and plausible, but also moderate, proposal. It is, however, is a far cry from the strong Content-Determination Thesis, that is, from the claim that every single representation causally mediating the fixation of the externalist content of a new mental representation represents a bodily experience or a property of the physical world experienced in a distinctively bodily manner.

11.3.3. Narrow Content

It might be better to think of the Content Thesis as a claim about internalist content, rather than as a claim about externalist content or the way it gets fixed.[4] On this view, the Content Thesis pertains to internal associations holding among various atomic mental representations (and various nonintentional physical mechanisms) and their role in cognitive processing. It matters little how we locate this role in relation to traditional discussions of content, sense, and reference (Block 1986). Nevertheless, it might be useful to call this a kind of sense or narrow content, according to which the conception (not the concept) of As is supposed to help to explain causally the behavior produced partly by the activation of the unstructured concept A. For instance, *being pulled behind a vehicle* is among the cluster of properties representation of which is internally associated with my unstructured concept TRAILER. As a result, if someone says to me she is going to buy a new trailer, I look to the back of her vehicle for a hitch. Here

---

4. This is a little misleading. The essential contrast comes between what a representation is about or refers to (externalist content) and what defines it, is grasped in connection with it, or is its conscious feel (internalist content). On this way of carving up the terrain, it is possible for a mental representation to have externalist content even though the representation is about an internal item, say, another thought or representation.

the embodied thesis may be at its strongest: in identifying aspects of the internal organization of, and relations among, those mental representations and nonintentional mechanisms that produce the behavior of interest in cognitive science.

Consider the kind of example that impresses many advocates of the embodied view. Perhaps an individual thinker's JUSTICE refers to an objective property of certain decisions or social structures. Assume also, however, that it is associated with various of the subject's other mental representations, including the compound concept EQUAL WEIGHT. Assume further that EQUAL WEIGHT is itself associated with a mental representation of a certain motor routine, maybe one that is used to balance objects, one on top of the other (cf. Karmiloff-Smith [1992, 82–87]). It is possible, then, that associations between JUSTICE and the representation of this motor routine, for which we may have no natural English expression, help to explain more about cognitive phenomena, analyses of court decisions, for instance, than one might have expected. Moreover, it might explain facts—reaction times, for example—about linguistic processing of sentences that include the word 'justice' (or synonyms).

Assume cognitive science is rife with such cases. What theoretical moral should be drawn? This does not by itself entail a new kind of content, mental representation, or cognitive processing, but suggests only that certain kinds of concepts (or nonintentional mechanisms) play a more significant role in cognition than might otherwise have been thought. This approach does not eliminate abstract concepts, external reference, computation, or any of the other supposed nastiness associated with orthodox cognitive science.

Think of this in terms of embodied reasoning. Lakoff and Johnson (1999, 54–55, 58, 65–66, 140–43) propose that we often reason metaphorically, guided by associations between two domains: a source domain and a target domain. Take time as our target domain and motion as our source. As one physically moves toward another person, the amount of motion required to make physical contact with the second person decreases. The amount of time it takes to reach the person also decreases. Thus, time becomes associated with motion through space, and the latter become a model for reasoning about the former; we begin to reason about the temporal domain by imposing structural features of the domain of motion through space onto the domain of time. For example, the subjects assumes that as some temporal interval, t_1 to t_2, elapses, the time between the subject and some further fixed time, t_3 (later than t_2), decreases—a projection from structure encountered in the spatial domain. Similarly for many other pairs of domains, such as positive feelings (target domain) and physical warmth (source domain).

Lakoff and Johnson's discussion is fascinating, as is similar, more orthodox research on, for example, learning by analogy (Gentner 2003). Nevertheless, it does not strike me as having the radical implications claimed by Lakoff and Johnson. First, a wealth of traditional cognitive science exploits the notion of association between experiences or cognitive states, and of course which associations form depends on the situations in which the subject finds herself.

Second, notice that the associations in question form between elements in two domains. These elements appear to be perfectly standard units in a computational model. After admitting that, yes, such elements do have an independent status (1999, 54–55), Lakoff and Johnson (1999, 59) downplay the importance of this fact: they claim that independent elements are bare-bones units from which nothing can be inferred. Okay, but that is a standard view (Fodor 1975, 1998), reflected in the distinction between atomic units and knowledge structures or between concepts and conceptions (Woodfield 1991). The subject can infer little from an atomic unit alone (although it might prime some other associated concept). Cognitive processing manipulates compound strings, and typically, the properties of compound strings help to account for behavior. Thus, it carries no dialectical weight to emphasize the relative inefficacy of individual bare-bones atoms.

Along these conciliatory lines, notice, too, that many of the illustrations given by Lakoff and Johnson involve abstract logical properties of such domains as motion and time—transitivity, for example (1999, 142). The ability to recognize such relations and to map them from one domain to another suggests a kind of logical facility typically associated with computational models of human cognition.

11.4. Vehicles, Realizers, and Apportioning Explanation

Sometimes supporters of the embodied view focus on the realizers of cognitive states (or what are often called the 'vehicles' of external content; for present purposes, I do not differentiate between the two). It is not entirely clear, though, how one might develop this focus on realizers into a substantive and important embodied thesis. Let us begin with an example.

When information is held in short-term memory, how is it coded? What is its representational format? Margaret Wilson (2001) summarizes various lines of evidence in support of an articulatory encoding hypothesis. On this view, stimulus items held in short-term memory are coded in a system the elements of which are marked by similarities and differences in the muscular processes controlling the articulation of words. One can think of this system in syntactic terms, as a kind of symbolic language; on the embodied view, though, it is of special importance that such encodings be realized by patterns of muscular activity of the sort that normally control articulation.

Assume that the articulatory encoding hypothesis is true. How does it stand in relation to computational orthodoxy? Articulation is a bodily process involving motor activity. Articulatory encodings of items in short-term memory do not normally cause the subject to speak. Thus, articulatory encodings are more like mental representations of motor activity, perhaps neural units that represent, say, combinations of Wicklephones (Wicklegren 1969), or whatever the primitive features of the articulatory process turn out to be. This yields a version of the Content Thesis. Bits of the articulatory code are embodied in the sense that they represent bodily actions or represent muscular activities that cause bodily actions. Yet, in the lines of experimentation reported by Wilson, these encodings represent the stimulus items, which need not have anything particularly to do with bodily activities. How do these patterns represent both the (suppressed or partial) commands to articulate and the stimulus items?

Here is a possibility. Articulatory encodings lead a double-life in the cognitive economy. When controlling the production of speech, they represent commands to produce certain phonemes. When, however, they are harnessed by short-term memory, these encodings represent the stimulus items. On this view, the cognitive architecture itself allows realizers to be used for different purposes when different higher-level functions are being implemented. This view strikes me as interesting and worth pursuing. It is not particularly unorthodox, however. Modern computers exhibit similar shifts, say, in the varying use of particular memory registers; the same code (analogous to a realizer) can have different content on different occasions of its appearing in that register. It can simply be part of one's model that when certain control structures are active, physical structures from a certain set realize representations from one domain (e.g., motor commands), and when different control structures are active, the same physical structures realize representations of properties from a different (perhaps more inclusive) domain.[5]

This view may seem more plausible the less robust the representational role played by articulatory encodings, qua their use in short-term memory. Consider, then, the possibility that the articulatory encodings represent stimulus items in an indirect way, as pointers (Newell and Simon 1997/1976, 86–87). On this view, they serve merely as intermediaries providing access to the concepts that represent the stimulus items, thus indirectly activating the conceptions of which those concepts are a part. The concepts designated may be linked to (and might even be identical to) mental representations of words in natural language, themselves associatively connected to ways of producing those words in speech. This provides a route from pointers in short-term memory, couched in an articulatory code, to the concepts themselves. This provides a very weak sense in which representations in short-term memory are action-oriented: they are realized by physical patterns that in some contexts control action.

The advocate for the embodied view might, however, have something more anatomical in mind, viz. that all mental representations are realized in distinctively sensory or motor cortex. On this view, the realizers of immediate motor or sensory representations provide a fundamental stock from which all other realizers of mental representations are drawn. Given the need for a

---

5. This helps to explain, within an orthodox computational framework, some of the kinds of context-sensitivity of representation discussed in chapter 10 in connection with the embedded view.

flexible architecture, though, the thesis on offer conflicts in no way with the orthodoxy. The standard view requires that a realizer must be capable of playing the right causal role, as described by the computational model; this restricts what can realize a given mental representation, but, beyond that, it does not tell us that the realizer must be *here* rather than *there*. If many realizers of not particularly sensory representations turn out to be in sensory or motor cortex—as defined anatomically—that will be of interest for certain purposes (say, predicting what cognitive damage a given lesion will cause), but does not tell us much about cognition itself. Furthermore, there is every reason to doubt that *all* realizers of mental representations appear in sensory or motor cortex; what is all of the rest of cortex doing when it lights up during cognitive activity?!

With respect to realizers that do appear in sensory cortex, one contested issue is their modal or amodal status at the cognitive level (Barsalou et al. 2003). The suggestion might be that, because realizers appear in distinctively sensorimotor cortex, the representations involved are distinctively sensory or motor in nature. This inference seems questionable, though. Recall the work on bimodally sensitive neurons, discussed in chapter 8 (Iriki, Tanaka, and Iwamura 1996; Iriki, Tanaka, Obayashi, and Iwamura 2001; cf. Graziano, Yap, and Gross [1994]). Such neurons plausibly represent the location of objects relative to the body, but not through a single modality; and a representation's being activated through more than one modality strikes me as a sufficient condition for its being amodal. Moreover, the representation is realized in what is arguably sensorimotor cortex. Thus, even if realizers of all mental representations were to appear in distinctively sensory or motor cortex, we would not have established any particularly unorthodox view of mental representation; it would depend on the cognition-related properties of the representations so realized.

Consider, too, the wealth of neurological evidence of the distribution of realizers throughout the brain, including nonsensory, nonmotor cortex. Neurons in the hippocampus and entorhinal cortex, for example, play a central role in the formation and storage of episodic (Vargha-Khadem, Gadian, Watkins, Connelly, Van Paesschen, and Mishkin 1997; Pastalkova, Serrano, Pinkhasova, Wallace, Fenton, and Sacktor 2006) and declarative memories (Fernandez, Effern, Grunwald, Pezer, Lehnertz, Dümpelmann, Van Roost, and Elger 1999), as well as spatial maps (Peigneux, Laureys, Fuchs, Collette, Perrin, Reggers, Phillips, Degueldre, Del Fiore, Aerts, Luxen, and Maquet 2004) , and representations of individuals (Quiroga et al. 2005). Mental representations of words and some related concepts are highly localized in nonsensorimotor cortex (Müller 1996, 623; Calvin and Bickerton 2000, 59–63), and some are highly distributed (Damasio and Tranel 1993; Pulvermüller 1999; Martin and Weisberg 2003) across areas that include nonsensorimotor cortex. Moreover, representations the realizers of which appear in prefrontal cortex appear to play a central role in attention, working memory, control, and awareness (Maia and Cleeremans 2005). Sensory cortex participates in the development of such units; one does not acquire a concept of, say, cows without some kind of sensory input. The question at hand, however, concerns what constitutes the realizers of representations, not their history of their formation; and here the answer runs clearly against the modally specific realizer thesis.

Some embodied theorists seem concerned that there is no neural evidence of amodal mental representations. Barsalou et al. (2003) ask, "Will direct evidence be found for amodal symbols in the brain?" (ibid., 89, and see also 87), suggesting that orthodox deployment of amodal symbols has no neuroscientific basis. What, however, would count as neural evidence of the use of amodal symbols (considered cognitively)? Evidence of the existence of nonsensorimotor realizers of some mental representations? If so, then the preceding paragraph puts paid to Barsalou et al.'s rhetorical challenge.

Barsalou et al. might, however, be asking for something else: evidence of neural realizers—somewhere, anywhere—of mental representations the content of which is amodal. We should expect there to be such representations, partly because we should doubt that the content of our mental representations reduces fully to sensory, motor, or bodily concepts. Assuming that materialism is true, such representations must be realized somewhere in the physical world. This seems enough to answer the challenge. We have independent reason to believe that human cognition employs concepts the contents of which do not reduce to bodily or sensorimotor concepts. We also have evidence that lots of mental representations are realized in areas other than distinctively sensory or motor cortex. Thus, the neuroscientific evidence, combined with independent arguments about content, provides strong evidence that the human cognitive system employs amodal representations.

I suspect, though, that Barsalou et al. would like more. In particular, I suspect they would like evidence that links the use of amodal representations to activity in nonsensorimotor areas of the brain. Such evidence exists, some of which is cited above (in particular, see Maia and Cleeremans [2005]). John Anderson and colleagues have reported activity in regions of posterior parietal cortex associated with the transforming of various kinds of information in abstract problem-solving (Anderson 2007, 76). This area may involve spatial representations, but, absent independent argument, there is no reason to think that spatial representations are modally specific. Or, consider the role of frontal cortex in representing contingencies in the Iowa Gambling Task (Bechara, Damasio, Tranel, and Damasio 2005), as well as numerous other decision-making tasks. It may be that emotion-related physiological activity plays some role in explaining behavior in such experiments, but this gives us no reason to think the representations involved in decision-making reduce to sensorimotor contents; and these representations are clearly realized in association cortex, not sensory or motor cortex.

These points about realization have important application to other embodiment-related issues. Let me digress for a few paragraphs, then, to emphasize the importance of keeping clearly in mind the distinction between cognitive models and claims about realizers. Mirror neurons become highly active both when the subject performs a certain kind of action and when the subject observes another person performing that kind of action—reaching, for example (Gallese, Keysers, and Rizzolatti 2004). Pronouncements about the theoretical implications of their discovery have run the gamut, but the existence of mirror neurons has frequently been used to support claims about embodiment.

Notice, though, that the orthodox view has a perfectly natural way to interpret the result; in fact, combined with standard views about realization, the orthodox view predicts the result. On the orthodox view, there is, at the cognitive level, a general symbol for reaching, and of course it becomes active when one thinks about one's own reaching and when one sees someone else reaching. The discovery of mirror neurons is nothing more than the discovery of the location of the realizers of amodal, subject-neutral concepts of actions, the existence of which is independently predicted by orthodox computationalism. That such realizers appear in areas of cortex near to where motor commands are issued, without themselves constituting the full-blown commands, is no surprise. We should not be surprised that the realizers of abstract representations of actions have easy causal access to commands to perform those actions; this is nothing more than efficient evolutionary engineering.[6] What is supposed to be one of the most radical and striking discoveries of cognitive neuroscience turns out to be relatively uninteresting, when one keeps in mind the distinction between cognitive models and their realizations.

I do not mean to dismiss the study of realizers and their properties. These are essential pieces of the larger cognitive scientific enterprise. In fact, the value of the embodied approach may be especially clear when seen in this light. Although I do not think embodied theorists want to endorse eliminativism, some of the embodied research shows that the explanation of cognitive phenomena is itself a mixed bag, or alternatively, that not all of what we thought of as cognitive phenomena are in fact cognitive. Many patterns of behavior (that the subject gave answer A rather than answer B) seem best explained by appeal to the content of representations involved. For example, speakers adjust the number and kind of gestures they make on the basis of beliefs about the presence and location of speakers, a relatively robust effect appearing across concrete experimental designs (Goldin-Meadow 2003, 137–40; also in this connection, recall the discussion of the false-belief task from chapter 3). Nevertheless, many aspects of human behavior—the amount of time it takes a subject to produce a response, for instance—may be best explained in terms of nonrepresentational aspects of the realizers.

---

6. Descartes would not have been surprised. In his Sixth Meditation, he argues that certain of the mind's important properties—its being subject to certain kinds of error—result unavoidably from engineering realities, to which even the most talented designer is subject.

This might be of special interest when a given representation, individuated in terms of its content, is realized in substantially different ways in the brain. Which realizer of concept A is activated (is it the mental representation of the word used to express that concept? a visual image of a typical instance of that kind?) may explain as much as the mere fact that some realizer or other of A was activated. More generally, realizers have properties that cause effects, and we attend to some of these effects when we study cognition. This may well lead to a kind of apportioning of explanatory work, a fragmented science of sorts (which might be exactly what we find in the domain of any higher-level or special-science). Some of the phenomena of interest cannot be reduced to physical types—the patterns are too abstract, and they are multiply realizable. At the same time, some aspects of the phenomena of interest are best explained by fine-grained physical properties of the systems in which the higher-level explananda appear; in the case of cognition, an investigation of embodiment may uncover these fine-grained properties.[7]

11.5. The Symbol-Grounding Problem

A general dissatisfaction with the notion of a symbol runs through the literature on embodied cognition. Talk of symbols seems too dry and removed from the complexity of actual human cognition. To the extent that computational symbols have meaning, it seems interpretation-based: meaning is merely in the eye of the beholder—the programmer, for instance (Searle 1980; Harnad 1990; Varela, Thompson, and Rosch 1991, 99; Wheeler 2005, 82; Gibbs 2006, 159). This complaint can be developed in at least three distinct ways, having to do with consciousness, reference, or real-time engagement with the world. In effect, the first was discussed in connection with the Chinese room argument. In this section, I focus on the remaining two.

11.5.1. Symbol-Grounding and Reference

As intuitive as the symbol-grounding complaint may seem, it is difficult to draw from these intuitions a compelling problem that the embodied approach solves. Consider one straightforward interpretation of the symbol-grounding problem. A necessary condition for a symbol's having genuine meaning is that it possess truth-conditions nonderivatively. Computational symbols, however, have truth-conditions only derivatively, that is, only insofar as some other thinker assigns truth-condition to them or interprets them as having truth-conditions.

---

7. Perhaps this is the case with imagistic properties of representations. As noted earlier, something with imagistic properties can function as the realizer of an atomic mental representation. Nevertheless, the fine-grained physical properties of the realizer of the image may help to explain certain aspects of subjects' responses.

Thus, computational symbols do not possess genuine meaning; as a corollary, the processing of computational symbols does not successfully model human thought.

This critique of the orthodox approach carries little weight; for it simply ignores the substantial literature on naturalistic theories of semantic content. I do not claim that there is a perfect naturalistic theory of representation on the table (a common state of affairs in the study of nearly any topic of interest), but plausible contenders populate the field (Dretske 1981, 1988; Millikan 1984; Fodor 1987, 1990—one approach [Rupert 1998] discusses reference-fixing specifically within an embodied framework, in terms of dynamical systems-based developmental theories). Moreover, at least one naturalistic semanticist, Fodor, explicitly states (1994, lecture 1) that his goal is to provide a naturalistic semantics for computational symbols.[8]

Notice, too, that the referential problem arises equally for the embodied view. Whether or not mental representations are modally specific or realized in sensory cortex or what have you, somehow they must get attached to their referents. Thus, the embodied approach does not seem to offer any special help with the grounding problem, as a problem about external content, beyond the approach to causal intermediaries discussed above.

The intuition to the contrary rests, I suspect, on a consciousness-based view: the idea that consciousness imbues symbols with meaning; this, however, simply changes the subject, taking as given one of the very phenomena—conscious experience—that cognitive science must explain. If the activation and manipulation of symbolic structures *constitutes* consciousness, then, given the existence of some conscious activity, it is impossible, on pains of regress, that conscious activity be required to imbue every symbolic structure with its meaning.

11.5.2. Symbol-Grounding and Narrow Content

Perhaps, however, the symbol-grounding problem pertains specifically to the narrow contents (or senses) of mental representations, the associated conceptions. On this view, in order that a thought have meaning, it (or its components) must be related to other thoughts (or their components) in appropriate ways. Orthodox computational symbols cannot alone possess the right sort of interrelations; for the meaning-conferring network must consist at least partly of connections to distinctively sensorimotor representations.

As Harnad presents it, though, the symbol-grounding problem is meant to be a problem for computationalism in general. Absent an argument that

---

8. Even when Fodor (1980) famously recommended that cognitive science ignore externalist content, his argument presupposed a general view about the external content of computational symbols—the causal view advocated by Putnam and Kripke, conceived of as a naturalistic theory of mental content.

the sensorimotor representations in question cannot be computational symbols, the problem loses steam. The computationalist will simply set to work modeling whatever are the requisite relations. It may be that for a subject's JUSTICE to be grounded, it must bear some important relation to a bodily concept or sensory image of balancing. If this relation can be modeled computationally, though, the symbol-grounding problem is certainly not a problem for computationalism.

What about the connection to real-time interaction, though. Perhaps the idea is that, for a symbol to be grounded, it must guide real-time interaction with the world and that only sensorimotor representations, processed in a distinctively analogue fashion, can guide real-time interaction. This may be true, but I am skeptical; and to the extent that the point is valid, it represents a point about empirical matters rather than a complaint about the nature of computational symbols. In what follows, I detail some of the reasons for this deflationary reading of the symbol-grounding problem.

First, the demand for connections to sensorimotor representations seems either unjustified or, if interpreted more liberally, the sort of thing that many orthodox computationalists accept. Consider a very demanding reading of the criterion at issue: For any mental representation C, there exists some proprietary set a of sensory or motor routines or representations, such that a subject cannot have C unless that mental representation causally interacts with members of a in the appropriate way. This view seems false: there simply is no reasonably sized set of specific sensory or motor experiences necessary for having a concept of justice or quarks or universities—or even palm trees, I suspect. The problem is cognitive holism, or at least the widespread connections holding among various mental representations and cognitive processes. One can have a reliable university detector that makes use of all sorts of sensory representations and motor routines—understood in terms of content or cortex—that do not have much at all in common with the set the next person uses.

In contrast, liberal readings of the demand seem true but dialectically inert, at least in the present context. Here is a sensible enough alternative: for any C, a subject must have at least one (or even some modest number of) sensory and motor experiences in order to acquire C. Notice the scope of 'some' here: you cannot acquire a concept while having no sensory or motor experiences whatsoever (or having only a paltry few). This may not be true; perhaps there are some exceptions. My point is that, if true, it does not conflict with orthodox cognitive science. Even those who advocate for innateness think that some causal interaction with or activity in the world is necessary for the acquisition of most, perhaps all, atomic concepts. This is not some idiosyncratically Fodorean view of concept acquisition. Philosophers who assign an important epistemological role to the a priori, from Plato to BonJour (1998, 9–11), allow that concept acquisition might require triggering interactions with the world, even where those concepts are highly abstract and participate in purely rationalist justificatory relations.

The proponent of the embodied approach might think I have missed the point about real-time interaction, but the same contrasting set of options, and the same diagnosis, recurs in the action-oriented context. The subject must have *some* sensory or motor connections in place in order to interact in a coherent way with instances of universities or justice; but there is no very particular set of such connections. In this case, the dialectically inert status of the former, less demanding reading follows from the standard view: in order for a cognitive science to be fully explanatory, it must include, somewhere in its models, an account of perception and motor control.

Second, it is not so clear that computationalism fails to account for connections between various nonsensory, nonmotor units and certain of our sensory routines. It is one thing to show that sensory and motor properties have an effect on processing; it is quite another to show that these effects involve the mapping of inputs to outputs of noncomputable functions. (Computer graphics are pretty impressive, after all.) Of course, the anticomputationalist embodied thinker would be happy to show merely that humans do not, in fact, solve the problems in question algorithmically, but that has not been done. The fallback position for many who oppose orthodox computationalism holds that the functions may be computable, and that in some technical sense humans may be implementing algorithms to compute them, but that the computational analysis is unilluminating—and that something else, say, dynamical-systems-based analysis is. This view, however, has to date been mostly promise and little product (see chapter 7).

Some of Harnad's remarks (1990, 336–37) suggest a certain view of computational symbols that orthodox theorists frequently reject: that a computational symbol must be part of a single homogenous system that explains cognition. This interpretation of orthodox computationalism may derive from claims made about general intelligence: the Church-Turing Thesis and sweeping claims about the connection between physical symbol systems and general intelligence (Newell and Simon 1997/1976). Such claims notwithstanding, the point of orthodox cognitive psychology has not been to formulate some perfectly general system that produces, or is capable of producing, all possible cognitive phenomena. Rather, the data to be modeled come from real subjects, and the architectures employed—SOAR, ACT, EPIC—aim to produce matching response profiles. The best way to account for the human data may invoke relatively computationally isolated modules (Marr 1982; Fodor 1983; Pinker 1997; Anderson 2007), including perceptual ones. The idea of proprietary codes for different modules or of the relative causal isolation of symbols used by a particular module hardly violates orthodox thinking. It is no moving criticism of the orthodoxy if one says "symbols in central processing cannot directly guide real-time behavior," when orthodox modelers rig the symbols in central processing to modules specifically to allow modules to guide real-time behavior.

We must grant the following to those concerned about symbol-grounding. If there is to be successful cognitive science, the processing posited must be rich enough to account for actual behavior, and this richness will include at least some connections to sensorimotor routines or representations. This does not mark an in-principle shortcoming of computational modeling. What kind of connections and how many depend on the data and the details of the models. Thus, I conclude by stating a theme that runs through this chapter. The embodied approach appears to offer a modest and important corrective to the orthodoxy, but not a sea change or principled departure.

12

Summary and Conclusion

Proponents of the situated approach in cognitive science have drawn striking theoretical morals from that program. My brief here has been to evaluate these claims. Of greatest interest has been the hypothesis of extended cognition: the claim that human cognition literally includes elements beyond the boundary of the human organism. The claim is surprising enough on its own; add the relatively uncontroversial assumption that a human's cognitive processing constitutes part of her mind and self, and radical implications follow: the human mind and self spread into the environment beyond the organism.

I have urged the rejection of the extended view, at least given the current state of the evidence. Cognitive-scientific results do not distinctively support the hypothesis of extended cognition, and extant philosophical arguments show, at best, that it is possible that cognition be extended—a thesis too weak to be of much interest in the philosophy of cognitive science and empirically oriented philosophy of mind. In arguing for this diagnosis, I have appealed to a positive vision of cognitive-scientific success and its methodology and to an associated principle of demarcation. With regard to both aspects of my reasoning, a comparative element is indispensable. It is not simply that I have argued for a systems-based approach to cognitive demarcation; it is also that the proponents of the extended view offer no plausible and useful alternative. It is not that my systems-based approach is the only way to account for the successes of traditional cognitive science; it is that the extended view does so only by offering trivial variants on the standard approach.

I have critically examined the embedded and embodied research programs as well. Here, however, my treatment differs significantly from my treatment of the extended case. Empirical findings support substantive versions of both the embedded and embodied theses. Yet, although these empirical findings reflect important trends in experimental design and in the modeling of cognitive processes, the theoretical import of such findings has been substantially oversold. Regarding the role of such central theoretical constructs as computation and representation, the embedded and embodied approaches offer little reason for revision. The most compelling embedded models of cognitive processing either explicitly adopt a computational approach or at least cohere with such a view. Using fewer representations or less elaborate computational routines does not amount to a rejection of computation or representation, particularly not if, as I have argued, the representations involved do not depart in a principled way from those used in orthodox computational modeling.

Similar comments apply to the embodied view. Many advocates for this approach criticize orthodox computationalist cognitive science, as well as the associated functionalist vision. In rejoinder, I have argued that no plausible version of the embodied thesis supports these claims. Unlike the embedded thesis, the embodied view tends to take less precise form; thus, much of my work involved sorting through possible interpretations of the embodied claim. Nevertheless, on plausible interpretations of the embodiment thesis, functionalism, the arbitrariness of symbols, the realization-relation, and the representation-relation all remain a central part of the cognitive-scientific endeavor. The embodied program helps us to home in on which functions the human brain computes and how human mental representations get into the content-determining relation to things in the external world, but such contributions are friendly supplements to the orthodox view, not departures from it.

In sum, then, I have argued that we are not undergoing the revolution promised by situated theorists and their philosophical interpreters. We have no reason to think cognition extends into the environment, and insofar as embedded and embodied cognition go, it appears that we face more of a nudging than a coup—a push toward different kinds of algorithms that may exploit different representational formats, perhaps computational architectures that both extract information from distinctively modal representations and use such representations as computational atoms.

I close with a few positive points, including some suggestions concerning the connection between philosophical topics and future work in the situated paradigm. First, as noted above, both the embedded and embodied approaches have much to offer cognitive scientists interested in the details of cognitive modeling. My deflationary discussions have focused on philosophical claims attached to the situated program. Nevertheless, with regard to active design of experiments and models, embedded and embodied research should proceed full steam ahead. Here, differences in degree can, for the purposes of working modelers, add up to a difference in kind, even if abstract philosophical picture remains relatively unchanged.

Second, the embedded and embodied programs can offer substantial insights to the philosophers as well. Many theories of representation premise mental (and linguistic) content on the kind of relation the human bears to things referred to or represented. The body provides the means to get into that relation, and thus facts about how the body contributes, in its fine details, to the human's relation to the world can inform theories of representation. An investigation of embodied and embedded cognition might help us to see how a given theory of mental content applies to humans; or more surprisingly, it might show us that our concepts have contents other than what we have thought. Along similar lines, given commitment to the possession of concepts with certain contents, the investigation of the body-as-mediator might serve to disqualify certain candidate theories of content. Assume we know that we represent P, but theory T cannot, given the facts about our bodily relation to the world, account for how we get into what T says is the content-fixing relation to P; then we might reasonably reject T.

Third, the embedded and embodied views might have implications for central debates in the metaphysics of mind (Hanna and Maiese 2009). Of long-standing interest to philosophy of mind is the question of so-called type–type identity theory: the idea that mental state-types match up with (in fact, are literally identical to) certain types of physical structures. The prominent philosopher of mind and metaphysician Jaegwon Kim has published a series of papers and books (1993, 1998, 2005) arguing that, in certain respects, the functionalist individuation of mental properties—even the fine-grained functionalism discussed here—is deeply flawed. As Kim himself has suggested, one might respond to his critique of functionalism by embracing a form of type–type identity theory, in particular, by identifying mental properties with species-specific physical properties, so that, for example, a desire for food in one species may simply be a different property from the property associated with foraging, eating, and like in another species, such that there is no single property present in both cases. Perhaps, in the end, situated cognitive science will support such reductions. By making clear the importance of fine-grained bodily details to the explanation of cognitive phenomena, the embodied and embedded views may help to soften resistance to a type–type reduction. A common objection to species-specific type–type reduction is that, for example, there *must* be something that human pain shares with, say, chimpanzee pain. An embodied reduction might show in detail what these two distinct properties do, and more importantly do not, have in common, thus showing that it is not so implausible that *being in human pain* and *being in chimp pain* are not the same properties.

Fourth, think about the way the situated program might inform work in naturalistic epistemology (Quine 1969; Kornblith 1993). If knowledge is a natural kind, partly a relation between the subject and the environment, the situated program promises to contribute to our understanding of it. By showing how we successfully interact with our environments, embedded and embodied models might help us to see what knowledge-conferring justification demands, or perhaps more to the point, does not demand.

Lastly, we should not forget that the empirical field is open, and as a result, none of my negative conclusions is meant to be anything like a final pronouncement. I have been taking stock of twenty years of situated research and philosophical theorizing about it. It may take a hundred more years to get a clear picture of the workings of human cognitive processing. As a naturalistically minded philosopher, though, taking stock from where we stand is precisely what seems appropriate. Doing so might help to direct investigation down the most fruitful path or merely to prevent premature misinterpretations of current research. One tradition holds that philosophical truths are eternal, and that philosophical results should aim to be likewise. I have no such aspirations. The actual truth may be eternal, but we, in the mix, must rock Neurath's boat to see what we can of the truth from where we are; and it is a big boat with many parts. Often, the best results we can arrive at in this situation take the form, "Given such-and-such data, it appears most likely that P." We could do a lot worse, and I have not yet come across reasons for thinking we can do much better.

References

Adams, F., and Aizawa, K. (2001). The Bounds of Cognition. *Philosophical Psychology* 14: 43–64.

———. (2007). *The Bounds of Cognition*. Malden, MA: Blackwell.

———. (2009). Why the Mind is Still in the Head. In P. Robbins and M. Aydede (eds.), *The Cambridge Handbook of Situated Cognition* (pp. 78–95). Cambridge: Cambridge University Press.

———. (forthcoming). Defending the Bounds of Cognition. To appear in R. Menary (ed.), *The Extended Mind*. Cambridge, MA: MIT Press.

Aizawa, K. (2007). Understanding the Embodiment of Perception. *Journal of Philosophy* 104, 1 (January): 5–25.

Anderson, J. R. (2000). *Learning and Memory*, second edition. New York: John Wiley & Sons.

———. (2007). *How Can the Human Mind Occur in the Physical Universe?* New York: Oxford University Press.

Anderson, J. R., Bothell, D., Byrne, M., Douglass, S., Lebiere, C., and Qin, Y. (2004). An Integrated Theory of Mind. *Psychological Review* 111: 1036–60.

Anderson, J. R., and Bower, G. (1973). *Human Associative Memory*. Washington, D.C.: Winston and Sons.

Anderson, J. R., Douglass, S., and Qin, Y. (2005). How Should a Theory of Learning and Cognition Inform Instruction? In Healy (ed.), pp. 47–58.

Armstrong, D. (1978). *Universals and Scientific Realism*, vol. II: *A Theory of Universals*. London: Cambridge University Press.

Astington, J. (1993). *The Child's Discovery of the Mind*. Cambridge, MA: Harvard University Press.

Baddeley, A. (1999). *Essentials of Human Memory*. East Sussex: Psychology Press.

Bahrick, H. P. (1979). Maintenance of Knowledge: Questions about Memory We Forgot to Ask. *Journal of Experimental Psychology: General* 108: 296–308.

———. (1984). Semantic Memory Content in Permastore: Fifty Years of Memory for Spanish Learned in School. *Journal of Experimental Psychology: General* 113: 1–29.

Ballard, D., Hayhoe, M., Pook, P., and Rao, R. (1997). Deictic Codes for the Embodiment of Cognition. *Behavioral and Brain Sciences* 20: 723–42.

Barlow, H. (1972). Single Units and Sensation: A Neuron Doctrine for Perceptual Psychology? *Perception* 1: 371–94.

Baron-Cohen, S. (1995). *Mindblindness: An Essay on Autism and Theory of Mind.* Oxford: Oxford University Press.

Baron-Cohen, S., Leslie, A., and Frith, U. (1985). Does the Autistic Child Have a "Theory of Mind"? *Cognition* 21: 37–46.

Barsalou, L. (1999). Perceptual Symbol Systems. *Behavioral and Brain Sciences* 22: 577–609.

Barsalou, L., Simmons, W. K., Barbey, A., and Wilson, C. (2003). Grounding Conceptual Knowledge in Modality-Specific Systems. *Trends in Cognitive Sciences* 7: 84–91.

Bartlett, G. (2008). Whither Internalism? How Internalists Should Respond to the Extended Mind Hypothesis. *Metaphilosophy* 39, 2: 163–84.

Batterman, R. (2000). Multiple Realizability and Universality. *British Journal for the Philosophy of Science* 51: 115–45.

Bechara, A., Damasio, H., Tranel, D., and Damasio, A. (2005). The Iowa Gambling Task and the Somatic Marker Hypothesis: Some Questions and Answers. *Trends in Cognitive Sciences* 9, 4: 159–62.

Bechtel, W., and Mundale, J. (1999). Multiple Realizability Revisited: Linking Cognitive and Neural States. *Philosophy of Science,* 66: 175–207.

Beer, R. (1995). Computational and Dynamical Languages for Autonomous Agents. In Port and van Gelder (eds.), pp. 121–47.

———. (2003). The Dynamics of Active Categorical Perception in an Evolved Model Agent. *Adaptive Behavior* 11: 209–43.

Bickle, J. (1998). *Psychoneural Reduction: The New Wave.* Cambridge, MA: MIT Press.

Biederman, I. (1990). Higher-Level Vision. In D. Osherson, S. Kosslyn, and J. Hollerbach (eds.), *An Invitation to Cognitive Science: Visual Cognition and Action,* vol. 2 (pp. 41–72). Cambridge, MA: MIT Press.

Birch, S., and Bloom, P. (2003). Children Are Cursed: An Asymmetric Bias in Mental-State Attribution. *Psychological Science* 14: 283–86.

Block, N. (1978). Troubles with Functionalism. In C. Savage (ed.), *Perception and Cognition. Issues in the Foundations of Psychology, Minnesota Studies in the Philosophy of Science,* vol. 9 (pp. 261–325). Minneapolis: University of Minnesota Press.

———. (1980a). Introduction: What is Functionalism? In Block (ed.), 1980b, pp. 171–84.

———. (ed.) (1980b) *Readings in the Philosophy of Psychology,* vol. 1. Cambridge, MA: Harvard University Press.

———. (ed.) (1981). *Imagery.* Cambridge, MA: MIT Press.

———. (1986). Advertisement for a Semantics for Psychology. In P. French, T. Uehling, and H. Wettstein (eds.), *Midwest Studies in Philosophy: Studies in the Philosophy of Mind,* vol. 10 (pp. 615–78). Minneapolis: University of Minnesota Press.

———. (1990). Can the Mind Change the World? In G. Boolos (ed.), *Meaning and Method: Essays in Honor of Hilary Putnam* (pp. 137–70). Cambridge: Cambridge University Press.

———. (2005). Review of *Action in Perception* by Alva Noë, *Journal of Philosophy* 102: 259–72.

Block, N., and Fodor, J. (1972). What Psychological States Are Not. *Philosophical Review* 81: 159–81.

Bloom, P. (2000). *How Children Learn the Meanings of Words*. Cambridge, MA: MIT Press.

Bloom, P., and German, T. (2000). Two Reasons to Abandon the False Belief Task as a Test of Theory of Mind. *Cognition* 77: B25–B31.

BonJour, L. (1998). *In Defense of Pure Reason*. Cambridge: Cambridge University Press.

Boolos, G., Burgess, J., and Jeffrey, R. (2002) *Computability and Logic*, fourth edition. Cambridge: Cambridge University Press.

Borrett, D., Kelly, S., and Kwan, H. (2000). Phenomenology, Dynamical Neural Networks and Brain Function. *Philosophical Psychology* 13: 213–28.

Bower, G. (2000). A Brief History of Memory Research. In Tulving and Craik (eds.), pp. 3–32.

Brooks, R. (1999). *Cambrian Intelligence: The Early History of the New AI*. Cambridge, MA: MIT Press.

Burge, T. (1979). Individualism and the Mental. In P. French, T. Uehling, and H. Wettstein (eds.) *Midwest Studies in Philosophy* IV (pp. 73–121). Minneapolis: University of Minnesota Press.

———. (2003). Replies. In M. Fráppoli and E. Romero (eds.), *Meaning, Basic Self-Knowledge, and Mind* (pp. 243–96). Stanford, CA: CSLI Publications.

Butler, K. (1998). *Internal Affairs: Making Room for Psychosemantic Internalism*. Boston, MA: Kluwer.

Calvin, W., and Bickerton, D. (2000). *Lingua ex Machina: Reconciling Darwin and Chomsky with the Human Brain*. Cambridge, MA: MIT Press.

Carroll, L. (1895). What the Tortoise Said to Achilles. *Mind* 4: 278–80.

Carruthers, P. (2002). The Cognitive Functions of Language. *Behavioral and Brain Sciences* 25: 657–74.

Carruthers, P., and Boucher, J. (1998a). Introduction: Opening up Options. In Carruthers and Boucher (eds.), 1998b, 1–18.

———. (eds.). (1998b). *Language and Thought: Interdisciplinary Themes*. Cambridge: Cambridge University Press.

Chalmers, D. (1994). On Implementing a Computation. *Minds and Machines* 4: 391–402.

———. (1996a). *The Conscious Mind: In Search of a Fundamental Theory*. Oxford: Oxford University Press.

———. (1996b). Does a Rock Implement Every Finite-State Automata? *Synthese* 108, 3: 309–33.

———. (2008). Foreword to Andy Clark's *Supersizing the Mind* (see Clark [2008b]).

Changeaux, J. P. (1997). *Neuronal Man*. Princeton, NJ: Princeton University Press, second edition, 1997; first edition, 1983/85.

Chi, M., Feltovich, P., and Glaser, R. (1981). Categorization and Representation of Physics Problems by Experts and Novices, *Cognitive Science* 5 (April–June):121–52.

Chomsky, N. (1980). *Rules and Representations*. New York: Columbia University Press.

Churchland, P. M. (1981). Eliminative Materialism and the Propositional Attitudes. *Journal of Philosophy* 78, 2 (February): 67–90.

———. (1998). Conceptual Similarity across Sensory and Neural Diversity: The Fodor/Lepore Challenge Answered. *Journal of Philosophy* 95: 5–32.

———. (2005). Functionalism at Forty: A Critical Retrospective. *Journal of Philosophy* 102, 1 (January): 33–50.

Churchland, P. S., Ramachandran, V., and Sejnowski, T. (1994). A Critique of Pure Vision. In C. Koch and J. Davis (eds.), *Large-Scale Neuronal Theories of the Brain* (pp. 23–60). Cambridge, MA: MIT Press.

Churchland, P. S., and Sejnowski, T. (1992). *The Computational Brain*. Cambridge, MA: MIT Press.

Clark, A. (1989). *Microcognition: Philosophy, Cognitive Science, and Parallel Distributed Processing*. Cambridge, MA: MIT Press.

———. (1995). Moving Minds: Situating Content in the Service of Real-Time Success. In J. Tomberlin (ed.), *Philosophical Perspectives: AI, Connectionism, and Philosophical Psychology*, vol. 9 (pp. 89–104). Atascadero, CA: Ridgeview.

———. (1997). *Being There: Putting Brain, Body, and World Together Again*. Cambridge, MA: MIT Press.

———. (1998). Magic Words: How Language Augments Human Computation. In Carruthers and Boucher (eds.), pp. 162–83.

———. (2001). *Mindware: An Introduction to the Philosophy of Cognitive Science*. Oxford: Oxford University Press.

———. (2003). *Natural-Born Cyborgs*. Oxford: Oxford University Press.

———. (2004). Is Language Special? Some Remarks on Control, Coding, and Co-ordination. *Language Sciences* 26: 717–26.

———. (2005). Intrinsic Content, Active Memory and the Extended Mind. *Analysis* 65: 1–11.

———. (2006a). Language, Embodiment, and the Cognitive Niche. *Trends in Cognitive Sciences* 10: 370–74.

———. (2006b). Material Symbols. *Philosophical Psychology* 19: 291–307.

———. (2007). Curing Cognitive Hiccups: A Defense of the Extended Mind. *Journal of Philosophy* 104, 4 (April): 163–92.

———. (2008a). Pressing the Flesh: A Tension in the Study of the Embodied, Embedded Mind. *Philosophy and Phenomenological Research* 76, 1: 37–59.

———. (2008b). *Supersizing the Mind: Embodiment, Action, and Cognitive Extension*. Oxford: Oxford University Press. Page numbers refer to uncorrected proofs.

———. (forthcoming). Memento's Revenge: The Extended Mind, Extended. To appear in R. Menary (ed.), *The Extended Mind*. Cambridge, MA: MIT Press.

Clark, A., and Chalmers, D. (1998). The Extended Mind. *Analysis* 58: 7–19.

Clark, A., and Toribio, J. (1994). Doing without Representing? *Synthese* 101: 401–31.

Cleeremans, A., Destrebecqz, A., and Boyer, M. (1998). Implicit Learning: News from the Front. *Trends in Cognitive Sciences* 2, 10 (October): 406–16.

Cooper, R. (2007). The Role of Falsification in the Development of Cognitive Architectures: Insights from a Lakatosian Analysis. *Cognitive Science* 31: 509–33.

Copeland, J. (1996). What Is Computation? *Synthese* 108: 335–59.

Cowie, F. (1999). *What's Within: Nativism Reconsidered*. Oxford: Oxford University Press.

Cummins, R. (1996). *Representations, Targets, and Attitudes*. Cambridge, MA: MIT Press.

Damasio, A., and Tranel, D. (1993). Nouns and Verbs Are Retrieved with Differently Distributed Neural Systems. *Proceedings of the National Academy of Sciences of the USA* 90, 11: 4957–60.

Dennett, D. (1984). *Elbow Room: The Varieties of Free Will Worth Wanting*. Oxford: Oxford University Press.

———. (1991). *Consciousness Explained*. Boston, MA: Little, Brown and Company.

———. (1996). *Kinds of Minds: Toward an Understanding of Consciousness*. New York: Basic Books.

———. (2005). *Sweet Dreams: Philosophical Obstacles to a Science of Consciousness*. Cambridge, MA: MIT Press.

Donald, M. (1991). *Origins of the Modern Mind: Three Stages in the Evolution of Culture and Cognition*. Cambridge, MA: Harvard University Press.

Dowty, D., Wall, R., and Peters, S. (1981). *Introduction to Montague Semantics*. Dordrecht: D. Reidel.

Dretske, F. (1981). *Knowledge and the Flow of Information*. Cambridge, MA: MIT Press.

———. (1988). *Explaining Behavior: Reasons in a World of Causes*. Cambridge, MA: MIT Press.

Dreyfus, H. (1992). *What Computers Still Can't Do: A Critique of Artificial Reason*. Cambridge: MIT Press. Originally published as *What Computers Can't Do: A Critique of Artificial Reason*. New York: Harper and Row, 1972.

———. (2005). Overcoming the Myth of the Mental: How Philosophers Can Profit from the Phenomenology of Everyday Experience. *Proceedings and Addresses of the American Philosophical Association* 79: 47–65.

Driver, J., and Mattingly, J. (1998). Parietal Neglect and Visual Awareness. *Nature Neuroscience* 1: 17–22.

Eagleman, D., and Holcombe, A. (2002). Causality and the Perception of Time. *Trends in Cognitive Sciences* 6: 323–25.

Edelman, G. (1987). *Neural Darwinism: The Theory of Neuronal Group Selection*. New York: Basic Books.

Egan, F. (1994). Individualism and Vision Theory. *Analysis* 54, 4 (October): 258–64.

———. (1999). In Defence of Narrow Mindedness. *Mind & Language* 14, 2 (June): 177–94.

Ehrsson, H., Holmes, N., and Passingham, E. (2005). Touching a Rubber Hand: Feeling of Body Ownership Is Associated with Activity in Multisensory Brain Areas. *Journal of Neuroscience* 25: 10564–73.

Elman, J. (1995). Language as a Dynamical System. In Port and van Gelder (eds.), pp. 195–225.

Ericsson, K., and Kintsch, W. (1995). Long-Term Working Memory. *Psychological Review* 102: 211–45.

Ericsson, K., and Simon, H. (1980). Verbal Reports as Data. *Psychological Review* 87: 215–51.

Ernst, G., and Newell, A. (1969). *GPS: A Case Study in Generality and Problem Solving*. New York: Academic Press.

Fernandez, F., Effern, A., Grunwald, T., Pezer, N., Lehnertz, K., Dümpelmann, M., Van Roost, D., and Elger, C. (1999). Real-Time Tracking of Memory Formation in the Human Rhinal Cortex and Hippocampus. *Science* 285: 1582–85.

Fodor, J. (1974). Special sciences. *Synthese* 28: 77–115.

———. (1975). *The Language of Thought*. Cambridge, MA: Harvard University Press.

———. (1980). Methodological Solipsism Considered as a Research Strategy in Cognitive Psychology. *Behavioral and Brain Sciences* 3, 1: 63–73.

———. (1981a). *Representations*. Cambridge, MA: MIT Press.

———. (1981b). The Present Status of the Innateness Controversy. In Fodor (ed.), (1981a), pp. 257–316.

———. (1983). *The Modularity of Mind*. Cambridge, MA: MIT Press.

———. (1987). *Psychosemantics: The Problem of Meaning in the Philosophy of Mind*. Cambridge, MA: MIT Press.

———. (1990). *A Theory of Content and Other Essays*. Cambridge, MA: MIT Press.

———. (1991) A Modal Argument for Narrow Content. *Journal of Philosophy* 88: 5–26. Reprinted in C. MacDonald and G. MacDonald (eds.), *Philosophy of Psychology: Debates on Psychological Explanation* (pp. 206–25). Oxford: Basil Blackwell, 1995. Page references are to the reprinted version.

———. (1994). *The Elm and the Expert: Mentalese and Its Semantics*. Cambridge, MA: MIT Press.

———. (1998). *Concepts: Where Cognitive Science Went Wrong*. Oxford: Oxford University Press.

Fodor, J., and Lepore, E. (1999). All at Sea in Semantic Space: Churchland on Meaning Similarity. *Journal of Philosophy* 96, 8: 381–403.

Fodor, J., and Pylyshyn, Z. (1981). How Direct Is Visual Perception? Some Reflections on Gibson's "Ecological Approach." *Cognition* 9: 139–96.

———. (1988). Connectionism and Cognitive Architecture: A Critical Analysis. *Cognition* 28: 3–71.

Fu, W., and Gray, W. (2006). Sub-optimal Tradeoffs in Information Seeking. *Cognitive Psychology*. 52: 195–242.

Gallagher, S. (2002). Experimenting with Introspection. *Trends in Cognitive Sciences* 6: 374–75.

———. (2005). *How the Body Shapes the Mind*. New York: Oxford University Press.

Gallese, V., Keysers, C., and Rizzolatti, G. (2004). A Unifying View of the Basis of Social Cognition. *Trends in Cognitive Sciences* 8, 9: 396–403.

Gathercole, S., and Baddeley, A. (1993). *Working Memory and Language*. Hillsdale, NJ: Lawrence Erlbaum Associates.

Gentner, D. (2003). Why We're So Smart. In Gentner and Goldin-Meadow (eds.), pp. 195–235.

Gentner, D., and Goldin-Meadow, S. (eds.). (2003). *Language in Mind: Advances in the Study of Language and Thought*. Cambridge, MA: MIT Press.

Gergely, G., Nádasdy, Z., Csibra, G., and Biró, S. (1995). Taking the Intentional Stance at 12 Months of Age. *Cognition* 56: 165–93.

Gernsbacher, M., and Robertson, D. (2005). Watching the Brain Comprehend Discourse. In Healy (ed.), pp. 157–67.

Gibbs, R. (2006). *Embodiment and Cognitive Science*. Cambridge: Cambridge University Press.

Gibson, J. J. (1979). *The Ecological Approach to Visual Perception*. Boston: Houghton-Mifflin.

Gigerenzer, G. (2000). *Adaptive Thinking*. Oxford: Oxford University Press.

Gillett, C. (2002). The Dimensions of Realization: A Critique of the Standard View. *Analysis* 62: 316–23.

———. (2003). The Metaphysics of Realization, Multiple Realizability and the Special Sciences. *Journal of Philosophy* 100: 591–603.

———. (forthcoming). Hyper-Extending the Mind? Setting Boundaries in the Special Sciences. *Philosophical Topics* 35.

Glenberg, A. (1997). What Memory is For. *Behavioral and Brain Sciences* 20: 1–19.

Goldin-Meadow, S. (2003). *Hearing Gesture: How Our Hands Help Us Think*. Cambridge: Belknap Press/Harvard University Press.

Goldin-Meadow, S., and Zheng, M. (1998). Thought before Language: The Expression of Motion Events Prior to the Impact of a Conventional Language Model. In Carruthers and Boucher (eds.), 1998b, pp. 26–54.

Gray, W., and Fu, W. (2004). Soft Constraints in Interactive Behavior: The Case of Ignoring Perfect Knowledge In-the-world for Imperfect Knowledge In-the-head. *Cognitive Science* 28: 359–82.

Gray, W., Sims, C., Fu, W., and Schoelles, M. (2006). The Soft Constraints Hypothesis: A Rational Analysis Approach to Resource Allocation for Interactive Behavior. *Psychological Review* 113: 461–82.

Graziano, M., Yap, G., and Gross, C. (1994). Coding of Visual Space by Premotor Neurons. *Science* 266: 1054–57.

Griffiths, P., and Gray, R. (1994). Developmental Systems and Evolutionary Explanation. *Journal of Philosophy* 91: 277–304.

———. (2004). The Developmental Systems Perspective: Organism-Environment Systems as Units of Development and Evolution. In K. Preston and M. Pigliucci (eds.), *Phenotypic Integration: Studying the Ecology and Evolution of Complex Phenotypes* (pp. 409–31). Oxford: Oxford University Press.

Griffiths, P., and Stotz, K. (2000). How the Mind Grows: A Developmental Perspective on the Biology of Cognition. *Synthese* 122: 29–51.

Grush, R. (1997). The Architecture of Representation. *Philosophical Psychology* 10: 5–23.

———. (2003). In Defense of Some 'Cartesian' Assumptions Concerning the Brain and Its Operation. *Biology and Philosophy* 18: 53–93.

———. (2004). The Emulation Theory of Representation: Motor Control, Imagery, and Perception. *Behavioral and Brain Sciences* 27: 377–96.

Halle, M. (1990). Phonology. In D. Osherson and H. Lasnik (eds.), pp. 43–68.

Hanna, R., and Maiese, M. (2009). *Embodied Minds in Action*. Oxford: Oxford University Press.

Harnad, S. (1990). The Symbol Grounding Problem. *Physica D* 42: 335–46.

Harvey, I., Husbands, P., and Cliff, D. (1994). Seeing the Light: Artificial Evolution, Real Vision. In D. Cliff, P. Husbands, J.-A. Meyer, and S. Wilson (eds.), *From*

Animals to Animats 3: Proceedings of the Third International Conference on Simulation of Adaptive Behavior (pp. 392–401). Cambridge, MA: MIT Press.

Haugeland, J. (1995). Mind Embodied and Embedded. In Y. Houng and J. Ho (eds.), *Mind and Cognition* (pp. 3–37). Taipei, Taiwan: Institute of European and American Studies, Academia Sinica.

Healy, A. (ed.) (2005). *Experimental Cognitive Psychology and Its Applications.* Washington, D.C.: American Psychological Association.

Holmes, N., Calvert, G., and Spence, C. (2004). Extending or Projecting Peripersonal Space with Tools? Multisensory Interactions Highlight Only the Distal and Proximal Ends of Tools. *Neuroscience Letters* 372: 62–67.

Horgan, T. (1993). From Supervenience to Superdupervenience: Meeting the Demands of a Material World. *Mind* 102: 555–86.

Horgan, T., and Tienson, J. (1996). *Connectionism and the Philosophy of Psychology.* Cambridge, MA: MIT Press.

Houghton, D. (1997). Mental Content and External Representations. *Philosophical Quarterly* 47: 159–77.

Hurley, S. (1998). Vehicles, Contents, Conceptual Structure, and Externalism. *Analysis* 58: 1–6.

———. (2001). Perception and Action: Alternative Views. *Synthese* 129: 3–40.

———. (forthcoming). Varieties of Externalism. To appear in R. Menary (ed.), *The Extended Mind.* Cambridge, MA: MIT Press.

Husbands, P., Harvey, I., and Cliff, D. (1995). Circle in the Round: State Space Attractors for Evolved Sighted Robots. *Robotics and Autonomous Systems* 15: 83–106.

Hutchins, E. (1995). *Cognition in the Wild.* Cambridge, MA: MIT Press.

Iriki, A., Tanaka, M., and Iwamura, Y. (1996). Coding of Modified Body Schema during Tool Use by Macaque Postcentral Neurones. *NeuroReport* 7: 2325–30.

Iriki, A., Tanaka, M., Obayashi, S., and Iwamura, Y. (2001). Self-images in the Video Monitor Coded by Monkey Intraparietal Neurons. *Neuroscience Research* 40: 163–73.

Jack, A., and Roepstorff, A. (2002a). Introspection and Cognitive Brain Mapping: From Stimulus-Response to Script Report. *Trends in Cognitive Sciences* 6: 333–39.

———. (2002b). The 'Measurement Problem' for Experience: Damaging Flaw or Intriguing Puzzle. *Trends in Cognitive Sciences* 6: 372–74.

Karmiloff-Smith, A. (1992). *Beyond Modularity: A Developmental Perspective on Cognitive Science.* Cambridge, MA: MIT Press.

Keijzer, F. (1998). Doing without Representations Which Specify What to Do. *Philosophical Psychology* 11: 269–302.

Kelly, S. (2001). *The Relevance of Phenomenology to the Philosophy of Language and Mind.* New York: Garland.

Kelso, J. S. (1995). *Dynamic Patterns: The Self-Organization of Brain and Behavior.* Cambridge, MA: MIT Press.

Kim, J. (1993). *Supervenience and Mind: Selected Philosophical Essays.* Cambridge: Cambridge University Press.

———. (1998). *Mind in a Physical World: An Essay on the Mind-Body Problem and Mental Causation.* Cambridge, MA: MIT Press.

―――. (2005). *Physicalism, or Something Near Enough*. Princeton: Princeton University Press.

Kirsh, D., and Maglio, P. (1994). On Distinguishing Epistemic from Pragmatic Action. *Cognitive Science* 18: 513–49.

Kitcher, P. (1984). Species. *Philosophy of Science* 51: 308–33.

Klatzky, R. Pellegrino, J., McCloskey, B., and Doherty, S. (1989). Can You Squeeze a Tomato? The Role of Motor Representations in Semantic Sensibility Judgments. *Journal of Memory and Language* 28: 56–77.

Kornblith, H. (1993). *Inductive Inference and Its Natural Ground: An Essay in Naturalistic Epistemology*. Cambridge, MA: MIT Press.

Kripke, S. (1980). *Naming and Necessity*. Cambridge, MA: Harvard University Press.

Lakoff, G. (1987). *Women, Fire, and Dangerous Things*. Chicago: University of Chicago Press.

Lakoff, G., and Johnson, M. (1999). *Philosophy in the Flesh: The Embodied Mind and Its Challenge to Western Thought*. New York: Basic Books.

Landauer, T., Foltz, P., and Laham, D. (1998). Introduction to Latent Semantic Analysis. *Discourse Processes* 25: 259–84.

Laurence, S., and Margolis, E. (2002). Radical Concept Nativism. *Cognition* 86: 25–55.

Lettvin, J. (1995). On Grandmother Cells. In M. Gazzaniga (ed.), *The Cognitive Neurosciences* (pp. 434–35). Cambridge, MA: MIT Press.

Levin, M. (1997). Putnam on Reference and Constructible Sets. *British Journal for the Philosophy of Science* 48: 55–67.

Lewis, D. (1970). How to Define Theoretical Terms. *Journal of Philosophy* 67: 427–46.

―――. (1973). Causation. *Journal of Philosophy* 70: 556–67.

―――. (1983). New Work for a Theory of Universals. *Australasian Journal of Philosophy* 61: 343–77.

―――. (1984). Putnam's Paradox. *Australasian Journal of Philosophy* 62: 221–36.

―――. (1986). *Philosophical Papers*, vol. II. Oxford: Oxford University Press.

Linser, K., and Goschke, T. (2007). Unconscious Modulation of the Conscious Experience of Voluntary Control. *Cognition* 104: 459–75.

Loftus, E., and Bernstein, D. (2005). Rich False Memories: The Royal Road to Success. In Healy (ed.), pp. 101–13.

Lovett, M., Daily, L., and Reder, L. (2000). A Source Activation Theory of Working Memory: Cross-Task Prediction of Performance in ACT-R. *Journal of Cognitive Systems Research* 1: 99–118.

MacDonald, C. (1990). Weak Externalism and Mind-Body Identity. *Mind* 99: 387–404.

Mackie, J. (1965). Causes and Conditions. *American Philosophical Quarterly* 2: 245–64.

Maia, T., and Cleeremans, A. (2005). Consciousness: Converging Insights from Connectionist Modeling and Neuroscience. *Trends in Cognitive Sciences* 9, 8 (August): 397–404.

Majid, A., Bowerman, M., Kita, S., Haun, D., and Levinson, S. (2004). Can Language Restructure Cognition? The Case for Space. *Trends in Cognitive Sciences* 8, 3: 108–114.

Marcus, G. (1999). Connectionism: With or without Rules? Response to J. L. McClelland and D. C. Plaut. *Trends in Cognitive Sciences* 3, 5 (May): 168–70.

Marcus, G., Vijayan, S., Rao, S., and Vishton, P. (1999). Rule Learning by Seven-Month-Old Infants. *Science* 283, 1 (January): 77–80.

Margolis, E. (1998). How to Acquire a Concept. *Mind and Language* 13, 3: 347–69.

Markman, A., and Brendl, C. (2005). Constraining Theories of Embodied Cognition. *Psychological Science* 16: 6–10.

Markman, E. (1989). *Categorization and Naming in Children*. Cambridge, MA: MIT Press.

Marr, D. (1982). *Vision*. New York: W. H. Freeman and Company.

Martin, A., and Weisberg, J. (2003). Neural Foundations for Understanding Social and Mechanical Concepts. *Cognitive Neuropsychology* 20: 575–87.

Martin, C. B. (1997). On the Need for Properties: The Road to Pythagoreanism and Back. *Synthese* 112: 193–231.

McClamrock, R. (1995). *Existential Cognition: Computational Minds in the World*. Chicago: University of Chicago Press.

McClelland, J., and Plaut, D. (1999). Does Generalization in Infant Learning Implicate Abstract Algebra-like Rules? *Trends in Cognitive Sciences* 3, 5 (May): 166–68.

McGinn, C. (1989). *Mental Content*. Oxford: Basil Blackwell.

Meltzoff, A. (1995). Understanding the Intentions of Others: Re-enactment of Intended Acts by 18-month-old Children. *Developmental Psychology* 31: 838–50.

Menary, R. (2006). Attacking the Bounds of Cognition. *Philosophical Psychology* 19: 329–44.

Millikan, R. G. (1984). *Language, Thought, and Other Biological Categories: New Foundations for Realism*. Cambridge, MA: MIT Press.

———. (1993). *White Queen Psychology and Other Essays for Alice*. Cambridge, MA: MIT Press.

Minsky, M. (1967). *Computation: Finite and Infinite Machines*. Englewood Cliffs, NJ: Prentice-Hall.

Müller, R. (1996). Innateness, Autonomy, Universality? Neurobiological Approaches to Language. *Behavioral and Brain Sciences* 19: 611–31.

Newell, A., and Simon, H. (1997). Computer Science as Empirical Inquiry: Symbols and Search. In J. Haugeland (ed.), *Mind Design II: Philosophy, Psychology, and Artificial Intelligence* (pp. 81–110). Cambridge, MA: MIT Press. Reprinted from the *Communications of the Association for Computing Machinery* 19 (March 1976): 113–26.

Nichols, S., and Stich, S. (2003). *Mindreading: An Integrated Account of Pretence, Self-Awareness, and Understanding Other Minds*. Oxford: Oxford University Press.

Nilsson, N. (ed.) (1984). Shakey the Robot. Technical Note 323, Stanford Research International Artificial Intelligence Center.

Nisbett, R., and Wilson, T. (1977). Telling More than We Can Know: Verbal Reports on Mental Processes. *Psychological Review* 84: 231–59.

Noë, A. (2004). *Action in Perception*. Cambridge, MA: MIT Press.

Obayashi, S., Tanaka, M., and Iriki, A. (2000). Subjective Image of Invisible Hand Coded by Monkey Intraparietal Neurons. *NeuroReport* 11: 3499–505.

O'Regan, J. K. (1992). Solving the 'Real' Mysteries of Visual Perception: The World as an Outside Memory. *Canadian Journal of Psychology* 46: 461–88.

Osherson, D., and Lasnik, H. (eds.) (1990). *An Invitation to Cognitive Science*: *Language*, vol. 1. Cambridge, MA: MIT Press.

Palmer, S. (1999). *Vision Science: Photons to Phenomenology*. Cambridge, MA: MIT Press.

Papineau, D. (1993). *Philosophical Naturalism*. Oxford: Basil Blackwell.

———. (2001). The Rise of Physicalism. In Gillett and Loewer (eds.), *Physicalism and Its Discontents* (pp. 3–36). Cambridge: Cambridge University Press.

Pastalkova, E., Serrano, P., Pinkhasova, D., Wallace, E., Fenton, A., and Sacktor, T. (2006). Storage of Spatial Information by the Maintenance Mechanism of LTP. *Science* 313: 1141–44.

Patterson, S. (1991). Individualism and Semantic Development. *Philosophy of Science* 58: 15–35.

Peigneux, P., Laureys, S., Fuchs, S., Collette, F., Perrin, F., Reggers, J., Phillips, C., Degueldre, C., Del Fiore, G., Aerts, J., Luxen, A., and Maquet, P. (2004). Are Spatial Memories Strengthened in the Human Hippocampus during Slow Wave Sleep? *Neuron* 44: 535–45.

Pereboom, D. 2002. Robust Nonreductive Materialism. *Journal of Philosophy* 99: 499–531.

Perner, J., Leekham, S., and Wimmer, H. (1987). Three-year-olds' Difficulty with False Belief: The Case for Conceptual Deficit. *British Journal of Developmental Psychology* 5: 125–37.

Perry, J. (1979). The Problem of the Essential Indexical. *Noûs* 13: 3–21.

Petitot, J. (1995). Morphodynamics and Attractor Syntax: Constituency in Visual Perception and Cognitive Grammar. In Port and van Gelder (eds.), pp. 227–81.

Piccinini, G. (2008). Computers. *Pacific Philosophical Quarterly* 89: 32–73.

Pinker, S. (1997). *How the Mind Works*. New York: W. W. Norton.

Polger, T. (2004). Neural Machinery and Realization. *Philosophy of Science* (*Proceedings*) 71: 997–1006.

Port, R. F., and van Gelder, T. (eds.) (1995). *Mind as Motion: Explorations in the Dynamics of Cognition*. Cambridge, MA: MIT Press.

Prinz, J. (2002). *Furnishing the Mind: Concepts and Their Perceptual Basis*. Cambridge, MA: MIT Press.

Pulvermüller, F. (1999). Words in the Brain's Language. *Behavioral and Brain Science* 22: 253–79.

Purves, D., Augustine, G., Fitzpatrick, D., Katz, L., LaMantia, A., and McNamara, J. (eds.) (1997). *Neuroscience*. Sunderland, MA: Sinauer.

Putnam, H. (1967). Psychological Predicates. In W. Capitan and D. Merrill (eds.), *Art, Mind, and Religion*. Pittsburgh: Pittsburgh University Press. Reprinted in H. Putnam, *Mind, Language, and Reality: Philosophical Papers*, vol. 2 (pp. 429–40). Cambridge: Cambridge University Press, 1975.

———. (1975). The Meaning of 'Meaning'. In H. Putnam (ed.), *Mind, Language, and Reality: Philosophical Papers*, vol. 2 (pp. 215–71). Cambridge: Cambridge University Press.

———. (1981). *Reason, Truth and History*. Cambridge: Cambridge University Press.

———. (1988). *Representation and Reality*. Cambridge, MA: MIT Press.

Pylyshyn, Z. (1981). The Imagery Debate: Analog Media versus Tacit Knowledge. In Block (ed.), pp. 151–206.

Pylyshyn, Z. (1984). *Computation and Cognition: Toward a Foundation for Cognitive Science*. Cambridge, MA: MIT Press.

Quartz, S., and Sejnowski, T. (1997). The Neural Basis of Cognitive Development: A Constructivist Manifesto. *Behavioral and Brain Sciences* 20: 537–96.

Quine, W. V. (1969). Natural Kinds. In W. V. Quine (ed.), *Ontological Relativity and Other Essays* (pp. 114–38). New York: Columbia University Press.

Quiroga, R., Reddy, L., Kreiman, G., Koch, C., and Fried, I. (2005). Invariant Visual Representation by Single Neurons in the Human Brain. *Nature* 435: 1102–7.

Ramachandran, V. (1995). Anosognosia in Parietal Lobe Syndrome. *Consciousness and Cognition* 4: 22–51.

Ramachandran, V., and Blakeslee, S. (1998). *Phantoms in the Brain: Probing the Mysteries of the Human Mind*. New York: William Morrow.

Rees, G. (2007). Neural Correlates of the Contents of Visual Awareness in Humans. *Philosophical Transactions of the Royal Society B* 362: 877–86.

Repacholi, B., and Gopnik, A. (1997). Early Understanding of Desires: Evidence from 14 and 18 Month Olds. *Developmental Psychology* 33: 12–21.

Richardson, D., Dale, R., and Spivey, M. (2007). Eye Movements in Language and Cognition: A Brief Introduction. In Gonzalez-Marquez, Mittelberg, Coulson, and Spivey (eds.), *Methods in Cognitive Linguistics* (pp. 323–44). Amsterdam: John Benjamins.

Robbins, P., and Aydede, M. (eds.) (2009). *The Cambridge Handbook of Situated Cognition*. Cambridge: Cambridge University Press.

Roediger, L., and Gallo, A. (2005). Associative Memory Illusions. In R. Pohl (ed.), *Cognitive Illusions: A Handbook on Fallacies and Biases in Thinking, Judgment and Memory* (pp. 309–26). Oxford: Oxford University Press.

Rosenbloom, P., Laird, J., Newell, A., and McCarl, R. (1991). A Preliminary Analysis of the Soar Architecture as a Basis for General Intelligence. *Artificial Intelligence* 47: 289–325.

Rowlands, M. (1997). Teleological Semantics. *Mind* 106: 279–303.

———. (1999). *The Body in Mind: Understanding Cognitive Processes*. Cambridge: Cambridge University Press.

———. (2006). *Body Language: Representation in Action*. Cambridge, MA: MIT Press.

Rumelhart, D., McClelland, J., and the PDP Research Group. (1986). *Parallel Distributed Processing: Explorations in the Microstructure of Cognition*, Vol. 1, Foundations. Cambridge, MA: MIT Press.

Rupert, R. (1996). The Best Test Theory of Extension. Ph.D. dissertation, University of Illinois at Chicago.

———. (1998). On the Relationship between Naturalistic Semantics and Individuation Criteria for Terms in a Language of Thought. *Synthese* 117: 95–131.

———. (1999). The Best Test Theory of Extension: First Principle(s). *Mind & Language* 14, 3: 321–55.

———. (2001). Coining Terms in the Language of Thought: Innateness, Emergence, and the Lot of Cummins's Argument against the Causal Theory of Mental Content. *Journal of Philosophy* 98: 499–530.

———. (2004). Challenges to the Hypothesis of Extended Cognition. *Journal of Philosophy* 101: 389–428.

———. (2005). Minding One's Cognitive Systems: When Does a Group of Minds Constitute a Single Cognitive Unit? *Episteme: A Journal of Social Epistemology* 1: 177–88.

———. (2006a). Functionalism, Mental Causation, and the Problem of Metaphysically Necessary Effects. *Noûs* 40: 256–83.

———. (2006b). Review of *Embodiment and Cognitive Science* by Raymond Gibbs, in *Notre Dame Philosophical Reviews*, August 20, 2006.

———. (2008). Frege's Puzzle and Frege Cases: Defending a Quasi-syntactic Solution. *Cognitive Systems Research* 9: 76–91.

Ryder, D. (2004). SINBAD Neurosemantics: A Theory of Mental Representation. *Mind and Language* 19, 2 (April): 211–40.

Samuels, R. (2002). Nativism in Cognitive Science. *Mind and Language* 17, 3 (June): 233–65.

Schöner, G., and Thelen, E. (2006). Using Dynamic Field Theory to Rethink Infant Habituation. *Psychological Review* 113: 273–99.

Schooler, J. (2002a). Re-representing Consciousness: Dissociations between Experience and Meta-consciousness. *Trends in Cognitive Sciences* 6: 339–44.

———. (2002b). Establishing a Legitimate Relationship with Introspection. *Trends in Cognitive Sciences* 6: 371–72.

Searle, J. (1980). Minds, Brains, and Programs. *Behavioral and Brain Sciences* 3: 417–24.

Segal, G. (1997). Review of *Cartesian Psychology and Physical Minds: Individualism and the Sciences of the Mind* by Robert Wilson. *British Journal for the Philosophy of Science* 48: 151–56.

Shapiro, L. (2000). Multiple Realizations. *Journal of Philosophy* 97: 635–54.

———. (2004). *The Mind Incarnate*. Cambridge, MA: MIT Press.

———. (2007). The Embodied Cognition Research Programme. *Philosophy Compass* 2, 2: 338–46.

Shoemaker, S. (1981). Some Varieties of Functionalism. *Philosophical Topics* 12: 93–118.

———. (2003). Realization, Micro-realization, and Coincidence. *Philosophy and Phenomenological Research* 67: 1–23.

Silverman, M., and Mack, A. (2006). Change Blindness and Priming: When It Does and Does Not Occur. *Consciousness and Cognition* 15: 409–22.

Simons, D., and Levin, D. (1997). Change Blindness. *Trends in Cognitive Science* 1: 261–67.

Smith, E., and Medin, D. (1981). *Categories and Concepts*. Cambridge, MA: Harvard University Press.

Spivey, M., Richardson, D., and Fitneva, S. (2004). Thinking Outside the Brain: Spatial Indices to Visual and Linguistic Information. In J. Henderson and F. Ferreira (eds.), *Interfacing Language, Vision, and Action* (pp. 161–89). San Diego, CA: Academic Press.

Spivey, M., Richardson, D., and Zednik, C. (forthcoming). Language Is Spatial, Not Special: Using Space for Language and Memory. In K. Mix, L. Smith, and M. Gasser (eds.), *Spatial Foundations of Cognition and Language*. Oxford University Press.

Sterelny, K. (2004). Externalism, Epistemic Artefacts and the Extended Mind. In R. Schantz (ed.), *The Externalist Challenge: New Studies on Cognition and Intentionality* (pp. 239–54). Berlin: de Gruyter.

Sterelny, K. and Griffiths, P. (1999). *Sex and Death: An Introduction to Philosophy of Biology*. Chicago, IL: University of Chicago Press.

Stillings, N., Weisler, S., Chase, C., Feinstein, M., Garfield, J., and Rissland, E. (1995). *Cognitive Science: An Introduction*, second edition. Cambridge, MA: MIT Press.

Storms, M., and Nisbett, R. (1970). Insomnia and the Attribution Process. *Journal of Personality and Social Psychology* 16: 319–28.

Swinburne, R. G. (1980). Properties, Causation, and Projectibility: Reply to Shoemaker. In L. J. Cohen and M. Hesse (eds.), *Applications of Inductive Logic* (pp. 313–20). Oxford: Clarendon.

Thelen, E., Schöner, G., Scheier, C., and Smith, L. (2001). The Dynamics of Embodiment: A Field Theory of Infant Perseverative Reaching. *Behavioral and Brain Sciences* 24: 1–34.

Thelen, E., and Smith, L. (1994). *A Dynamic Systems Approach to the Development of Cognition and Action*. Cambridge, MA: MIT Press.

Tiffany, E. (1999). Semantics San Diego Style. *Journal of Philosophy* 96, 8 (August): 416–29.

Townsend, J. T., and Busemeyer, J. (1995). Dynamic Representation of Decision-Making. In Port and van Gelder (eds.), *Mind in Motion: Explorations in the Dynamics of Cognition*. pp. 101–20.

Tulving, E., and Craik, F. (eds.) (2000). *The Oxford Handbook of Memory*. Oxford: Oxford University Press.

Tversky, A., and Kahneman, D. (1971). Belief in the Law of Small Numbers. *Psychological Bulletin* 2: 105–10.

van Fraassen, B. (1977). The Pragmatics of Explanation. *American Philosophical Quarterly* 14: 143–50.

van Gelder, Timothy (1991). Classical Questions, Radical Answers: Connectionism and the Structure of Mental Representations. In Terence Horgan and John Tienson (eds.), *Connectionism and the Philosophy of Mind, Studies in Cognitive Systems*, vol. 9. Dordrecht: Kluwer Academic Publishers, 1991.

————. (1995). What Might Cognition Be, If Not Computation? *Journal of Philosophy* 92: 345–81.

Varela, F., Thompson, E., and Rosch, E. (1991). *The Embodied Mind: Cognitive Science and Human Experience*. Cambridge, MA: MIT Press.

Vargha-Khadem, F., Gadian, D., Watkins, K., Connelly, A., Van Paesschen, W., and Mishkin, M. (1997). Differential Effects of Early Hippocampal Pathology on Episodic and Semantic Memory. *Science* 277: 376–80.

Vera, A., and Simon, H. (1993). Situated Action: A Symbolic Interpretation. *Cognitive Science* 17: 7–48.

Walsh, D. (1998). Wide Content Individualism. *Mind* 107: 625–52.

Wegner, D. (2002). *The Illusion of Conscious Will*. Cambridge, MA: MIT Press.

Weiskopf, D. (2004). The Place of Time in Cognition. *British Journal for the Philosophy of Science* 55: 87–105.

————. (2008a). Patrolling the Mind's Boundaries. *Erkenntnis* 68, 2: 265–76.

————. (2008b). The Origins of Concepts. *Philosophical Studies* 140, 3: 359–84.

Wellman, H., Cross, D., and Watson, J. (2001). Meta-analysis of Theory-of-Mind Development: The Truth about False Belief. *Child Development* 72: 655–84.

Wheeler, M. (2001). Two Threats to Representation. *Synthese* 129, 2: 211–31.

————. (2004). Is Language the Ultimate Artefact? *Language Sciences* 26: 693–715.

————. (2005). *Reconstructing the Cognitive World: The Next Step*. Cambridge, MA: MIT Press.

Wheeler, M., and Clark, A. (1999). Genic Representation: Reconciling Content and Causal Complexity. *British Journal for the Philosophy of Science* 50: 103–35.

Wicklegren, W. (1969). Context-Sensitive Coding, Associative Memory, and Serial Order in (Speech) Behavior. *Psychological Review* 75: 1–15.

Wilson, Margaret (2001). The Case for Sensorimotor Coding in Working Memory. *Psychonomic Bulletin & Review* 8, 1: 44–57.

————. (2002). Six Views of Embodied Cognition. *Psychonomic Bulletin and Review* 9: 625–36.

Wilson, Mark (1985). What Is This Thing Called "Pain"?—The Philosophy of Science behind the Contemporary Debate. *Pacific Philosophical Quarterly* 66: 227–67.

Wilson, R. (1999). The Individual in Biology and Psychology. In V. Hardcastle (ed.), *Where Biology Meets Psychology: Philosophical Essays*. Cambridge, MA: MIT Press.

————. (2001). Two Views of Realization. *Philosophical Studies* 104: 1–30.

————. (2004). *Boundaries of the Mind: The Individual in the Fragile Sciences*. Cambridge: Cambridge University Press.

Wilson, R., and Clark, A. (2009). How to Situate Cognition: Letting Nature Take Its Course. In P. Robbins and M. Aydede (eds.), pp. 55–77.

Wimmer, H., and Perner, J. (1983). Beliefs about Beliefs: Representation and Constraining Function of Wrong Beliefs in Young Children's Understanding of Deception. *Cognition* 13: 103–28.

Winograd, T. (1971). Procedures as a Representation for Data in a Computer Program for Understanding Natural Language. MAC-TR-84, MIT Project MAC.

Woodfield, A. (1991). Conceptions. *Mind* 100, 4 (October): 547–72.

Woodward, A. (1998). Infants Selectively Encode the Goal Object of an Actor's Reach. *Cognition* 69: 1–34.

Index